Th

OAK

To Dan from Bill

Based on a true story

1st Book Sold

WILLIAM T. WALRAVEN

Fulton Books, Inc.
Meadville, PA

Published by Fulton Books 2020

ISBN 978-1-64654-371-7 (paperback)
ISBN 978-1-64654-372-4 (digital)

Printed in the United States of America

CHAPTER 1

⳨

The air filled with music of singing birds, the soft new grass, and the blue skies with high white clouds announced the new life of spring. The sounds of lowing cattle in the distant meadow didn't interrupt Eric's deep thoughts. Sitting on top of a hill, he accepted these familiar sounds around him. In this picturesque landscape of flowing hills, spotted with rich farmland, and woods located in the most Southern party of Holland, Eric grew up.

He was now in his early twenties, his slim but strong built body, blue eyes, and light-brown hair made him a sharp contrast with the green grass. Rolling a cigarette, he kicked off his wooden shoes, which rolled a couple of feet down the hill. This spot, overlooking all that was dear to him, was his spot. Many times, he sat here, trying to find answers to the thousands of questions that arose in the mind of a young man.

Nico, his closest friend, had been the only one who had shared this place with him. Here, where they had opened up to each other their deepest thoughts and feelings, would become past. Eric felt lonely. Within a couple of days, he would emigrate to Canada, leaving all this behind. Question after question, impossible to answer, shot through his mind. Why was he leaving all this? He could make a living here. Going to the other end of the world as a complete stranger to people with a different language (he spoke only a few words of English) and likely with different habits scared him. From the other side, the excitement of traveling and meeting the unknown had always been in his blood. Even as a young boy, his blood had urged him to find out and experience all that was beyond his vision,

3

strength, and endurance. He welcomed the feeling of unmatched powers that the release of adrenaline gave his body in occasions of danger or excitement. But always after every experience, there was this place called home. All through his young life, it had cradled him. It was a hard decision to make, but after all, farming in this area was a poor existence, and working in the deep coal mines of this district was hard and with no future except early retirement.

He spent five years in one of those coal mines, which had not only strengthened his body but also made up his mind to get away from Holland. If he had to leave this area and try to start a new life in another part of Holland, he could just as well travel to a country that supposedly had better opportunities for willing and hard-working young men. Once he left this nest, he would be a stranger anyway.

A sparrow landed on a thin branch within an arm's reach of him, perfectly balancing its tiny body against the gentle swaying of the branch, which accepted this added load. For a moment, it sat there nervously, twitching its head in all directions, until it noticed the presence of Eric. It made a shrieking sound and hastily left this danger zone. The sound broke Eric's thoughts, and with a deep sigh, he pushed his cigarette butt into the soft ground beside him. On the other side, looking down the hill, he could see his village lying like a jewel with its red-shingled roofs and white-walled houses between sloping hills.

On his left in the distance was the coal mine, the only industry in this area, spitting out large clouds of smoke and steam from its chimneys.

The sound of the church bell made him look back to the village again. He would never forget his village and all its people. They were good, decent, hard-working people, and somehow, sitting here, he loved them all. He also knew that some of them he would never see again, at least not in this lifetime.

The village where Eric grew up and spent his young years was an old village with some of the relics dating back to the twelfth century. One of the houses still displayed a date of 1737 in one of the walls. It is located in one of the most beautiful provinces of Holland, a province called Limburg, where in this area the famous—or rather infamous—Limburger cheese originated. It is one of the smaller provinces and extends like a tail on the southern part of the country. This tiny strip is bordered by Germany on one side and by Belgium on the other. It is at the most, thirty miles wide, and since on each border a different language is spoken (German and French), many different dialects are spoken. Nearly every village, some only a couple of miles apart, had its own dialect ranging from low German to low French. Proper Dutch was only spoken in schools.

Eric's village, located on and practically surrounded by the German border, had a low German dialect, which Eric would never lose, even after decades of living in English-speaking countries.

Eric's parents were raised in villages on the Belgium border before they got married, and they had a flat French accent, which haunted them for many years for being strangers in his village. Anyone who visited or moved to a village and had no close family bonds with anyone in that village was not accepted and were handled as total strangers. Anyone having a different accent was practically an outcast. It was also nearly impossible for Eric's parents, who moved to this village when Eric was one year old, to get to know the villagers. Everyone was called by a series of first names instead of their surnames.

A name like John from Pete and Mary from the Cross was very normal and, for the villagers, no problem. It meant that John was the son of Pete and Mary (everyone knew Pete and Mary) living close by the old iron cross at the outskirts of the village. It could even go a step further. If John married and had a child called Tilly, anyone asking, "Who is that child?" would get an answer like "Oh, that is Tilly, from John from Pete and Mary from the Cross." All these villages were like close-knit families living there for generation after generation. Everyone was somehow related to others through centuries of intermarriage. Through this interbreeding, the percentage of misformed, lame, blind, and all sorts of handicapped people was very high over the whole district.

Feuds between villages was very common, and it was practically impossible for a young man to start courting a girl from another village. Naturally, it happened, but both young people, besides being in love, had to have the willpower and determination to withstand the abuse rendered to them by their villagers for not choosing one of their own kind. If after they were married, they moved to one of the two villages, it was half as bad, but if the two moved to another village, it would be a long time before they were accepted in that village.

Besides the deep coal mines and everything related to it, farming and growing of vegetable seedlings, which were sold in bunches at the neighboring marketplaces, was the only industry in many villages. Most farms were small, everyone having no more than one horse and four or five cows. Anyone having more than that was considered a large farmer.

More than half the working men in Eric's village were coal miners. The closest mine, the largest one, was within an hour's ride by bicycle, the bicycle being the only transportation at the time. Only the well-to-do who lived in the cities could afford a car as a means of transportation.

Eric's parents were from good old stock. His father, John Oosterbeek, was a medium-built man and was the second oldest in a family of ten children. At the age of thirteen, John's father had died between the bumpers of two railroad cars while his youngest child was just one year old. With only six years of grade school behind him, Eric's father and his older brother of one year had to find a job to keep the rather poor family on their feet.

His first job was in a glass-blowing factory. In an unbelievably hot and smoke-filled factory, he was put to work as a glass blower. He dipped the long hollow rod into the hot liquid glass and blew his lungs out until his eyes nearly popped out of their sockets while turning the rod between his hands—twelve hours a day, six days a week. It made him grow up fast. The job was too hard for him. His lungs had not the volume of a mature man, and many times the red-hot glass would cool off too fast before entering the mold and would brake. He'd then receive more kicks under his behind from the forever drunken foreman. He had to take all this because in those days, a job was hard to find. His young heart, however, would burn from the unfair handling he had received for trying his utmost. Finally, he was transferred to the fine crystal-grinding section. After about three or four years with the only thing to show were his hands full of scars, the leftover cuts of the broken crystal, he found a job in a large laboratory connected to the coal mine.

Eric's mother, Martha, was raised in the village two miles from Eric's father. They lived above a grocery store, while her father also worked at the railroad. Her mother, Eric's favorite grandmother, operated the store besides raising four children.

At a very young age, Martha found herself a job as a live-in maid for a very wealthy family in her village. She was a hard-working young woman, and her love for the kitchen and preparing food for the family and the many parties, made her in no time the chef cook. Her knowledge of cooking never left her, and she was well-known in Eric's village after they moved there. She was many times asked to cook at weddings, parties, and funerals.

Martha met John with a bang. John, now twenty-four years old, went with some friends one Sunday by bicycle to Martha's village to have some fun in the local bars. After a few hours and in a good mood, they chose to return home as unexpected bad weather was approaching the village. Before they reached the end of the village, however, the rain came down in buckets, and lightning and thunder blasted the skies above them. Quickly they decided to find cover and wait until the rain had subsided. John found cover in the hallway of the store operated by Martha's parents. As good-hearted, down-to-earth villagers at that time, Martha was sent downstairs to invite the young man in the hallway to come upstairs out of the rain and have a warm cup of coffee. At the moment when Martha, now eighteen years old, met John, a lightning bolt lit the sky, followed immediately by the exploding sound of thunder, and that was how Eric's parents met. Two years later, they married and moved to a small village close to John's job. In the three years that they lived in the village, Martha gave birth to two sons. First came Johann and, two years later, Eric.

The laboratory, which was part of the coal mine where John was employed as a general laborer, manufactured large amounts of ammonia, one of the many products made from coal, to be used in the manufacturing of fertilizer. It created an impossible smell in the village when the wind blew from the wrong direction. For this reason, they moved when Eric was one year old to the village where Eric spent his young years.

Six years later, Martha gave birth to another son, Paul. Another six years later, Eric's only sister was born, Ellie. For two years, they lived in a very small house on the main street of the village.

Eric was only three years old but still remembered them moving into a larger house. His father was moving the furniture piece by piece with his heavy wheelbarrow, while his mother was packing and unpacking the smaller articles. He remembered having a hard time pedaling his little tricycle up the loose white gravel-covered driveway of the new home. Constantly, the little wheels of the tricycle got stuck. It drove him into a tantrum. His father, noticing the misery his little son had created for himself, picked him and his tricycle up with one arm and, with a couple of large steps, put him down on a flat concrete walking path behind the house. Eric never forgot this incident because at that moment, he realized how strong and powerful his father was.

The new house had a very large kitchen, his mother's paradise, and a huge living and dining room with very high ceilings separated by two unbelievably hard-to-move sliding doors. Upstairs were three large bedrooms; only two were occupied—one by his parents and the other by Eric and his brother, Johann. The third was used for storing space.

The reason that Johann and Eric slept together in one large bed was to preserve body heat in the wintertime; central heating in homes was unheard of at that time. The only room that was heated by a coal stove was the kitchen and once in a while, on a special occasion, the stove in the living room was used.

Eric could not remember if the dining room was ever used. Everyone had a room like that. It had the best furniture and was only used as a showroom. Eric always got a scary feeling whenever he walked into this room. The forever-shining massive table surrounded by chairs stood there like a statue, and the big heavy framed pictures of his grandmothers and heavy-mustached grandfathers without a smile on their faces would watch every move he made. Even if he moved from one side of the room to the other, it seemed that their eyes were always following him. At one time, he even stuck his tongue out to one of his grandfathers, and he was positive that one of the moustaches moved slightly. It scared him so much that for many weeks, he didn't dare go back into this room again.

Sleeping with Johann in the same bed had its problems. Johann had in his young years the nasty habit of bed watering, with the result of Eric waking up many times as wet as Johann was, depending on what side Johann was sleeping when the accident occurred. Johann's or, for that matter, Eric's misfortune didn't promote brotherly love, because many times Eric would use in their arguments the striking word "bed pisser."

Across the road from their new location was a farm—one house and an animal stall, with one horse, two cows, three or four pigs, and some chickens. This farm became Eric's home away from home, and Willem, the farmer's son, who was in his early thirties and still a bachelor, became his second father. They became pals for life. Working at this farm with the animals and working the fields introduced in Eric at a very young age the beauty and feelings for animals and the outdoors.

Within a couple of years, Eric could handle very easily the huge Clydesdale horse named Max, and Max and Eric were the closest of friends for many years. Many times, Eric would share a sandwich with him, and gently with his big lips and huge teeth, Max would take this gift out of his small hand while giving him with his big brown eyes a warm feeling of understanding.

At this farm, Eric learned the beauty of the animals—their courting, reproduction, birth, and the close relationship in these matters between man and beast.

Besides school, Willem was his teacher for everything you couldn't find in books. If a cow would behave quite oddly in the meadow, then Willem would explain that nature's forceful urge of mating had entered her. In a noneducated but beautiful way, Willem would tell Eric while sitting on the large wooden feedbox in the cow stall the story of life and reproduction. Shortly thereafter, they would walk with this cow a couple of miles over many small field pads to the only farmer who could afford to have a bull. Eric was too young to be allowed to enter the large barn to see the mating of these two animals, but Willem would direct Eric to a window where he, with eyes possibly larger than the bull, would witness the beauty and power of mating and the start of a new life. On the way back, they seldom talked, both full of their own thoughts and feelings. The cow walked behind them in grace, once in a while grasping for a patch of juicy grass.

Behind Eric's house separated by a huge old private hedge was the village school. From the first through the seventh grade, Eric spent seven aggravating years here (aggravating because it took his valuable time away from Willem and the farm). Who needed all that baloney about arithmetic and language? And who cared about the old people in history who were already dead for many centuries? Sitting in this classroom filled with the stinking smoke of the teacher's forever-burning pipe while listening to the music of the horse-drawn farm wagons and the sound of the cattle in the nearby meadows made schooling an aggravation.

He liked some of the teachers, but in general, they were not his kind of people. They were the master. They would give you with their soft, ladylike hands a likken for no reason at all, or worse, they would give you for punishment a hundred sentences to write, like "I will not interrupt the classes during schooltime," to be handed back to them the next morning. This punishment was really rude, because besides giving him a sore hand and wrist, it took his freedom away. No, schooling was not for him. It was all the teachers' fault. They were the reason of his lost freedom in nature's beauty. If there were no teachers, there wouldn't be any schools.

One of his neighbors was an old grouchy lady who didn't like Eric too much because he would throw small stones at her skinny dirty chickens. Willem's chickens were a lot better, whiter, and he would listen with pleasure to the early morning cries of the big red and brown rooster, the undisputable master of Willem's chickens.

At the end of the street was the village cemetery. This sinister place surrounded by high walls and a steel gate was the most gruesome place for Eric in the whole village. In daytime, he would avoid it as much as possible, but in no way would he dare to pass or come even close to this place during early evening or darkness. Surely not after his mother had told him that if someone would hit or kick his own parents, his hand or foot would protrude above the grave after this person was dead and buried. The first time after this shocking news came to him, he visited the cemetery in procession with the village pastor on All Souls' Day. His eyes were shooting from grave to grave, looking for these members. He was quickly put at ease when he couldn't detect one in the whole graveyard. Coming home, he requested an immediate answer to this grave lie. His mother's serious answer was that this only happens at night and when daylight breaks through, these members would disappear again. He decided he would never pass this place at nighttime, because with his inquisitive mind, he would hear these arms and legs plopping out of the ground.

The other end of his street crossed the Main Street, which encircled the village to find its way back to the only street leading approximately two miles through fields and meadows to the closest city. At this crossing point was the village church and across from this church was a large stoop in front of a small general store at one corner. This was the only evening gathering place for young and old to hear the latest on everything, including who was sick or died or stranger in town. Many stories were told by old farmers and coal miner, and Eric, sitting between them, could listen for hours about the dangers of coal mining and the stories of old farmers about werewolves and ghost they had seen around the old farms. Many nights, Eric could not sleep because there were ghosts all around him. The south part of Holland was predominantly Roman Catholic and the rest Protestant, including the Dutch royal family. These southern villages were very fanatic about their religion, because anyone not being of the Catholic faith was automatically branded as a heathen and was not accepted in the village.

Eric's pastor was the tallest man in the village. Not only was he the tallest man, who automatically demanded respect, but as pastor, he was also the most knowledgeable and most powerful man. He was the spiritual advisor for the local soccer team, brass band, and drum-and-flute corps. Between these tough but good village people, he was the man of God with power to spare.

Weather permitting, he would walk every midmorning back and forth in front of his church, everyone passing him paying respect by nodding their heads and greeting him, "Good morning, Mr. Pastor." Always he would walk with his hands loosely together at his back, the outer hand repeatedly opening and closing. Eric, at about four years old, had watched this procedure for days, maybe weeks, while sitting at the big corner stone at the crossing on his street. One day, it got the best of him. This opening and closing, slightly squeezing of this hand began to work on his nerves. A farm wagon went by, and the horse beautified the street with some fresh droppings. For a moment, he observed the fresh droppings and the squeezing hand. The rest is village history… Before he realized what he was doing, he sneaked behind Mr. Pastor and dropped the still-warm round droppings in his hand at the precise moment of squeezing. For a second, he was awarded the most unforgettable sight. However, this triumph was short-lived.

The next thing he remembered was a sound of disgust, an unbelievable quick turn of such a big man, and a lightning-fast hand dazzling his head. Next with his dirty hand, he grasped Eric by his clean shirt (remember, it was still morning) and, with steps a mile long, dragged him while screaming over his lungs for mercy in the direction of Eric's home, passing bystanders with a look in their eyes that no good would come from this kid. His mother, hearing his alarming cries, came running toward them. After some, he guessed, unpleasant words between the two, he was handed over into the safe hands of his mother. After coming home, his entire body still shaking and gasping for air, his mother gave him a couple of good lickens on his behind and sent him for further punishment to his bedroom for the remainder of the day. Lying on his bed, he hated Mr. Pastor and his mother for this harsh and unfair punishment for nothing at all. When later that day his father came home from work, he gave him another good and hard talk about his deed. When leaving Eric's room, however, he could not prevent a weak smile on his face. One thing was sure—Eric had gotten rid of his frustration and Mr. Pastor of his squeezing habit.

John, Eric's father, was a hard-working man and very caring for his family. He was a wise man and a forever optimist and loved fun in his life. However, sometimes he would go overboard, like that one time when Eric went with him to the High Mass on Sunday. During the service, they had to stand up and kneel constantly, which Eric found ridiculous. He cheated sometimes by not kneeling. One of the times when they had to stand up, his father let a fart go that sounded like a cannon shot.

Eric got very embarrassed even more so when his father turned around and said to a very old lady sitting behind them, "You should be ashamed of yourself."

When they walked home, Eric confronted his dad. "How could you do such a thing to that poor old lady?"

"Well, let me tell you," answered his father. "It was unfortunate, and it happened too fast. Everyone was looking in our direction, so I made a quick decision. When a very old person farts in church, nobody will blame her because of her age. However, if they all suspected that it was me, the whole village would talk about this for a couple of weeks. Don't tell Mother anything about this."

Eric felt better, and they continued home.

Holland located on the North Sea, that part of the ocean between England and Europe, has a sea climate. The summers are mild but with a lot of rain when the wind comes from the west from the sea, spring and fall is beautiful, and winters are very raw. In general, however, the temperature in winter doesn't drop too far below the freezing point, and the snow was not more than five or six inches at the most at one time, but the icy cold winds filled with ice crystals played havoc with any unprotected part of the body. It was winter again and getting closer to St. Nicholas and Christmas. The raw, howling winds would whistle tunes in the chimney flute, and Eric, sitting on the heavy cast iron coal box beside the kitchen stove, could listen for hours while watching his mother preparing the evening meal.

"I noted that your carrot was still in your shoe this morning," said his mother without looking at him. "You know that is a reminder from St. Nicholas and Black Peter."

Eric was shocked. He didn't know that his mother noticed it, too, this morning. It took him by surprise, because he had woken up very early and sneaked down the stairway to see what had happened to his wooden shoes and his brother Johann's. A terrible feeling came over him when he discovered that the carrot was gone from Johann's shoes but was still in his. What had he done to deserve this? He was in disgrace with St. Nicholas, and that meant no presents on St. Nicholas Day. He didn't feel the cold in the kitchen but sat there in the kitchen chair, in deep thought, trying to find out what he did wrong.

Could it have been the incident with Kathy yesterday at the kindergarten? He had pulled a little too hard on her hair so that she'd started crying when he ran into her while playing with the other boys on the playground. These dumb girls were constantly in the way. They were only good for playing with dolls or playing house. But surely, they weren't rough enough to play with the boys. He was lucky enough that his parents had chosen him to be a boy. What would have happened if he were a girl? Just terrible!

Or was it that he had forgotten last night to bring the kindling inside the house and put it neatly underneath the kitchen stove for his mother to light the kitchen fire the next morning? It was his job, but he had been playing too long outside last night with the children, and when he came home, it was so late that his mother reprimanded him. He had been angry about that because he felt he really wasn't that late, but surely, he wouldn't go and get kindling for her now after she spoiled the happy mood he was in. She must have done it herself because he noticed the kindling underneath the stove.

This St. Nicholas certainly was a holy man if he knew all that had happened this quickly. Somehow, he had to set things right today with his mother and with Kathy. Otherwise, it was no use for him to put out his wooden shoes again tonight.

His thoughts were interrupted when he heard his mother coming down the steps. Quickly he took the carrot out of the wooden shoe and hid it in the garbage can. He couldn't let his mother know because she would ask questions about why the carrot was still in his shoe, and he was not in the mood to answer any of them this early in the morning.

When his mother entered the kitchen, she looked in surprise at Eric. "What are you doing up so early? You must be freezing down here in the kitchen."

"Well, I just woke up early this morning, and I couldn't sleep any longer," answered Eric.

"Come on, go upstairs and quickly put your clothes on before you catch a cold," she said while kindly pushing him out of the kitchen door in the direction of the stairway.

While Eric was gone, his mother noticed the missing carrot out of Eric's shoe, and a faint smile came onto her face. She knew her youngster. He would be worried all day, but he would try to make up for whatever he thought he did wrong.

That day, he pushed an apple into Kathy's hands, a real shining apple, because he had rubbed it for quite some time on his trousers. Kathy had a surprised look on her face, but Eric was gone already before she could ask a question.

He was really surprised to see the look on his mother's face when the carrot was gone out of the shoe that morning. How could she know? He was up before her, but then he had experienced in many situations that mothers seemed to know everything, and he didn't ask the question that was on the tip of his lips. Without saying a word, he got up and went to the stall, found a carton, and filled it up to the top with kindling. It was so heavy that when he finally reached the kitchen, he was out of breath.

"Here, Mother," he uttered. "This will surely be enough for two days."

"Eric, you shouldn't have," replied his mother. "That was too heavy for you." But then she picked her youngster up, hugged him, and kissed him on both cheeks. Somehow Eric knew at that time that his carrot would be gone the next morning.

Already more than a month before St. Nicholas Day, the sixth of December, the younger children were kept in line by the constant warning of their parents that they would tell St. Nicholas all about their bad deeds. Night after night, they had to place their wooden shoes filled with fresh straw, a carrot, some bread, and a piece of paper filled with their wants—if possible, in their own handwriting—as they awaited the arrival of St. Nicholas on a white horse and his helper, Black Pete.

The carrots and the straw in the wooden shoes were a gift for the horse. If the wooden shoes of some of the children in one family were emptied the next morning and some were not, that meant that Black Pete had come that night, gone down the chimney (hence the name Black Pete), and would deliver the message of the good, behaving children to the saint. But the untouched wooden shoes were a warning for their owners that a lot of catching up and good deeds had to be done.

The story of St. Nicholas was as follows: Some centuries ago, Nicholas, a bishop of Madrid, Spain, was walking one evening through his city and found the massacred bodies of a couple of children in a barrel. The bishop was so shocked by this cruel and bizarre scenery that he fell on his knees and prayed to the Lord to return life to these bodies. The Lord granted his wishes, and the children came to life again. This story, true or false, made this bishop a saint and was chosen in Holland as the saint for the children. St. Nicholas was dressed as a bishop. He had his staff, high pointed hat, and long white beard and mustache, and he sat on a white horse. Black Pete dressed in colorful clothing with short bulging pants and a cap on his head and a large plumb feather leading the horse. They made a trio that demanded respect even by the rowdiest of the youngsters.

Black Pete was a young man who had colored his face and hands black because of the lack of colored people at that time in the villages of southern Holland. Ringing a hand bell or rattling a chain, he drove many tiny tots into a tantrum or drove the wide-eyed, panic-stricken older ones behind their father or mother, holding on for life to their legs, when this trio passed through the village to the local school grounds a couple of days before St. Nicholas Day.

Seated on a golden throne in one of the classrooms, the friendly, smiling saint would welcome the children one after the other. The quiet ones could sit on his lap, but the screaming little ones, who by now were carried on their father's or mother's arm into the room, squeezing the daylights out of the already embarrassed parent, would only be patted by the white gloved hand of the saint, which drove their little bodies even further into life-saving jerks that many times completely closed the windpipes of the bulging-eyed parents trying to utter at least a few friendly words in apology. Quickly, Black Pete, who had a big gunny sack filled with candies, cookies, and little presents, would push a handful of these goodies into the hands of the parent. Trying to ease the situation, Black Pete would smile at the youngster, which most of the time ended up into the cliché of the event.

Seeing only the white of the eyes and teeth of the smiling Black Pete made the youngster scream at the top of his lungs and would hasten the embarrassed parents through a maze of anxious onlookers who still had to follow that same path. At the exit, the youngster, heaving for breath and losing his grip, would calm down.

The older children who could sit on the old man's lap were asked all kinds of questions, like "Do you help your parents?" "Are you good in school?" "Do you do your homework well?" and so on. Naturally, with innocent eyes keeping Black Pete in line of view and with hefty nodding of their heads, the children would answer, "Yes, Sainter Klaas [a short form of Saint Nicholas]" to all questions. In the child's mind, everything was going in the right direction, and they could expect some nice gifts, but most of the time, the parents would drive a spoke through the wheel by mentioning a couple of misbehaviors of the youngster. This information would make Black Pete angry. Rattling his heavy chain and rolling his eyes would cause the child to portray a deep sorrow or to defend this outrageous interference when everything was going so well.

Eric was in many such situations and discovered already at an early age that his mother was more likely to go along with his answers than his father. At times when his father had an afternoon shift and Eric was only accompanied by his mother, he would end up a winner.

A few years in a row, Eric noticed that a month or so before St. Nicholas Day, his small wheelbarrow was gone. But he received a beautiful new one (in a different color) as the main part of his presents. Some years later, he found out when a big paint chip broke off, how many colors of paint this wheelbarrow had received from his father during his early years. Christmas was always a day to remember, because Christmas and the days leading up to it were always very special to Eric.

On the day before Christmas, when his father sharpened the ax and put his heavy winter jacket on, Eric knew the time had come for him and his father to pick out a Christmas tree in the woods surrounding the village. Eric was kind of stocky in build, and he loved to work with his father, while Johann was slender in build and hated already at a very young age anything that had to do with manual labor.

Eric walked behind and tried hard to step in the same footsteps his father left behind in the soft snow to prevent the snow from entering his wooden shoes. With heavy knitted shawls around their necks and heads, the twosome made their way silently through the harsh cold, windy landscape. The silhouette of his father in front of him with the ax over one shoulder made Eric think of the story of the *Woodcutter in the Black Forest* his mother had read to the children on one of the longer winter evenings.

Sometimes his father asked if he could carry him, but Eric refused. He wanted to be just like him. Walking behind his father, trying to make the bigger steps, made him breathe heavily, his breath changing to steam just like he saw his fathers'.

Arriving in the woods, his father wiped the snow off a fallen tree, and together side by side, they took a rest from the long journey. Silently, they sat there listening to the eerie sounds of the wind through the trees, the cracking and rubbing of cork dry branches, followed by a tranquil stillness when the wind ebbed. Eric heard the sometimes backbone-shivering sounds, but sitting beside his father, he wasn't afraid and could feel the strength, closeness, and warmth of his father. Together, out of many, they chose the right tree, and with a couple of powerful cuts by his father's ax, the tree slowly moaned and groaned as if protesting. Finally subsiding, it fell into the snow. As always, it was a beautiful young tree, seven to eight feet tall. Eric stood there looking at the fallen youngster of the woods.

His love for nature made him sad. This young tree that had taken years to develop in this harsh climate didn't even have a chance to grow up like its neighboring huge masters of the woods. His father, knowing his son's feelings, interrupted his thoughts by telling him that it was good for these wild woods to be thinned out so that more sunlight would reach other young trees, who would then have a chance to become giants.

When Eric got cold, his father put him on his lap, opened his jacket, and let Eric nestle himself against the warm body of his father. While putting his arms around him, Eric noticed how rough and big his father's hands were. He also noticed that one of his fingers was quite crooked on the tip, and he questioned his father about it.

"Oh," his father replied, "that happened when I was a youngster like you. I got my finger stuck between the heavy doors of the church, but at that time, there was no money in the family for doctors, so my mother put a bandage around it, torn off from an old sheet, and that was it. I guess the finger must have been broken and grew together crooked. It never bothered me. Remember, Eric, in that time, we were really poor. Every penny counted, and there surely was no money to go to a doctor for just a finger."

His father tied a loop around the base of the tree and put Eric on it so that his wooden shoes could keep him in balance, while his father pulled the tree home.

On his way back, his father stopped a couple times to catch his breath from the heavy pulling and to wipe at the same time the drip off his nose with the top of his rough hands. Eric followed the same gesture as if he had pulled the tree. As they arrive home, the tree's bottom branches were removed and used all throughout the house behind pictures and wall plaques. The tree itself was planted in a big pail filled with wet sand and moved to the corner of the living room, where for generations his ancestors stood. Now it really was Christmas.

Within a few hours, the whole family filled the house with the Christmas spirit—shining decorations, small candles on the tree, white angel hair, silver paper strips, and the pine smell. Not only the rooms but also the people in it were filled with wonderful Christmas feelings.

The manger (made by his father from rough birch wood), the sheep and shepherds, the donkey, the ox, and the Holy Family all found their places under the tree. The three wise men were located a distance away from the manger and were moved every day a little closer until the thirteenth day after Christmas—the day, as the legend went, they arrived at the manger.

That same evening, the whole family gathered in front of the tree. As they sang Christmas songs, the candles were lit, while all the other lights were dimmed. The sparkling of candlelight into the youngsters' eyes and the glow on their faces made Christmas in these villages what it was supposed to be—peaceful. Eric was too young yet to go to midnight Mass, but he would stay awake in bed and listen to the village people passing by in subdued voices, walking in their wooden shoes through the snow. The bedroom was cold as only the coal stove in the kitchen and living room was used in the daytime, but Eric cuddled in the warm blankets and didn't feel this cold. It was Christmas, and with his young head still full of the happenings of the day, he fell into a deep, restful sleep. Christmas Day was not only a day to always a beautiful peaceful day for the villagers. It was a family day; the married sons and daughters would come home in the later afternoon to have a big family dinner.

Before the High Mass started at ten o'clock in the morning, Eric was already at the church so he could spend some time looking at the big manger in front of the church's altar. It was a big manger, nearly as big as a real stall. The Christ child the size of a real baby lay there in the straw with his arms spread and with a big smile on his face. Mary and Joseph were kneeling beside the child, and Mary, with beautiful rosy cheeks, had a smile on her face, which reminded Eric of the face of his own mother. Shepherds and sheep were all over the place, and the huge ox and donkey lay in the back of the manger, supposed to heat the child with their breath. At least that was what his mother told him. Eric noticed something strange about the ox, and after careful inspection, he came to the conclusion that a chip had come off the ox's head and it was missing one eye. Someone had painted the whole spot just black, but it looked quite odd to Eric, and he had to laugh at the whole situation.

All through the Mass, they were singing beautiful songs, and whenever Eric knew a song, he did his utmost to sing as hard as he could until one of the nuns who sat behind, watching the children, came over to him and, with a kind of subdued voice, demanded Eric to stop.

When they came home after the Mass, the radio was playing Christmas songs. His mother was preparing for the big Christmas dinner, Johann was reading a book beside the kitchen stove, and his father, sitting in the living room, was talking to one of the neighbors while sipping on a small glass of Dutch gin for Christmas cheer. All in all, it was a real Christmas Day, but for Eric, it was a very boring day. He couldn't even play that day with Nico, his best friend and neighboring boy, who only was a couple of months younger than Eric. Somewhere around the house was a picture showing the two of them in a baby carriage taken in a meadow. It was impossible for Eric to understand why he had to stay home all day.

Why couldn't he play with Nico, or why couldn't Nico come over to their place? He questioned his mother repeatedly.

"This day of all days, you stay home, and Nico stays home also. To stay home one day a year isn't too much to ask, is it?" his mother frowningly replied.

"Why don't you play a game with Johann?" his father called out from the living room. "That will keep you busy for a while."

"I'm reading!" Johann shouted back. "And I don't want to play with him anyhow."

This was all right with Eric because he was not too crazy about his older brother anyhow, and he knew that in no time, they would be in fights. So he just as well had to make the best of it that day.

In the winter, John had afternoon shift twice a month. Martha, after the children went to sleep, enjoyed the quiet evening sitting beside the warm kitchen stove, reading her history books, which she loved. In the evenings, she always wore slippers with a large "pom" on top. If she sat very still, a small mouse would come through a hole in the corner and nestle itself in one of the poms.

When she told Eric about this, he did not believe her. So she said, "Okay, Eric, this evening, instead of going early to bed, you can lie on the couch, but you have to be very still." After some time, very boring to Eric, a mouse came out of the hole. It was twitching its head nervously in all directions to make sure that the surroundings were safe. Then it nestled itself in one of the poms. Eric was amazed at the sight, and he watched it a for a while. The next thing he heard was his mother telling him to go to bed. He must have fallen asleep and had moved.

Martha told John about it. He was not particularly crazy about having mice in the house, and when after some time more mice visited the kitchen, he closed the hole with cement. That was the end of the visiting mouse.

CHAPTER 2

⊹

It was early May 1940. Eric woke up at the break of dawn. It was a crisp morning but promised to turn into a beautiful spring day. He lay there, daydreaming, while listening to his brother Johann's deep breathing beside him. He finally got up and opened the window and looked down at the street to the crossing of his and the Main Street. It was very peaceful, except for Willem's chicken rooster across the street, informing the neighborhood that he was awake. Eric was looking across the street, trying to find the rooster, when his right eye caught a movement at the crossing. When he turned his head, he saw a soldier in a strange green uniform crawling around the corner and, with his short automatic machine gun, looked up at the flat-roof house across from him.

At that time, he noticed Eric and very quickly pointed his gun in his direction. Eric had no idea what was happening and just waved at him. The soldier took a few seconds and then made a sign to someone to follow him. Soon two then three and then more followed around the corner. Eric watched for some time the passing of the soldiers until an eardrum-breaking racket from the very low flying German bombers made him jump back from the windowsill and run screaming into the upstairs hallway.

His mother rushed to him; grabbed him and his brother, Johann; and calmly but quickly helped them down the stairs. In the meantime, she tried calming them down while explaining that war had broken out. Eric was about six years old at the time, and the only airplane he had ever seen was a small two-decker high up in the sky. These big bombers must have scared the living daylights out of the whole district. Maybe this was the intention of the Germans, because except for a couple of shots fired and a few Dutch soldiers killed, the war—or better, the resistance of the Dutch forces in that part of the country—was over.

After the first wave of airplanes passed over the village, the sound changed to the noise of armored vehicles and thousands of boots of the marching German soldiers hitting the Main Street in the direction to the close by city. This marching went on for hours.

The children had quieted down by now, and after Martha made sure it was all right for them to go outside, Eric grabbed a quick sandwich and ran down the street and joined Nico and other children at the corner of the street to watch the soldiers marching by. He didn't know what war all was about, but for the children, it was exciting. They waved and saluted the soldiers, and some of them smiled and waved back. One of the soldiers pushed a small puppy, which must have been a couple of weeks old, into Eric's hands. He took it home and showed it to his mother. She immediately noticed that the puppy was covered with lice, so she washed him with warm soap and water. She dried him in a towel and gave him back to Eric. After some discussion with Nico, they called him Prince. This puppy grew up to a beautiful large shepherd and, besides Max, the horse, became Eric's closest friend in many adventures during the wartime years.

When marching subsided, an uneasy calmness came over the people. They clustered together, discussing this abrupt event. One family, thinking that the Germans would take all the food supplies, went with a big round washbasin to one of the village bakers and had it filled full of loaves of bread. This gesture exploded the villagers, and everyone rushed to the stores, buying everything they could lay their hands on, not realizing that the food would spoil without the availability of refrigerators or freezers at that time in the homes. The only cool place was a very humid basement with dirt floors, where potatoes and apples, besides preserves, were kept for the winter months. The result was that after a week or so, most of this food ended up in the garbage. However, this incident made the war a reality and was the start of a nearly five-year-long cruel World War II.

The Dutch Armed Forces, however small, fought bravely for five days against the overwhelming German forces. These few days gave England time for their defensive actions and allowed the Dutch queen and her family to escape to England. After a few days of fighting, the Germans demanded that the Dutch surrender. If Holland didn't surrender, they would bomb and flatten one city at a time. The German high command kept their word. They bombed Rotterdam flat, killing roughly thirty thousand people, and promised to come back the next day to give Amsterdam the same fate. Holland surrendered. Within weeks, a large part of Western Europe fell to the mighty German masters.

After Holland surrendered, the first item on their forever-growing list was the confiscation of all radios (TVs were not yet in existence). This was easy because in Holland, a radio was a luxury item, and consequently, everyone possessing a radio would pay taxes for it. It was only a small task for the Germans to obtain these lists. Everyone on this list was notified to deliver their radio to the nearest specified location.

Eric's father, noticing that the German soldiers didn't inspect these radios, dismantled the inner radio parts, tightened a rock in the inside chassis to give it some weight, and got his name off the list. He mounted his radio in an old couch in the kitchen, and all through the war years, it was never discovered. Many evenings after the children were in bed, some of the trusted neighbors supposedly played cards in the kitchen but were actually listening to Radio Orange, the voice of the Dutch queen in England. Also, coded messages were transferred back and forth from the Dutch resistance group.

Another proclamation forbade anyone from being on the roads after 8:00 p.m. Only people with special permits, like coal miners or anyone going to or coming back from their jobs at night, had to wear a yellow band on their left arm, permitting them on the roads. If caught, it meant automatic prison or, worse, being shot on the spot. Naturally, this was no problem for the inventive Dutch people. Holes were made in private hedges, and fences were torn down in their backyards, which made an effective network of new communication roads. Also, local resistance people used this network for a quick getaway during the many razzias held by the Germans. Many of the Dutch National Socialistic Party members collaborated with the Germans after the surrender of Holland and became the Dutch's most fierce enemies. They worked closely together with the German Gestapo (short for Secret State Police) and the well-known SS. Through this trash of Dutch people, thousands of fellow Dutchmen (Jews and resistance members alike) found their dead in one of the German concentration camps or were shot instantly.

The first few years of the war didn't change Eric's life at all. The world and its problems seemed to go over the heads of the village children. His first love was still the farm. Except for plowing the fields, which was done with a single blade plow pulled by Max and where a sturdy and strong hand was needed to guide the plow and the other hand for the reins, Eric was now a full-fledged farmhand. Feeding the animals and milking the cows in his free time was a chore, but he loved it.

Prince, now fully grown, followed him like a true friend wherever he went. Being a good German shepherd, he quickly learned to drive the cows together in the meadow when it was milking time. Generally, Prince was a good-hearted dog and could withstand some abuse from the children. Only on occasions when Eric got into trouble with another boy would Prince show his teeth and, with a deep growl, let the intruder know that he had gone far enough.

Eric loved the game of soccer and played it every time he had a chance between school and working at the farm. The only problem was that soccer shoes were practically impossible to get; only the teenagers who belonged to the local soccer team had real leather soccer shoes. The younger village boys would tie a rope around the wooden shoes and the ankle for playing soccer in the streets. Eric, who was tall for his age, most of the time took the position of goalie. Many times, his reactions had to be unbelievably fast when one of the attackers broke the string while kicking the ball with all the power available to him in Eric's direction. Both wooden shoe and ball arrived instantaneously.

Slowly and surely, the German SS and Gestapo closed in on the helpless Jewish race all over Europe. Holland, which had a large

Jewish population, realized too late how the German plan to terminate their hated Jews worked. With the utmost secrecy and precision, they went to work. All the governmental agencies down to the village elders were already replaced by Germans or German collaborators. Everyone above the age of eighteen was notified to go to their local city hall to update their civil records. Without suspicion, the Dutch people assisted the cruel Germans in the first step to massacre their own relatives, neighbors, and friends. Simple questions were asked, like name, age, occupation, religion, and religion of living and non-living relatives, parents, grandparents, etc. It was only a matter of time and elimination, and the Germans had a perfect record of everyone having only the slightest amount of Jewish blood.

Within a couple of months, everyone of Jewish blood, young and old, had to wear the yellow Star of David and was destined for destruction. It was now only a matter of time for the shrewd, devilish masterminds to close the net. They promised by relocation a promised land for the Jews. Beautiful films were shown about the settling of new Jewish communities in Poland where young and old worked together and had accommodations with flower gardens. This false advertising produced such a rush of Jewish people for their promised land that many of them sold all their belongings and paid outrageous prices on the supposedly black market for tickets on the special trains to their new and promising destinations.

Actually, for a while, only the well-to-do Jews could afford these prices. Only after thousands and thousands had freely left Holland and found instead of beauty the misery of the by-now well-known concentration camp or death in the forever-operating gas chambers did the Dutch people realize the monstrous games the Germans were playing. The shockwaves of this realization were felt by every Dutch citizen, and the hatred for everything that ever sounded German surpassed its borders. The peaceful and friendly Dutchmen had unknowingly sent part of its own people like lambs to the slaughter. Still, some Jewish families didn't believe these rumors, and for some time, the half-filled trains rolled over the border into Germany. This slow down action didn't agree with the German SS high command and soon the up-to-now-friendly actions were replaced by the most monstrous, cold-blooded, and beastly operations the world had seen in modern times.

A German SS command would close a whole city block, driving everyone, young and old, with bayonets and clubs to an open area. Everyone on their list being of Jewish blood were driven like cattle into waiting trucks and, from there, to the train stations. These actions, called razzias, were feared by the Dutch people to the end of the war because this was the beginning of some tactics to also capture people in the Dutch resistance. The hatred for these bloodthirsty Germans brought the brave Dutch people closer together and developed in Holland the cleverest and highly sophisticated resistance organization known. The resistance organization spread like wildfire through Holland and the rest of Europe and was the most feared organization the Germans had to contend with. Through these brave people with their vast network of communication, the lives of thousands of Dutchmen and, later, captured allies alike were saved. Also, it gave Holland new life and hope for its suffering people, and once again, Holland was strong.

Many Jewish children who were playing in other city blocks during these razzias escaped the hands of the Germans and were picked up by the friendly non-Jewish neighbors. Quickly and in an orderly manner, the resistance would take care of these children and relocate them into small border villages right under the noses of the SS border commands. The friendly and very brave villagers who took care of these children received false papers from the resistance movement. In most cases, the papers showed the children as orphans from their dead non-Jewish relatives of the bombing of Rotterdam. Eric's parents also received a Jewish child a couple of years younger than Eric. All through the rest of the war, Piet (his real name was David), who, for the children's sake was introduced as Eric's cousin from an uncle who had died, stayed with his family. Eric accepted him as a family member, but Piet, with his proper Dutch language (Eric's dialect was more German) and being very weak and sickly, didn't fit in with Eric's bloom of life.

However, when anyone was teasing or trying to start a fight with his cousin, he would step in between and receive his shared of cuts and bruises instead of his helpless new family member. Only after the war did Eric realize that Piet was not his cousin and that his real name was David. It was after the Dutch Red Cross had located relatives of the youngsters and reunited the many leftover families. For these down-to-earth folks like Eric's parents, all that they and hundreds of others had done was not considered bravery, just decency. The good and brave deeds of many Dutchmen during World War II was not praised in many books; nevertheless, this quiet bravery made Holland and its people outlast its most cruel enemies through the centuries.

Eric was around seven years old when one particular Easter Sunday, it all happened. Easter Sunday was one of the highest religious days in the Catholic Church in the southern part of Holland. All villagers went to church on that day—not only for religious reason, but more so to show off their new outfits. This high Sunday falls in early spring and the once-a-year time for new clothing. The young ladies would show off their colorful new spring dresses, and the young men walked like peacocks in their new suits with new shirts and ties, not able to turn their heads from the starch-stiffened collars on their shirts.

On this day, a very religious family like Eric's would send their children three times to church—the seven o'clock early Mass to go to communion, the ten o'clock High Mass, and the three o'clock afternoon Vespers. Eric didn't mind the early Mass because, after all, he had the day before gone to confession and stood in line for more than an hour between all those people gliding a rosary through their fingers before he could confess his sins. While standing there, he had figured out that it was impossible for some of these elderly ladies to pray Holy Mary or Our Father as fast as they moved the rosary between their hands. He had tried it. At his fastest way of praying, they had moved already to the next bead before he was halfway through the Holy Mary. He guessed that they were only showing off but in the meantime were trying to figure out what sins Peter Van Der Bink or Marie Van't Aaltje had committed.

This early morning Mass was worthwhile because he could go to communion. Sticking his tongue out as far as possible to Mr.

Pastor gave him a good feeling because he still had a grudge for him since the squeezing-hand incident. While giving the host, Mr. Pastor never noticed Eric's real intent. It surely was not the host.

After the first Mass, Nico, Eric's friend, was waiting for him outside the church, and together they walked in the direction of home, discussing the unfairness of the parents sending the children three times on one day to church. They should know better. Kneeling on hard wooden benches a couple of inches off the floor until their knees had no feeling anymore or standing straight, shifting their weight from one leg to another, unable to talk or even whisper to the boy beside them because of the watching eyes and ultrasharp ears of the schoolmaster behind the children's benches, was too much for every healthy young boy.

If the schoolmaster caught them whispering to their neighbor or trying to exchange some marbles, he would walk between the benches toward them, passing the other children with a scared look on their faces of "Not me! It wasn't me!" Their heart would stop beating when he stopped behind them, and with a demanding but whispering voice, he would tell them to keep quiet—in the mean-time, punishing them by pinching their arms black and blue. They wouldn't dare to give a sound, scared that the punishment would be worse. The worst punishment would be that they were pulled, with a lot of noise, out of the bench and had to sit all alone in front of the whole church on the always cold white marble communion bench. The shame was unbearable, and it was followed automatically by further punishment on the next school day.

Eric and Nico had made their decision. They would play hooky during the ten o'clock High Mass. Coming home that morning, he saw his mother and father setting the breakfast table with the best plates and cups and a white tablecloth. Today, Easter Sunday, would normally be the day of finding colored eggs outside in their yard, but it was wartime, and eggs were nearly impossible to get. Still his father had managed to get two eggs the day before on the farm where he had helped out after work. The smell of the two eggs mixed with a lot of milk to fill the bottom of the frying pans at the kitchen stove, combined with the brewing of some real coffee saved for this special day, and the early morning sun reflecting on the white breakfast plates made this morning, Easter Sunday, the promise of a beautiful day.

After breakfast, Nico walked in with an extra loud "Happy Easter, everyone!" He knew that at least he would receive a handful of candy eggs out of the filled glass bowl on the living room table for such happy greetings. Normally, on a day like today, the big church bell would carpet the village and neighboring fields with its beautiful heavy sound, announcing the High Mass. Today, however, this familiar sound was exchanged with the silver sound of a tiny bell. Erick and Nico found the exchange amusing but quickly were stopped in their laughter when Eric's mother sadly explained that the Germans in the last couple of weeks had removed all the big bells of the churches in Holland to be melted down for ammunition.

With the sturdy warning of "You two behave yourselves," the two left for church, both kind of nervous on how to play hooky without being noticed by the villagers who were quietly talking as they walked in the same direction. The nervous tension overwhelmed both boys when they noticed Eric's father and Johann were catching up behind them. Something had to be done fast. Across the church was Jansen's farm with an extended old wall on one side of the farmhouse. The street between the church and this farmhouse by now was filled with the villagers wishing one another "Happy Easter!" Slowly but surely, Eric moved in the direction of that wall, and Nico followed his footsteps. Without daring to look if anyone noticed them, they quickly stepped behind the wall. They stood there breathless and heavily perspiring, waiting for the moment when Eric's father or, for that matter, any villager, would discover their plan. They stood there behind the wall, looking at each other, too nervous to talk and wondering if it was all worth it.

The sound of the wooden shoes on the street and the talking of the villagers slowly ebbed down and was replaced with the soft music of the organ in the church being transmitted through the big stained-glass windows. The two could breathe a little easier, and they waited another five or ten minutes more so as not to run the chance of still being detected by the latecomers. When everything seemed safe, both came out of their hiding place, jubilant over their success, but still with kind of a heavy heart. The covered hall across the front of the church was filled with wooden shoes, neatly arranged side by side, large and small, painted ones and older ones freshly scrubbed for the day. It was not that wooden shoes were not allowed in the church, but a couple hundred people walking on a marble hallway, trying to get to their seats on wooden floors, would probably tear the paint off the vibrating walls.

Today, both boys seemed to be tuned in to each other. While both were looking at this vast array of wooden shoes, Nico brought up a brilliant idea. "What about we mix up all the shoes?" It would probably be fun to watch all these people coming out of church and not finding their shoes. Eric agreed, and within a few minutes, the deed was done. Still full of excitement, both ran into the woods and found themselves an open spot to grasp the warm spring sun. Still puffing of all the happenings, they lay down in the fresh new grass and filled their lungs with the overwhelming smell of the pine trees.

When the arms of the church tower clock moved closer to eleven o'clock, they got up and slowly walked back to something they didn't expect at all. The noise of the air filled with furious shouts stopped the boys in their tracks. With their hearts bouncing in their throats, they walked on, too nervous to talk to each other. Coming by the church, they witnessed a mass of shouting, pushing, and crawling people. Some developed into fist fights that would upset the normal peaceful village for weeks to come. Words passed between friendly families that harmed their relationship forever. The boys were shocked. The grounds normally used before church for friendly meetings and Easter well-wishing had changed into a battleground the village would never forget. The fury went on for hours. Some of the older more aggressive villagers walked home in their socks, cursing and promising that if they ever got their hands on these bandits who played such a dirty trick and that on Easter Sunday, they would pull their limbs from their bodies. Mr. Pastor, who had tried to calm the people down, fell over a couple of fighting youngsters and lost his glasses in the mess. Shouting and pushing, he finally found them. His classic, pinch-on-the-nose, expensive glasses had lost their usefulness.

An hour before the afternoon Vespers, the village announcer stopping at different points in the village while ringing his loud handbell, declared the cancellation of the Vespers for this day. This was a smart move from Mr. Pastor. In the following week, a meeting was held by the village elders, and it was unanimously decided that this could not have been done by the youngers of this village. A grave letter was sent to the elders of the neighboring village a couple of miles down the road, which raised the sometimes-hostile tension between these two villages to its limits. Eric and Nico, realizing the enormous impact of their deed, made a lifetime commitment to each other to never let anyone know that they had committed this deed, which is still branded in the village's history.

Eric's village mainly consisted of farmers and coal miners. The shortness of food supplies in the northern part of Holland was not felt by these southern villages. The winter of 1942–1943 was one of the coldest winters Holland had witnessed for years, and many Dutchmen living in the northern cities were left without food and coal to heat their houses. Thousands died from starvation or froze to death. Whole families left the cities on foot or by bicycle on their long journeys to the farm districts of the south with nothing but the clothes on their bodies. Only the strongest reached the south; many died a lonely and cold death along the many roads.

The first groups to arrive received shelter, food, and clothing from the helpful southerners, but when the stream of starving people kept flooding the south, there was nothing left to give. The farmers were on rations themselves, because the German inspectors would only leave the farmers enough of their produce to feed their own families; the rest was carried off for the German forces. Still, most of the farmers were able to hide some of their produce and, in the cover of night, would freely assist the remaining villagers or anyone who needed food. Some farmers, however, were not that kind and robbed many hungry countrymen of their last possessions—not so much their own neighbors, but more so the starving northerner who would give anything, even their wedding rings, for a loaf of bread. These farmers became very wealthy during that time, but most of them were punished for their deeds after the war. Most of the villagers, however, had their own garden for fresh vegetables, and they assisted the farmers during the harvest; instead of money, they received rye and wheat for their labor.

Eric's father was a good provider for his family, and all through the war years, they had no shortness of the basic foods. Everything was rationed by the Germans, but these rations were too small to live on and were getting smaller and smaller when the war lingered on. Eric's father had at least an acre of land already before the war, and he converted it into a very high-producing vegetable garden. Leftovers and scraps from the kitchen and horse and cow manure scraped from the roads and garden leftovers were thrown into a pit and, when decayed, were used as fertilizer to be mixed by shovel into the garden again. Eric, who had a stronger build than his older brother, Johann, spent many evenings and weekends helping his father in his garden. It was hard work for a youngster of his age, and he preferred working at Willem's farm more than this gardening, but working together with his father, whose strength and endurance he admired, had its privileges. Many times, his father gave him some extra pocket money on Sundays.

Meat, like beef and pork, was practically nonexistent, but Eric's father raised a whole stall full of rabbits, and his mother would prepare them in many different ways. Also, he would exchange his tobacco and liquor rations for rye or wheat at the farms and then milled it by a hand-operated grinder in the stall behind the house. A twenty-five-pound bag of rye would take hours to mill, and turning the handle of the grinder would lame Eric's arms.

Also, the thick cream of the fresh milk received from Willem's farm, when left overnight, was gathered for a week and then poured in a big ceramic jar. A plunger that extended through a hole in the cover of the jar was moved up and down by hand until the butterfat separated into butter. This butter, a bit sour tasting, on a slice of still-warm fresh white bread baked in his mother's kitchen oven, was a real delicacy. Rye was burned in a dry frying pan on top of the stove whose smoke made the eyes tear and was used as a coffee substitute. Coffee beans were impossible to get. The same way, the petals of the tulips were prepared as a tea substitute.

One day John and Willem, the farmer, butchered a small pig the German inspector had overlooked in the stall behind John's house. Willem had tied the pig's legs together and used another piece of rope around its mouth. Late in the evening, when it was already dark, he had carried the pig across the road to Eric's place. Willem's family was too afraid of the Germans, and they didn't want anything considered illegal to happen on their property. Everything went as planned. The pig was lying on a table in the stall. Willem would cut the pig's throat with a butcher knife, and John stood ready with a pan to catch the blood that later would be prepared into blood sausage, a delicacy in Holland. However, at the moment the knife entered the pig's throat, the pig jerked, and the rope around its mouth came loose. It started to scream like a "stepped pig." The animal couldn't have done a better job to alarm the Germans. Grinding rye and butchering pigs without a permit meant automatic jail sentences. This screaming must have been heard all over the village. The jerking motions of the pig covered both men with its blood. The shock of being discovered by the Germans paralyzed them for a moment until Willem made a slash at the pig's throat with such force that he nearly cut its head off. The screaming stopped, and quickly they turned off the light. There they stood waiting for the inevitable, too scared to talk or to breathe. In the dark, they heard the blood flowing from the table onto the floor and felt the last life jerks from the pig. At any moment, they expected the Germans to rush into the stall and take them prisoner. For a long time, they stood there, heavily perspiring and listening to every sound in the neighborhood, but nothing happened. With a sigh of relief and still heavily breathing, they continued to butcher the by-now-lifeless pig. This was the first and the last time Eric's dad butchered a pig in his stall during the war.

After WWI, Germany had paid off huge war debts to many countries and was broke. Nearly 50 percent of the population had no jobs, and a large number of workers were involved with the communist union. All this was the reason that a person like Adolph Hitler, by promising a radical change for all of Germany, became their new leader. When Hitler started as führer (leader), he made many changes in Germany, all for the better at that time. He provided jobs, and the unemployment rate dropped. Germany, who was in a great depression, saw a bright future again. However, one large part of the population was Jewish. The Jews were the bankers, businesspeople, etc., and they controlled most of the wealth Hitler needed to reach his dream of a united Europe (the Third Reich). With his two companions, Goring and Himmler, the day was set for the barbaric destruction of the Jewish population.

It should be mentioned, however, that not all Germans were barbaric and mean. It was only these special groups—the Gestapo, some sections of the SS, and the NSB (Dutchmen who collaborated with the German). This last group was most feared because it could be anyone, even your own neighbor. Most of the regular German forces consisted of men who were forced to join and came from all ranks of life, from city dwellers to farm boys, and they hated these special forces. Some of the agricultural inspectors, most of them farmers themselves in their homeland, were reasonable people, and when handled fairly, they would many times knowingly miscalculate the produce to the farmer's advantage. If some of the farmers, after several warnings, still tried to make a fool out of an inspector, they took drastic steps, and the punishments were harsh. It was the greediness of some of the farmers who made it harder and harder for the other farmers to assist their neighbors when the war lingered on.

The German dictators were cruel in many ways, but they also changed many things in Europe for the better. Particularly, changes were made for the workmen and the younger generation. For the labor force, anyone who worked overtime got extra pay, and if Sunday work was involved, they got also extra rations of food, cigarettes, and a small bottle of gin. Also, the Germans believed that after they won the war and changed all of Europe into one Germanic master race, their hopes of success lay in the younger generation. Most of the Dutch people are of the German race, so the younger generation had to be strengthened not only mentally but also physically. For the first time, weekly sports and gymnastics were introduced in the curriculum of the schooling system. Also, vitamin C or oranges were supplied to the schools in wintertime and once a week were given to the children.

Also, youth groups were organized, like the Hitler Jugent (Hitlers Youth) for boys and girls in the ages from ten to sixteen years old. The uniforms of the boys consisted of white shirts, black tie, and black short pants; the girls were similarly dressed, except with a black skirt. All carried armbands with a swastika, the symbol of Nazism, imprinted on it. The groups were organized like the Boy Scouts and had summer camps, where the basics of Nazism were taught. When they marched through the cities and villages, they sang beautiful German songs that made many youngsters envy them. Eric also wanted to join this group, because the uniforms, the singing, and the marching were to his liking. His parents, however, knew the real reason of the German minds and wouldn't hear of it. At that time, Eric couldn't follow their reasoning and didn't agree at all with their decisions, but then he was too young to understand and saw only the fun part of this German master plan.

One day the Germans advertised that Adolph Hitler would drive through a close-by town the following Saturday on his way back to Germany. All people were requested to cover all sidewalks. Eric and Nico went to the marketplace to see this Hitler. All side-walks were full of people, but both had no problem pushing their way to the front. In front of the people, on both sides of the road, were SS soldiers keeping the road clear. After about one hour, a large amount of motorcycles, followed by several cars, went by. In one of the cars was a rather small man dressed in yellowish brown uni-form, flat hat, and small mustache. Hitler stood with his right arm stretched sideways, saluting the crowd, who were supposed to give the same greeting back to him while shouting "Heil Hitler [Haile to Hitler]!" It took only a minute for him to pass, and both boys did not know what all the fuss was about.

Within a few years, most items and materials that could be used in the war were not available anymore. One of the first on the list were bicycle tires. Bicycles were the only form of transportation for most people. They would use old rubber hoses, which sounded like flip-flops because the ends were tied together with heavy staples, or they rode on bare rims, which made a hell of a noise. Nevertheless, it was transportation.

Of all the villagers who sat on the stoop at the corner of Eric's street in the evenings, one person was always the loudest and most talkative of the group. His name was Tom VanDer Wal, a farmer in his midfifties and strong as a horse. Tom always knew and could do everything better than anyone. It made many people angry. One time when he left after showing off again, the remaining men decided that they would teach him a lesson.

After discussing many different options, they decided on a bicycle race without tires around the village. They knew that normally he would win, but one thing Tom did not remember was that one of the villagers, Piet Vlodrop, had an identical twin brother, Alex, living about seventy miles away in another village. Both brothers had not been in contact with each other since early childhood; nobody knew about this. The next Saturday, Piet and another villager went by train to visit Alex, asking him if he would go along with the joke on bigmouth Tom. After listening to the two men, Alex decided to do it.

The plan went as planned.

One Saturday, in a few weeks, the race would be on, and all the racers would ride two times around the village. The first prize would be one hundred guldens; second, fifty; and the third, twenty-five.

This event was highly advertised by the village announcer, who, after ringing his big handbell about every one hundred yards, shouted the latest news. Naturally, this race would be quite an event, and when the day arrived, most of the villagers watched this spectacle. It was a beautiful summer day, and at 2:00 p.m., approximately twenty-five men arrived at the start line in front of the church.

One man shouted, "Get ready… Go!" And they took off.

Already since the announcement, Tom had shouted and proclaimed that he would be the winner. It would be a cinch. He quickly paddled to the front because he knew that at the first corner, some people would slip into one another. After the first round, Tom was ahead, as everyone expected. There were about ten riders left. The remaining fell around the corners or gave up.

Piet had started also, but halfway through the second round, he was far behind and drove into an open barn door, as planned. One man standing at the last corner would give his brother, Alex, a sign to get on his bicycle as soon as the racers came around the third corner. Alex was dressed identically as Piet. When Tom made the last corner, short of winning, he saw that "Piet Vlodrop" was in front of him.

Unbelievable! How could that have happened? he thought.

Perspiring very heavily and with his last power, Tom tried to beat Piet, but he finally lost by one bicycle length. He was so upset that he didn't even wait for his fifty guldens for the second prize winner and drove straight home. This was such a disgrace for him that he didn't join people at the stoop for several weeks. When he finally showed up, he was a changed man, and some of the organizers felt really sorry for him. But they decided not to tell him until many years later.

Eric, standing on the finish line, was also very surprised that Piet had won the race. He also didn't know what had really happened until some weeks later, when he overheard the whispering of some of the men.

By now, the Americans had entered the war and from their English bases, many night, the heavy bombers would fly over Holland to flatten cities in Germany. When the sirens blasted waves of back-chilling sounds over the village, everyone ran for cover to their basements. Eric's basement was very strongly built with steel beams in the ceilings, and every time the siren went off, Willem, his two sisters, and his father (Willem's mother had been dead for several years) would come over to hide out in the basement until the danger passed.

The basement had a stuffy, humid smell. It had a dirt floor, and besides the racks full of preserves, which his mother had made (some of them were years old), half of the basement was covered with potatoes and apples. Also, a big clay jar filled with brewing sauerkraut stood in a corner. This gave the air a sour smell.

Most of the time, it lasted an hour or so before the siren would blast again to deliver the message the danger had passed. But once in a while, the bombing came very close. Some of the German cities bombed were within forty-five kilometers or about thirty miles from Eric's village. The vibration of the heavy bombing made the jar of preserves shudder, and the thundering noise of the explosions made everyone plug their ears with their fingers. On most of these particularly dangerous nights, his father was not present, as he was working afternoon and evening shifts. But then Eric sat beside Willem on the wooden bench against the wall. Every time a heavy explosion occurred, Willem, who had his arm around Eric, would pull him closer against his body as if to protect him. Eric felt these automatic muscle spasms in Willem's arm and felt safe.

In the middle of the bombing, amidst the crying of the females and the loud praying of everyone involved, Johann's nervous bladder always gave way, and quickly he interrupted the whole shebang by standing there, jumping from one foot to the other, asking everyone gathered to find an empty jar or can for him to relieve himself of his agony. Paul, Eric's younger brother, was at that time only a few years old, and he sat most of the time on Martha's lap, not knowing of the dangers involved. He would yell at every explosion "Boom!" while looking as if he had discovered something new.

One evening, however, when the sirens again blasted the surroundings and Martha and her three sons were already in the basement, Willem opened the basement door and shouted, "Martha, come up and take a look! The whole neighborhood is lit up, and it looks like daylight. Look, these airplanes are throwing out white lighted balls on parachutes." This produced such a light that the whole neighborhood changed from darkness to nearly daylight. Within minutes, all hell broke loose. It rained bombs, and the earth shook so violently as if the world was going to end, nearly destroying all civilization. Crawling and falling over one another, they made it back into the supposedly safe basement. The constant eerie whistling of the bombs followed by tremendous explosions, which shattered and broke the jars of preserves, dumping their contents all over the floor, made this panic-stricken group of people scrunch so closely together, waiting for the inevitable. For the first time, Eric felt the seriousness of their situation and expected at any moment the final explosion. Even Eric's little brother, Paul, held tight on his mother's lap, felt and saw the panic. He scrunched himself so closely to Martha's body that later she witnessed pinch marks of his tiny hands all over herself.

Wave after wave of bombers came over, dropping their bombs. After about twenty minutes to a half hour, which seemed like an eternity, a stillness unequalled came over the area, and it was as if the earth was holding its breath for a last onslaught. Everyone sat there, not yet believing that as if by some miracle, they were safe. Only the candlelight was playing games with the shadows on the wall. The shock of stillness was broken when the door of the basement swung open, and John came stumbling down the steps. His whole body was shaking. He fell into Martha's arms and then collapsed onto his knees on the basement floor. His clothes had been torn to shreds, and he was bleeding all over his body. Cuts on his face and a deep gash on the side of his head had transformed his whole head into a bloody mess.

"Thank God you're all safe," he uttered, still out of breath. This incident broke the tension, and now everyone realized the bombing had stopped.

"My god, John, what happened? Are you badly injured?" Martha cried and, with Willem's help, pulled John to his feet.

"No, I think there are only cuts and bruises of the many times I fell down on the way home. They were bombing the coal mine. I had a feeling of what was going to happen when the whole area was lit up. I immediately left my job, jumped on my bicycle, and tried to make it home, but I guess I was too late. The bombs were falling all around me, and the shockwaves of the explosions threw me many times off the bicycle, besides falling over the residue of exploded houses. All around me, the buildings were on fire, and many times, I ran, fell, and got up again, carrying the bicycle when it was impossible to ride. It was hell, and I didn't believe I would make it home, but I had to. Somehow I had to."

When finally the siren signaled that the danger had passed, they came out of the basement and witnessed the red sky of the burning houses and buildings close by. Except for two barns and one elderly farmer killed, his village had miraculously escaped destruction. The villages around the mine were all aflame. Hundreds and hundreds of people were killed, and many parts of the surrounding villages were completely wiped out. It could have been a real disaster if some of the bombs had hit the main shafts of the coal mine. It would have trapped thousands of coal miners still working underground. It still took them nearly twenty-four hours before enough emergency repairs were made on top of the mine to get the lifts in operation again and bring the miners to safety and into the arms of their crying loved ones.

Not until years later after the war did the Dutch government finally get the answer to this bombing from the American government. It had just been a mistake. Instead of bombing the German coal mines on the other side of the border, they had bombed the Dutch coal mine.

Nearly every evening, Eric would help Willem by milking cows and feeding all the animals, including his best friend, Max, the horse. After the work was done, they would sit together in a stall on a large wooden feedbox, talking about the happenings of the day.

One evening in July 1943, Willem said, "Eric, you better go home. It is already dark outside, and you know that the Germans are very tough when you are still on the street after dark."

Eric looked around and answered, "Our house is only fifteen feet from yours."

"Yes," Willem answered, "but the Germans are very careful because of all the resistance movements are at nighttime."

Eric left and after saying "Good night." He started crossing the street. Everything was dark because all the windows had to be covered with black paper. He thought that he heard someone shouting, but it didn't register. At once, he saw a flash of light, heard a sharp sound, and felt a tremendous hit like a sledgehammer against his top right leg. The impact made him fall on the street. It was a very sharp pain, but quickly it changed into numbness. He tried to get up but couldn't. When he touched his leg, he felt warm blood. He screamed for his dad. John, who was home, heard the shot and Eric's screams. He ran into the street, grabbed his arm, and pulled him through the porch to safety. The Germans had shot twice at him but missed. Once inside the safety of the porch, John carried his son to the kitchen and laid him down on the couch.

He pulled down Eric's blood-soaked trousers. "You know that you've been shot. You should have come home earlier. I will bandage it, but we cannot go to the hospital until tomorrow morning."

Eric had a very painful and restless night. Early the next morning, Willem covered the horse-drawn wagon with straw, which would soften the bouncing of the wagon, which had two big wooden wheels and no springs. After they arrived at the hospital, he was laid down on a stretcher in the hallway. He had to wait because during that same night, a town just over the border had been bombed and many were wounded, soldiers and civilians alike. These people were divided over several hospitals in the area. After several hours, two medical assistants carried Eric to one of the operating rooms. They wanted to stop Eric's father from entering this room, but John did not want to hear of it, and he forced himself into the room.

The doctors looked very tired and had blood all over their uniforms. One doctor, seeing John's determination, told him to take a seat in the corner. When they removed Eric's bandage, they noticed that the bullet had also broken the thigh bone. One doctor looked carefully at the wound and said, "We have to remove that leg. An infection has entered it."

When John heard this, he immediately jumped up and said "No, you do not take his leg off!"

"It can turn into gangrene, and then his life will be in danger," answered the other doctor.

"How much time does he have before you have to remove his leg?" John asked. He would give his son every chance available.

Being very tired, the doctor shook his head and said, "Okay, it is now noon. We will remove the bullet, set the leg, and wait until midnight. If the color of his leg has changed for the worse, we will have to remove it from just above the wound."

"Let's give him that chance," John replied.

The last Eric remembered was that they put a mask over his face. He woke up several hours later and was in bed in a small room, with John sitting beside him. They had put some splint on his leg and some removable bandages over his wound.

Every time a nurse or doctor walked by, he heard his father say, "Come and look. The color is changing for the better." But all answered that he had to wait until midnight.

Finally, shortly after midnight, a doctor walked in and slowly removed the bandage. Eric's father, by now tired and very nervous, kept saying "See? It looks a lot better."

The doctor carefully inspected the wound. "I have to agree with you," the doctor answered. "It does look better. I think that the danger is gone. You better go home and have some sleep. You deserve it. The nurses will take over from here. I, too, will go home because all the wounded people kept us busy for nearly twenty-four hours straight."

John kissed his son on his forehead and said, "We did it, son. We did it. I will see you later." Then he left. He had not only saved his son's leg but also his future.

Willem and Nico visited him many times, and Nico mentioned, "Amazing what some people will do to get noticed."

After eight days in the hospital, Eric left by taxi with John and Willem. He still had to use crutches for a while, but his healthy body made him run around in no time.

Wednesday and Saturday were Eric's best days, because there was only a couple of hours of school in the morning. These two afternoons he was free and could enjoy everything this beautiful environment had to offer. Most of the time, at these mornings, the teacher would read for an hour to the children. The stories Eric was most interested in were adventure stories. Peary and the North Pole and Amundsen with his South Pole expeditions filled him with excitement and drove his adventurous and searching mind to its limits.

In November 1943, the German anti-aircraft guns shot down an American airplane. It fell like a fireball out of the sky and exploded over the border into Germany. The next day, the teacher read about Amundsen and the South Pole. At twelve o'clock, he dismissed the classes and let them go home. Eric and Nico, with their minds full of their new hero, Amundsen, made a quick decision. They would discover their own South Pole that afternoon.

Eric's father had made him from electrical pipes a big heavy sled. With Prince, Eric's dog, pulling the sled and choosing one of the soft-flowing hills around the village as the "South Pole," the afternoon was set. After their noon meal and a change of clothing, the two adventurers ingeniously put a harness of ropes and old belts together so Prince could pull the sled. It took them a while and some harsh words before he finally subsided to this unusual form of playing. After a couple of mistrials, wherein Prince got completely tangled in the ropes, they decided that Nico would lead the dog by pulling on his leash, while Eric would help by pushing the sled. Running down the street in the direction of the fields, they passed several German soldiers, who laughed at this unusual trio. Reaching the fields, they paused for a moment to give Prince and themselves a chance to catch their breath and to make their base camp like Amundsen had done. A couple of clumps of frozen clay with a stick standing up in the middle made a perfect camp and a direction finder for their return trip.

The latest snow had serenely carpeted the fields. The sky was clouded, and the gusting wind drove the loose snow-like waves over the frozen land. The boys didn't feel the cold. This was the most perfect weather for their imagination, precisely the harsh weather Amundsen had to withstand to reach his goal. The hill that was chosen for the South Pole was barely visible. The boys, knowing the area like the back of their hands, struggled against this blinding wind to their path of glory. The sled was gliding easily over the hard-blown snow, and Prince, who finally got used to the idea, transformed into a true sled dog.

Suddenly, Nico stopped and showed Eric something strange to the right in front of them. It was a bundle of white cloth slightly covered with snow. A heavy insulated boot of a man protruded, lifeless, from the bundle. For a moment, they stood there breathing heavily from this unexpected scary sight. After some doing of untangling wires and cloth, they came to the conclusion that it was an American pilot lying under his parachute. He was still alive but unconscious. His right leg was strangely lying underneath him. They quickly discovered that the top of one leg was broken. Part of the thigh bone had ripped his heavy pants and covered it with dark coagulated blood. There they stood, staring at this man who came from faraway, lying there helplessly. Amundsen and the South Pole were forgotten. The pilot was dressed in a heavy leather jacket, pants, and insulated boots. Part of the parachute was still connected to him; it had covered and protected him from the wind and the cold.

"What are you going to do with him?" Nico asked. "We just can't let him lie here to die!"

"Well, what do you think we should do?" replied Eric. "If we tell the Germans, they will take him to prison or maybe shoot him."

Both decided not to hand him over to the Germans.

By now, they knew all about the resistance movement, and somehow, they would get ahold of them... But how? After some discussion, they found the answer. They would bring him to the nuns' convent in the village. Sister Theresa was there; she was the only trained nurse in the village. She would help him and surely would not tell the Germans because that would be sinning and a nun could not sin. They had to work fast. This pilot must have been from that bomber that had crashed on the other side of the border. The poor man must have been lying there all night long. They decided that Eric would take the sled and go back to the village to get his friend Willem and together they would tie the big wooden feedbox, which stood in the cow stall, to the sled. Nico would keep Prince and watch the pilot from a distance so that if someone would see him, he wouldn't give away the location of their American hero.

Arriving at the farm, Eric came to the shocking conclusion that Willem had left for the city. Eric's father had also left already for his afternoon shift. There was no one else he could trust. Somehow, they had to do it by themselves. With some rope, he tied the box to the sled and went on his way back to the fields. Perspiring heavily, he began to realize the grave danger this mission could develop into if they were caught. He knew the rudeness of the German Gestapo. Torturing, concentration camp, being shot—these were words he heard daily during that time and not at all strange to Eric. Not only himself and Nico but his parents, the sisters, all of them—he was putting them in danger.

He stopped for a moment. The scared, squeezing feeling in his chest made breathing difficult. It was so easy to tell the Germans of their discovery, and it would be all over with. No one would find out, and even if they did, no one would blame them because they were only children. For a moment, he was panic-stricken, but then the peaceful face of the American made his decision final. Everywhere the rumors went that soon the Americans would come and once again free Holland from these unwelcome invaders. He really didn't know what freedom meant. For half of his young life, there had been war. How would it be—no more bombings, no more shouting commands on the streets? And how would a big bell in the church tower sound through the village if they would ever get one again?

For Eric, this American was the first real person with a message that peace once again would come. He calmed down a little bit and went on. No, he would not give up that easily. If he could help it, he would save this hero, maybe even save his life. Arriving at the scene, he found Nico practically frozen. Standing in this cold wind, his face and lips had turned purple. Prince barked a couple of times, happy to see his master, but he got awarded with a quick slap on his head, which stopped him in his tracks. This stupid dog could give them away.

Hastily they went to work now. It took them quite some time to get all these belts and small cables connected to the parachute off the wounded man. Neither one was afraid of a wounded person. By now, they had witnessed many wounded soldiers and civilians during the bombing periods. The wind caught hold of the parachute and bulged it out. The two had a hard time bundling it up and burying it in a close-by ditch and covering it with snow. Pulling the sled and box over to its side, they now carefully pushed and rolled the pilot into the box.

Pulling and pushing the box and sled up was another matter. It took all their power and energy to finally get it up straight. The wounded man moaned a little bit when the box and sled fell into position. He lay in an awkward position, and the wound on his leg opened up again. Eric took the front, and Nico pushed. Prince was jumping and running in all directions, happy of his freedom and knowing that the direction was home. Once in a while, they stopped, gasping for air, and gave their exhausted bodies a rest. The wound, still bleeding, was dripping into the white snow. While pushing the sled, Nico watched faithfully and ground each drop into the snow with his foot.

Coming closer to the villages, they noticed that the street where the nun's convent was located had filled up with German SS trucks and soldiers. Panic-stricken they knew this was the end. They would never be able to pass these soldiers without being detected. To protect themselves, the only thing to do was deliver their hero to the Germans. All their efforts had been for nothing. Now feeling exhausted by this unexpected let-down, they carried on, pulling and pushing the sled, now heavy as if it were filled with lead.

Suddenly, while passing a sugar beet pile, Eric stopped. A brilliant idea had flashed into his mind. In the late fall, the farmers would pile up sugar beets in the fields and cover them with straw and then dirt to make a natural protection for the winter feed for their cattle. The dirt would freeze, but the beets protected with this heavy layer of straw stayed fresh. In the winter, the farmer would open one end, and after he loaded his farm wagon, he would close off the opening with straw.

"Why don't we cover the pilot with beets and leaves? And if a German stops us, we tell him that we're bringing beets to the poor nuns?" Eric said to Nico while out of breath.

For a moment, they thought it over. Reserve energy, which young people were rich of, streamed through their bodies, and in no time, the box was partly filled with beets and leaves, covering the wounded man perfectly. The bleeding had luckily stopped by now, and with their last energy, they pulled this extra-heavy load past the soldiers. They did not dare to look up, scared that their eyes would give them away.

Stopping at the open wrought-iron gate of the convent, they discovered another unforeseen obstacle. The lane to the convent was way too steep for the boys. After a couple of minutes of indecision, Eric, who had become the leader of their expedition, made possibly the bravest steps in his life. He went straight up to a German SS officer and asked very politely if some of his soldiers could give them a hand, because they were bringing beets to the sisters. The officer smiled and, with a couple of commands, had some of the soldiers push the load to the back door of the convent. With a kind of weak smile, the boys watched as the soldiers left. When they were sure that no one was in sight, they rang the backdoor bell.

A sister opened the door. Seeing the two exhausted youngsters with a box full of beets made her smile. She thanked the two for their goodness but mentioned that these beets were not good for eating. Her rosy color and smile changed quickly when the two told her that they needed Sister Theresa because they had a wounded pilot underneath these beets. She mentioned something like "Oh my god!" and rushed off to get Sister Theresa. Within a minute, Sister Theresa and three or four other sisters came rushing in. In no time at all, the sisters moved the heavy sled and box into the hallway and closed the door behind them. While the other sisters were taking the beets out, Sister Theresa guided the two dead-tired youngsters into a small room and asked one of the sisters to bring some hot chocolate milk for them.

Inside the room, Sister Theresa very nervously told the boys of the danger they had put the convent in and if they would mention only one word of this to anyone, the Germans would find out and all the sisters would be sent to concentration camps. After making sure that the sisters would contact the resistance movement and not hand their hero over to the Germans, they both promised the sister never to mention anything to anybody, not even their parents.

Awfully tired but with a beautiful feeling, they left the convent. The hot chocolate milk felt good and had relieved their sore throats from the heavy breathing. The sled and empty box glided now, feather light, behind them like a silent witness. The sisters had removed the blood from the box and had covered the bottom with some straw. After disconnecting the box from the sled and putting the box back in the cow stall, the two sat down for a while, discussing proudly their deed now that the danger had passed.

A few weeks later, they found out from Sister Theresa that she had cleaned the wound and set the leg bone and that same evening, the resistance movement had picked him up and, within a couple of days, had gotten him over to safety in England. That was the last the two boys ever heard about their hero, but that was not important.

News broke through from the resistance movement that the Allied forces had landed in France. Even before this news finally broke through to the villagers, everyone knew that something had happened. The normal, peaceful village had changed into a nervous commotion of movement of German forces. Shouting officers, heavily roaring tanks and trucks, and marching soldiers made everyone aware that the end of the war was near. These were exciting days for Eric and Nico. Their schoolmaster had closed the school, and both could observe, sitting at the corner stoop at the end of the street, the tremendous mass movement of the German forces. It seemed that they were moving in all direction. This went on for days. Finally, their movement changed to one direction—the German border. The Germans were pulling back, and with it came the sounds of the still-faraway front line.

Months later, Radio Orange reported that thousands and thousands of Allied paratroopers had parachuted around the city of Arnhem, sixty miles to the north, to protect the important bridge over the Rhine River. Fighting was heavy, and loses on both sides were high. In the late seventies, a movie, *A Bridge Too Far*, was made about this battle. The once-proud and fearful German Army was crumbling. The chaos and pitiful sight of a defeated army was breathtaking. Hordes of dirty, exhausted soldiers stumbled by. Trucks, horse-drawn farm wagons, or even wheelbarrows carrying wounded soldiers pushed by dead-tired comrades as they passed through the villages over the German border. It was a sickening sight. Eric remembered the beginning of the war when the German forces marched through the village while singing marching songs. An older soldier pushing a wheelbarrow stopped right in front of Eric to give his exhausted body a rest. Eric noticed that the badly wounded soldier in the wheelbarrow was very young. He couldn't have been more than sixteen or seventeen years old. Eric's heart jumped in his throat.

This boy was not much older than he was. Eric walked over to the wheelbarrow and took the hand of the young soldier in his hands.

A weak smile came on the dirty and painful face of the youngster, followed by a tear that slowly ran off his right cheek. When the older soldier resumed the march, Eric held on to the hand and walked beside the wheelbarrow until the next street, feeling sad about this young man, who was his friend for this short duration.

When the stream of retreating soldiers ebbed, an eerie peace fell over the village except for the sounds of the exploding grenades coming closer, sounds from the Allied forces, who were now in full force pushing forward. Within a few days, the mortars came whistling over the village and exploded over the border on the German side. The village children, being used to and having grown up during the war, quickly learned that as the grenades gave off a whistling sound, they were still in their flight path but that as soon as it changed over into a kind of murmuring sound, they would fall flat to the ground. That was the sound of a grenade coming down. In no time, they became so used to these sounds that Eric and his friends played soccer at the village soccer field while the grenades whistled overhead. Only a couple of times was the game interrupted, and that was when the sound changed and they had to fall flat to the ground. When a few exploded in the village, it was high time to run home.

Martha was already with the other two children in the basement when Eric arrived. Utterly upset that her son was playing soccer in this dangerous time, she gave Eric a slapping on his head, which baffled him. While blurting his lungs out, the only defending words Eric could bring out was "But…but they were still whistling!" After the barrage of mortars stopped for a while, the explosion in the village had killed a few people and an older nun in the convent practically next door to Eric's. The nun, who was tired of constantly moving from her bedroom to the basement, was killed right in her bed. A shell fell through the roof, went through her body, and lodged without exploding into the basement floor.

On September 19, 1944, Eric woke up very early in the morning. Something had interrupted his sleep. The daylight was breaking through, and all the indications were there that it would be a sunny day. For the last couple of days, all Germans had left the village. Half awake, Eric heard the sound of running footsteps. Quickly he jumped out of bed and ran to the open bedroom window to find out what was going on. Leaning over the window, he noticed some movement at the corner of the street some fifty yards away. It was a strange-looking soldier with a rifle in his hands, ready to fire. He nervously looked around the corner, observing within seconds everything the experienced mind of a front-line soldier possibly could detect.

Eric remembered that this was practically the same scene he witnessed at the start of the war four years ago, except that these were possibly Americans. Quickly Eric pulled back, his body shaking with the excitement not only from what he just witnessed but also by instinctively knowing the danger he'd been in from the nervous finger of the ready-to-fire soldier. He realized that this was the first American soldier in his village because for the last few days, the villagers had known that the Americans were breaking through. Very carefully, he took another glimpse down the street. Now he saw more soldiers running from one hideout to the next.

Full of excitement, Eric woke up the rest of the family by shouting, "The Americans are here!"

In no time, he got dressed and wanted to run outside, but Martha quickly got ahold of him and warned him that it was too dangerous to go outside now. Eric was too excited to listen but was stopped short in his tracks when at once all hell broke loose.

The whole hillside on the north end of the village was covered with heavy American guns and tanks shooting at will over the village and into Germany. In seconds, the whole family ran for safety into the basement. The thundering noise of the heavy guns were ear-piercing. Martha, sitting beside John on a wooden bench, prayed loudly, a rosary was gliding through her fingers. For a moment, Eric, who was sitting on a big bag of potatoes, closed his ears with his fingers and thought about the wounded young German soldier and hoped that he was not on the receiving end of the mortars. For an hour or so, the shooting went on, but then except for a few guns, it stopped.

About a half hour later, the door of the basement swung open, and Willem shouted, "Come out. We are liberated! The Americans are here!"

Outside, the streets filled up with outrageously happy villagers. All over the village, the long-hidden Dutch flags were hung outside windows. People were shaking hands with one another, and it was perfectly normal for the young ladies to kiss every American soldier they could get their hands on. Soon the roaring noise of an American tank came rolling down the main street, already covered with flowers, followed by a whole stream of tanks.

Eric walked alongside one of the tanks and looked up with admiration and the highest respect to the tank commander, who was in control of this huge noisy machine of war. The tank commander waved back at the happy, well-wishing villagers, and when he discovered Eric, he took something out of his pocket and threw it to him. Not knowing what it was, Eric picked it up from the street, and while watching the commander, who tore off the wrapping paper and stuck it into his mouth, Eric did likewise. It tasted sweet and minty. After some hours, when Eric ran home, he mentioned to his mother, "These Americans have funny candy. You can keep on chewing, but it never gets less." It was the first chewing gum Eric ever tasted.

For days, the festivities went on. Dancing in the streets, the singing of the Dutch national anthem, and the noise of the drunken villagers gave the Dutch people a time of blowing off the anger, frustration, and depression they had kept inside for nearly five years. No one went to work. The days became wilder and wilder after the liberation. Constantly, the resistance movement, with bands on their arms with the letters "OD" (which stood for "resistance movement" in Dutch), drove trucks and cars, loudly blowing their horns through the villages and cities, followed by hysterical, screaming people to pick up not only German collaborators, their girlfriends and wives, but also innocent people. Someone had only to point a finger at you, and you were branded. Some innocent people in small communities never out lived the shame that was put on them.

Even Eric's father was pinpointed. One afternoon, a loud, horn-blowing car, followed by hysterically shouting villagers, stopped in front of the house. Not really understanding what was happening, Eric's parents ran to the dining room to look out the window. At that moment, rocks were thrown through the windows, and one rock cut Martha's forehead. One of the ODs came into the house and showed Eric's father that he was on the list of people to be picked up. Both men knew each other very well, and after they both discussed the situation, they decided that it must have been a mistake. Instead of going with the waiting auto, John promised that he would go the next morning to the city hall, where the OD headquarters were located, to clear his name. When the OD person went outside without Eric's father, the bloodthirsty crowd hurled more rocks through the windows and destroyed beautiful vases and pictures and his mother's pride and joy, the china cabinet with all the crystal once hand-ground by John in his younger years.

It took a couple of pistol shots in the air for the OD person to calm down the crowd and explain to them that this was all a mistake. Only when they drove away to his next victim did the crowd follow them, but they had left Eric's family in a state of shock. It took John only a couple of minutes the next morning to clear his name, but it took many years for the whole family to be fully accepted again by some of the villagers.

The five years of building up hatred for the Germans and everything that was connected with them made many of the normal, peaceful Dutchmen into wild, raving maniacs. True, many German collaborators who had assisted the German Gestapo in murdering thousands of Dutchmen deserved everything that was coming to them, but in times like this also, many innocent countrymen fell victim to this uncontrollable revenge-seeking mobs.

Eric went with Nico to a close-by city to witness the degradation of all women who were picked up for being wives or girlfriends of German soldiers or German collaborators. The marketplace in front of the centuries-old city hall was already filled with impatient people waiting for the main event. A loud roar went up when finally the autos arrived with the women, who were already in a state of shock. Rudely, like animals, they were pulled from the autos and pushed and pulled up the steps to the balcony of the city hall. Some women had been picked up early in the morning and were only wearing a nightgown under their raincoats. The events that followed made Eric and many decent people sick to their stomach.

Each woman was pushed forward to the railing. While protesting their innocence, they first got their hair shaven off in front of wildly shouting people. Some of these women fainted but were revived by a pail of cold water thrown over them. Next, they were painted black asphalt swastikas on their bald head. One fairly heavy woman fainted, and while hanging over the railing, one of her breasts protruded from her nightgown. The mob started shouting all kinds of obscenities; this became screaming when one of the beastly ODs painted the breast with tar. By now, many people, including Eric and Nico, had seen enough of this barbarism. They left for home, but their spaces were quickly filled with the latecomers, and the shouting and screaming went on into late in the afternoon.

After a couple of weeks of celebrating their liberation and also committing these outrageous brutalities, the Dutch people calmed down, and the healing of wounds and the clean-up and rebuilding of battle scars began. For Eric and Nico, the days that followed were times of excitement. The schoolhouse was taken over by American forces. All day long, the two practically lived with the American soldiers, and in no time, they picked up some of the English language. English—or, for that matter, the American language—sounded to a Dutchman like someone trying to speak with a hot potato in his mouth. "Chewing gum," "cigarettes for Papa," and "chocolate for Mama" were known after a few days, followed by "yes," "no," "thank you," and "okay."

On the other side of border, all the German villages were evacuated when the American forces broke through. All the farm animals that were left behind, like horses, cattle, sheep, goats, and heavy oxen, were driven over the border to the Dutch villagers to be taken care of. Most cows and oxen that came over the border to Eric's village were driven onto the village soccer field. Eric and many other youngsters who worked at farms knew that it was high time for these cows' overly full udders to be unloaded. Many days in a row, Eric, like the other boys, would carry a pail and a small three-legged stool to the soccer field to milk the cows.

One day, Theo, one of the village boys who had never worked at a farm, seeing Eric passing by day after day to the soccer field, wanted to be part of the group and followed him. Arriving at the field, Eric, knowing that Theo didn't know anything about farming, showed him how to milk a cow.

"Is that all there is to it?" said Theo, thinking that these farm boys made so much out of nothing. "Which cow should I take?"

A mean streak arose in Eric's mind. "Why don't you take the big fat one over there? Then you will have your pail full in no time," Eric replied.

Theo walked over to the huge animal, thinking how dumb Eric was, milking a meager cow and giving him the big one. Out of the corner of his eye, practically not able to keep from bursting out laughing, Eric watched Theo crawling all around the animal.

Finally, with a hopeless look on his face, Theo shouted, "I can't find it!"

"What can't you find?" replied Eric.

"The udder!" Theo shouted. At the same time, he got hit hard by the tail of the ox, who didn't agree at all with Theo's searching hands on his belly.

All the youngsters on the field, who had kept quiet while watching this setup, now let loose and laughed and teased Theo, following him down the field. Theo'd had forever enough of farming and had gained the nickname of Ox.

The younger teenagers quickly got used to the American soldiers and started looking for new excitement. One of the youngsters, Hans, who was the village roughneck, started a club. Actually, it was like a little army. Hans was the general. Their hideout was in one of the woods surrounding the village. Marching neatly in rows, using sticks for rifles and fighting an invisible German army in the woods, was a new excitement. Eric, too young but tall for his age, was accepted in this army, and Nico, who didn't want to be separated from Eric, was accepted as a Red Cross soldier. Secret pathways were laid out in the woods with markers showing misleading directions to the base camp to have intruders walk in the wrong direction for miles.

For a while, this playing satisfied them, but the constant search for excitement made them look to new avenues. It all started with a German rifle one of the youngsters found in the woods. It had a broken stock but otherwise was in good working condition. German ammunition could be found all over, and in no time at all, the rifle was ready for operation. The broken stock of the rifle held tightly against a big rock and the rifle tied down with metal straps elevated by rocks in the direction of a German village church tower opened up a new form of playing. Soon the boys knew the difference between regular rounds of ammunition and tracer bullets. Only a select few were chosen to load and fire the rifle, and Eric was one of them. In the early evening, this group set up the rifle. After connecting a long rope to the trigger, the boys loaded it at the command of the general, but the general would fire the rifle. This could only be done for a few rounds each evening at different locations to stay away from the American MPs.

All that still was not enough, and it went from bad to worse. They needed more excitement. Soon they went over to robbing American supply trucks. If one of the trucks was chosen to be robbed after days of watching what the load was all about, an evening was set for the daring deed. One or two boys would start fooling around in front of the truck, getting the attention of the soldier who was on guard. Once the coast was clear at the back of the truck, the remaining youngsters would rob everything they could get their hands on. Within a matter of weeks, the camp had a supply of rifles, ammunition (including hand grenades), boxes filled with canned foods, and even a box with surgery instruments enough to outfit an operating room.

Naturally, the parents of the youngsters didn't know about this and still believed that the kids were only playing innocent games. These supposedly innocent games ended up in near disaster for the general. One of the robbed boxes contained fuses and very small sticks of dynamite. This discovery gave the reckless, daring youngsters new ideas. They were going to explode their own bridge. It took them days to build a bridge from piece of wood, rocks, branches, and mud over one of the drainage creeks. The small dynamite sticks were inserted into the bridge, and the long fuses were laid over a higher ridge to be thrown into a small fire. The soldiers would hide behind the high ridge, while the general had his own hideout closer to the bridge. The raising of one hand of the general was the signal to fire. Then all went wrong.

Seeing a raised hand from the general, the boys quickly threw the bundles of fuses into the fire, not knowing that the general was only inspecting the bridge for the last time and, while trying to keep his balance, had raised his arm. After a loud explosion, they found their general unconscious and bleeding all over. The general was lucky, and after a few weeks in the hospital, with only a few broken ribs and numerous cuts and bruises, he could return home. It was also the end of their army because shortly after this incident, the village people, with the help of American soldiers, who by now had found out about the supposedly innocent games, destroyed the camp and punished the youngsters.

The village meadows, school, ballroom, and large homes were occupied by the American forces. Eric's home was completely filled with high-ranking officers and was used as a central location for the high command. Only his parents' bedroom was off limits to the forces. Two majors used the remaining bedrooms. The very sturdy basement was converted into a central communications station. A huge bundle of telephone cables protruded from the basement window. From there, the cables ran along the house over the roof and were tied down to the sturdy brick kitchen stove's chimney. From the chimney, the cable split up into all directions. The large living and dining room, with the open sliding door between the two, were used as high command's strategy rooms. Maps covered the walls and were spread over two connecting long tables at all times. A guard was posted at the front door and one in the hall between the basement and the living room.

The only city water tap was in the basement, which created a problem. Every time Martha needed water, it was the guard who had to get it for her. Eric and Johann slept between the soldiers on the kitchen floor, and Paul, who was only four or five years old at the time, slept in his parents' bedroom.

One early morning, while Eric and Johann were still sound asleep, curled up under the army blankets, it happened. It sounded like a direct hit from a mortar. The whole kitchen went black from the root in the chimney. Everyone jumped to the outside for safety. The noise of a heavy tank on the street superseded the shouted commands from the officers. When daylight broke through, the story unfolded. From one of the last counteroffensive actions, a German tank lost its way and ran right through the village. Turning a corner at too wide of an arc while trying to save his hide, the German tank ran right over the steel corner light post. One of the bundles of telephone cables coming from Eric's house chimney was connected to this light post and had pulled the chimney completely off the roof. The incident left the kitchen in a mess, but that was all.

A few days later, Eric noticed an armored wagon in front of the house with a small triangle green flag on the antenna. More guards were posted all over the house, and it seemed like everyone was more nervous than normal. It was clearly noticeable that someone very important was inside. It had rained for the last couple of days, and the village streets, broken up by trucks and tanks, changed over into mud a foot deep. The constant traffic of high-ranking officers made the house look like the street itself. Late in the afternoon, a group of very high-ranking officers left the basement, and instead of leaving through the hallway, they took the wrong turn and went through the kitchen to the outside. Martha, preparing the evening meal on the kitchen stove, smiled at the highest-ranking officer. While returning her smile, he said something to her while holding the outside door open for the other officers. Martha, feeling the moist, cold air entering the kitchen, said "Shut the bloody door!" while thinking that she had said, "Please shut the door." The high-ranking officer lost the smile off his face, but then looking at the warm smiling face of Martha, he returned the smile and hurriedly closed the door. The next day, one of the officers, who had Dutch parents and could speak some Dutch, explained to Martha that she had said "Shut the bloody door!" to general Bratley, the general commander of the American forces. She was very embarrassed and made her apologies but never forgot this incident.

The school had been closed because the American forces needed the space, and Eric and Nico had constantly visited them. The playground was at a slight incline to the school building. At the bottom of the playground was the inlet iron gate, and beside it were the girls' and boys' toilettes.

On most days, some American jeeps were parked against the school building, and for Eric and Nico, these were items to play with. Sitting behind the steering wheel, they imagined that they could drive this thing. One day, while playing in one of the jeeps, they released the brake by accident, and the jeep started to move slowly downhill, increasing in speed. The two did not know what to do, so Nico called out, "Eric, jump!" They both jumped onto the playground, and the jeep crashed into the toilet wall, making a big hole in it.

Hearing the crash, some of the soldiers came running out of the building and chased the two boys. They never did catch them, but from that time on, the big metal porch was closed to all visitors except the army.

For days, Frank, an assistant to an American major who used one of the bedrooms, had given Eric candies and big chocolate bars. One day he motioned to Eric to come upstairs because he had more chocolate. In the bedroom, Frank gave Eric a very large box of chocolate. Eric gave him a piece of it while sitting beside him on the bed. Frank put an arm around him and pulled Eric closer. Eric liked it because he was such a nice man. After a while of cuddling, Frank opened his own trousers and, while smiling, took Eric's hand and guided it into his trousers. Eric felt strange but also some kind of excitement. He felt that it was wrong, what he was doing, because his parents and the pastor had told him that touching himself or another person that way was not only wrong but sinful and that he would have to tell the pastor in his next confession.

But all these thoughts left him when Frank opened Eric's trousers and started playing with him. After some time, Eric felt his face blushing, and a strange but very pleasant feeling came over him. Shortly thereafter, this feeling became overwhelming, and he pushed Frank's hand away. Frank kept on stroking himself and made strange noises until he took a handkerchief out of his pocket and wiped himself clean. Both lay beside each other on the bed, and Frank, now very serious, made Eric understand not to tell anyone—for sure, not his parents.

It had been very strange for Eric (now nearly eleven years old), but it was also very pleasant, and Frank liked it. Many times, they spent time together until after about two months, this group of Americans moved on. Eric never thought that it had been wrong, and he missed Frank.

Some time later, he told Nico all about it and discussed it for a while. Nico did not agree with Eric and mentioned to him that he would have to confess all this to the pastor before he could go to communion again.

"I did notice that you did not go to communion for a while but thought nothing of it. Another problem is," said Nico, "how are you going to tell our pastor?"

"Oh yes," Eric answered, "this is a real problem."

But soon the they found the answer. Eric would drive by bicycle to a village some distance away, where no one knew him, and go to confession there.

"Okay," Nico answered. "I will go with you next Saturday afternoon because that is the time when priests hold confessions."

Arriving at this village, Eric and Nico went into the church and noticed a small line-up before the confession booth. When it was Eric's turn, he told the priest all about his supposed sins.

The priest looked at him through small holes in the sliding board separating the two and said, "Young man, you are not from this village. I know all the children here."

Eric was shocked. Would he still run into trouble? It was some time before he could answer, but then he lied. "I was driving by your church and want to go to communion tomorrow, so I thought to go to confession here."

"From which village are you?" the priest asked.

Eric mentioned a different village than his own. The priest gave Eric absolution, but he would have to pray a whole rosary for his sins.

When Eric left the booth, the priest said to him, "By the way, I also forgive you for lying about the village you said you came from."

On the way home, Eric mentioned the remark of the priest. "How did he know?"

"I don't know," Nico answered. "I guess he had this happen time and time again, but who cares? He forgave you for it anyway."

When the first group of soldiers left the village, a larger division of Americans arrived and moved into one of Willem's meadows. The large meadow beside the cemetery was covered with army tents, and no one besides army personnel was allowed to enter this meadow. Eric, always looking for a handout, noticed a pair of old worn-out leader army boots lying on the side of a huge pile of empty cans. For weeks, he watched those boots. Leather shoes were impossible to get and were too expensive. The only footwear the youngsters of the village had were wooden shoes. These old army boots would be worth their weight in gold for any youngster. Weeks and weeks went by, and it became an obsession for Eric. He had to have these shoes. Seeing it lying there for everyone to see drove him out of his mind. What about if another boy would notice them and sneak in? He would lose his shoes! Luckily, that a forever-growing pile of cans covered them. Eric, knowing where they were, tied a piece of rope on the fence wire to mark the exact location when the time lent itself for his acquisition of the shoes. Finally, the day came when the Americans moved on.

Eric watched sadly as the Americans packed up to leave. Many of the soldiers had become his friends, and he knew that he would never see them again. For that matter, the whole village was sad, for many of the soldiers had shared their kindness and food with the villagers in return for their living quarters. Many tears were shed when the soldiers climbed into the trucks to move.

Standing in the middle of the well-wishers, Eric remembered his shoes. As quick as he could run on his wooden shoes, he ran to the meadow. Just in time! A bulldozer had dug a big hole and was starting to push the whole pile into the hole when Eric arrived. He still was not allowed to enter the meadow. Watching with eagle eyes, he saw his shoes rolling over and over, finally ending up on top of the pile at one end of the hole. He could cry when the bulldozer covered it all with a thick layer of dirt. For a moment, he stood there. His shoes were gone. Slowly with his hands deep in his pockets, he walked home. What a sad day. Everything was going wrong for him.

At home, his father noticed the sad mood his youngster was in and, trying to reduce this sadness, mentioned, "Well, boy, sooner or later, your American friends had to leave."

"No, Dad, it is not only that," replied Eric and told his father the story of his lost shoes.

"Come on, boy. That's the best thing that could have happened to those shoes! No one will find them, and only you know the exact location under the dirt. Tomorrow morning, early, when all the soldiers have left, we will go together and dig them out."

Eric's face cleared up, and after quickly swallowing a sandwich his mother had prepared, he ran outside to watch the last trucks leaving the village. Now he didn't feel so bad at all anymore and could even smile at the thought of what they'd be doing the next morning.

It took both only a half hour or so the next morning to dig them out. After they returned home, his mother washed off the dirt and put some old socks in the toes of the shoes because they were a mile too big for Eric. Even so, these shoes were Eric's pride possession and were admired by every village boy. He walked around like Charlie Chaplin, but who cared? They were real leather shoes from his American friends.

To Eric's chagrin, when the American soldiers left, the village school reopened again. After for more than a month they had been totally free and "played around" with the American soldiers, Eric thought schooling was for the birds. He missed his American friends, but one thing was for sure. After he grew up, he would go to America. Sitting in the classroom again and listening to the teacher, who carried on as if nothing had happened, was too much to ask. It wasn't easy for the teacher at that time either to drill the now-wild youngsters into their daily routines again. The sturdy hands of the teachers, however, had a reverse affect, and it took them longer than necessary to get the rebellious youngsters back in line.

One day, after the Americans had left, they were followed by the English Eighth Army (called the Desert Rats) for a well-deserved rest after their fight against Rommel in Africa. All over, soldiers were moving into the houses in the village, and Eric ran home to find out if they had some English guests too. Coming home, however, he found a commotion going on in the long covered hallway between the house and stall. He was amazed seeing soldiers moving large boxes, kettles, pots and pans, and a long gasoline-operated stove with many burners from a large truck in front of the house and into that hallway. Eric didn't know what it was all about, but he sure was happy and wanted to make friends right away with one of the soldiers who was installing the large stove.

The soldier, however, having a terrible time putting the stove together, shouted when Eric came close by, "Get out of the way!" At the same time, he gave Prince a kick on the behind, which made the dog run into the garden, howling along the way. He stopped and looked back, questioning the reason for all this.

When the soldier, without saying anything more, continued with this installation, Eric thought, *What a mean son of a bitch! How dare this guy kick Prince and be so mean to him? He only wanted to be friends.*

Going into the kitchen, Martha explained to Eric in a happy voice, "Eric, we have the kitchen here for the English officers. Actually, they call it the officers' mess. From now on, we will have good food. The cook, the kitchen aides, and some of the officers are already moving in. Did you notice the big guy with his black beret hanging over one ear and an old broken pipe in the corner of his mouth? That is the cook, one of the soldiers told me."

Noticing Eric's lack of interest, she asked, "What's the matter with you? Aren't you happy? Isn't that good news?"

"I don't like the English soldiers," Eric replied, and then he told his mother what had happened.

"Well, I guess you two were in the way. It is already late in the afternoon. Dinner has to be ready by six o'clock, one of the soldiers explained to me, and the cook hasn't even installed the stove yet."

"I don't care. He had no right to kick Prince."

The rest of the evening, he kept himself occupied by watching the serving of the evening meal to the officers in the living room. Some of them smiled at him while passing by, but Eric ignored them. He didn't like the English and really missed his American friends. The following day, when Eric came back from school, he passed the cook again in the hallway. Stirring with a big spoon the contents of a large kettle, he looked and smiled at Eric. Not yet forgetting the events of yesterday, Eric passed him without answering his smile.

This man has an ugly face, Eric thought. *He even has a couple of teeth missing.* Yet there was something friendly in that smile that stuck in his mind. Maybe he had been wrong yesterday and had misjudged the man.

He knew his mother had a small bag of sugar cubes in the kitchen cabinet from which he would sneak one every once in a while. He was going to try again to make friends with the cook, and to show his goodwill, he would give him some of the sugar cubes. If that didn't work, that would be it. Then he would never try to make friends with this man again.

He could easily sneak some sugar cubes as his mother was getting a pail of water from the only water tap they had, which was in the basement. When Eric entered the cook's domain, his fists full of sugar cubes, he walked straight toward the cook and, without saying a word, pushed the cubes into his hands. For a moment, the man looked surprised, but then he smiled.

While rubbing his big dirty hands through Eric's hair, he said, "Thank you. I am Louis, the cook here." And continuing without taking the pipe out of his mouth, the rest of his words were lost.

Eric, now happy, smiled back at him and answered, "I am Eric."

Without further saying a word, Louis looked around for a moment and then took a big knife, cut a huge slice of white bread, covered it with marmalade, and offered it to Eric. Accepting this return gift of friendship, Eric sat down on a box. Smiling and licking his lips, he showed Louis how much he appreciated the gift and that it was delicious.

Then Louis noticed Prince standing at the end of the hallway, ready to jump out of the way if it would be necessary again. He cut off a piece from the side of bacon hanging from the wall and threw it to Prince, who, not knowing what came at him, jumped away a couple of feet.

"Come on, boy. Take it." Eric called Prince back.

Hearing his master's friendly words, Prince turned back and, after eating the handout, slowly yet carefully walked over to Eric and sat down beside him.

Louis petted the dog and said, "Good dog, good dog." While looking into Eric's eyes he knew that they had become friends. For the rest of the English occupancy, which would be five to six months, Louis took very good care of the rest of Eric's family, but for Eric and Prince, he would always do that little extra.

On Christmas Eve 1944, all day long Louis and his assistants had been cooking and baking all kinds of specialties for a Christmas party for the officers, and in the early evening, all ranks of officers were arriving from all over the neighborhood. The laughing, cheering, and singing went on late into the night. Early Christmas morning, the officers were so drunk they were falling all over the furniture. When finally most of them were gone and Martha had a chance to look into the room, she noticed that most of her beautiful furniture was lying in shambles on the floor. Furious and with tears rolling down her cheeks, she yelled at the remaining officers. They couldn't understand her, but it didn't take a brain to realize what she was saying. Louis, who had heard her hysterical screams, pushed her calmly but surely out of the room and tried to explain to her that he would take care of it.

John, who had finally fallen asleep after all the racket, woke up and, coming into the kitchen, found Martha standing by the kitchen stove, still crying.

"John," she said, "they ruined all the furniture. Go and look at it. It's a real mess."

Louis then turned to John and tried to explain to him what he would do about it, but John couldn't understand him. Two days later, after everything was cleaned up by the soldiers, a big army truck stopped in front of the house, and the most beautiful pieces of furniture were moved into the rooms. It was gorgeous and very expensive furniture with beautiful hand-cut wooden armrests.

Louis had fun when he saw the questions on John's and Martha's faces. "Germany," he said. "A lot of furniture in Germany." They had gone over the border by truck and robbed the home of a wealthy family who had evacuated anyhow and left their furniture behind.

In January 1945, Prince got sick. Listless, he would lie in the corner of the kitchen and wouldn't touch his food. Eric was helpless.

He tried everything to get Prince back on his feet again, but without results. Even Louis's best pieces of meat from the kitchen were left untouched. Shortly thereafter, Louis grabbed Eric by the hand when he returned from school and guided him to a spot in the garden.

He said, "Prince is dead. I'm sorry, so sorry."

For a moment, Eric stood there, looking at the spot, and then it dawned on him what Louis was telling him. Very upset, he ran into the kitchen and asked his mother what happened. Knowing her son was heartbroken, Martha explained to him as easily as possible that earlier in the morning, Prince had become so sick and was suffering quite a lot. Louis, seeing the suffering of Eric's friend, had carefully carried him into the garden and ended his misery with a bullet.

Both Nico and Eric were heartbroken for days. Their really true friend was gone, and it left a tremendous empty space. They had marked the spot with a wooden cross roughly nailed together, and many times even years later, they would return to this spot and talk about the many adventures he had been part of. He hadn't just been a dog. He had been a friend that would have given his life if necessary for his two comrades. Louis tried everything to relieve his young friend from his burden, but to no avail.

When the time finally came for the English soldiers to move on again, the rough and tough Louis hugged Eric as if he were leaving his own child and then, without looking back, stepped into the waiting truck and drove on.

Ironically, it was a German soldier at the beginning of the war who had pushed Prince as a puppy into Eric's arms. Now at the end of the war, he had been shot by an English soldier.

Shortly thereafter, the rest of Holland was liberated, and within months, Germany surrendered. But for Eric, the war had ended when Louis and his truck left the village.

In 1946, to the utmost happiness of Eric's parents, Martha gave birth to a daughter, Eric's only sister. Eric was now twelve years old. His brother Johan was fourteen, and Paul was about six years old. The newborn, called Elly, was for John and Martha a dream come true. After sixteen years of being married and having three sons, they finally had a daughter.

CHAPTER 3

✠

A t the front of the church at the crossing of the main street and Eric's street was one of the few streetlights the village possessed. Naturally, it was under these lights that the young and old gathered in the evening for their daily meetings. The farmers and coal miners would exchange the happenings of the day, while the young men mingled, whistling at and discussing the parading young girls, who welcomed the interest shown to them. Evening games were at most times played in the late fall when the air cooled down too much for the older generation to be outside. They gathered in warm cow stalls and around someone's fireplace, playing cards. The card players were the easiest to detect. Their loud discussions were heard outside the kitchens (the only place heated by a coal fire).

On one of the evenings, Eric was playing "kick the can" with some of the older boys. He was about twelve years old, but being tall for his age and besides being a fast runner, he was accepted by the teenagers. "Kick the can" was played as follows: After some kind of number game, one person was left to be the can protector. Everyone hated that job, but there had to be one. While standing with one foot on an old empty can, the can protector would count aloud to one hundred with his eyes closed, while the rest of the participants ran in all directions to hide in the many dark places and shadows that one streetlight would provide.

The protector would then try to find each one, discover them, and try to outrun them to the can. If he touched the can first, the other player was out and had to wait until the game was over. If the protector beat everyone to the can, the game was over, and the first player out became the new protector. However, if only one of the players outran him, he would then kick the can as far as he could. All out players would run away, and the protector had to pick up the can and start all over again.

Eric had played this game many times, and most of the time, he was fast enough to outrun the protector when caught. This one time, however, while he was protecting the can, an older farm boy constantly outran him. While taking the wooden shoes in his hands, running on his thick woolen socks, he would bypass Eric and kick the can a mile far. This game went on for a couple of evenings, Eric constantly being beaten to the can. Everyone made fun of him. He didn't mind losing, but this laughing made him angry. He had to do something and fast before he became the laughingstock of the village.

His eye caught a rock lying on the side of the road. It was just large enough to fit in the can. While everyone had found their positions, Eric quickly put the stone in the can and went on as if nothing had happened. After counting out a couple of players, Eric walked slowly in the direction of home. While counting, he had heard this farm boy running and hiding in the same direction. In the dark, he saw the branches of a bush in his neighbor's yard move, and with a jump, the farm boy was on his way to destruction. This time, Eric didn't follow him, but he ran as fast as possible home. Just before he reached the big porch door, the jubilant laughter of the out boys were stopped by an immense cry of sharp pain and an unbelievable knowledge of God and saints in heaven, which woke up some of the already-sleeping neighborhood.

For many months, Eric wouldn't bypass this boy's farm because the boy would have broken Eric's neck if he could have gotten ahold of him. But with two broken toes, the boy's speed was reduced to less than half for quite some time. Eric, instead of being the laughingstock, became someone for his friends to look up to. The younger ones practically worshipped him, for he had to be very brave to do something like that to that strong and powerful farm boy. Only the older generation, including his parents, didn't agree at all with his devilish deed. But then, they were the old folks. What did they know?

Every village had its own village electrician employed by the local power company. Tony Koren, a middle-aged bachelor, not only repaired and installed the electrical wiring in the houses but also had to install the tall wooden poles and power lines through the village. He was respected very highly by the villagers because of his knowledge of working with such a mysterious and dangerous technology.

Eric watched with interest how Tony could climb these poles when he was extending the power lines at the end of the street. With his heavy safety belt around the pole and his heavy leg wear with pins protruding from it, Tony would climb the poles as if there was nothing to it.

One day while working on top of the pole, he looked down and noticed Eric standing underneath it, watching every move he made.

"Hey, you down there! Are you stupid or something? If I'd drop a screwdriver from way up here, it would enter your head and come out through your toenails."

Eric laughed at the way he said it, but he quickly moved out of the way.

"Aren't you Eric from John and Martha down the street?" Tony asked, and without waiting for an answer, he continued, "Do you mind giving me a hand for a moment?"

"Sure," said Eric. "What do you want me to do?"

"Do you see that loose wire lying on the road there? Why don't you pick it up and pull on it as hard as you can? Then I can tie it up to the insulators here."

It was Wednesday afternoon with no school, and Eric didn't mind helping Tony all afternoon until dinnertime. Eric would pull the wires, and Tony would climb the poles to tie them to the insulators. Once in a while, they took a rest, and while sitting on the side of the road, Tony explained to Eric what his job was all about.

"Not only are you a good worker, but you like what you are doing. Will a couple of guldens be enough for all the work you have done this afternoon?" Tony said while reaching for his wallet.

"No, Tony, I really enjoyed it, and I don't want any money. But maybe I can work with you more often and learn this trade. I'm very interested in it."

"It's a deal." Tony replied. "From now on, I'll let you know whenever I'm working, and if you have some time, just come over."

Tony and Eric didn't know it at that time, but that afternoon changed Eric's interest for the rest of his life. Before that day, his only interest was farming and caring for the animals, and working the fields seemed to have been his destination. Surely Willem and the farm were very close to him, and handling Max, the horse, was a real enjoyment. But even Willem had told him many times that small farming was really a poor existence. Eric spent more and more time with Tony, and within a year, he became quite knowledgeable of the practical side of that trade. Still, whenever Willem needed him, he was always happy to give a helping hand; and many times, while sitting at the wooden feedbox in the stall, Eric would tell Willem all about what he had learned and experienced in the dangerous, though no longer mysterious, electrical trade.

At the age of fourteen, Eric had learned so much that he practically rewired his whole house and added many lights and receptacles all throughout the village. Nico had also gotten interested, and in no time at all, Tony had two assistants. Therefore, it was no mystery to the parents of the youngsters when both Nico and Eric decided after finishing their years of grade school to enroll in a two-year electrician course at the technical high school in the city close by.

After graduation, Eric found employment in the huge hydro-electric central generating station on top of the coal mine named Maurits, owned by the Dutch government. This generating station produced with its many large steam turbo generators the high electrical power (10,000 volts) necessary not only for the coal mine but also for the southern part of Holland. It could connect through a large switching station and network of underground cables the needed electrical power to parts of Germany and Belgium in case of an emergency. Nico also found a job in the large electrical repair shop on top of the mine. They had the same shift, from 8:00 a.m. to 5:00 p.m., including a half-hour lunch. Although they couldn't contact each other during working hours, they could still ride their bicycles together to and from the mine.

Eric was assigned to Arnold Mueller, a master electrician. Arnold was a soft-hearted, friendly man and was a top-rate and respected electrician who was in charge of the maintenance at this big power switching station. This station, being part of the generator building, was divided into two large rooms. One room, where the switchboard operators were located, was filled with large electrical panels covered with all colors of indicating lights and switches, overlooking the main hall of the massive generators. The second room was divided into a lower fuse room and an upper switching room. Underneath this section of the building was the cable cellar, which was completely filled with rows of large high-power steel-covered electrical cables, some four to five inches in diameter, which conveyed the power underground to its destinations.

He really enjoyed working with Arnold in the superclean switching station and showed his appreciation by coming early to work and making coffee before Arnold would arrive. Eric was amazed with all this enormous electrical equipment, and his heart pounded when Arnold, who was visibly pleased with his young assistant's excitement, mentioned Eric's progress to management.

Five years had gone by since the end of World War II, and the rebuilding of Europe had begun. Eric's village tried to return to its peaceful existence, but without success. The deep wounds left in many who had lost someone dear to them or lost their belongings had changed the village people. Also changed were the values of these people, who had been for years under depression. It seemed as though everyone had lost some of their feeling for high morals, and the rate of divorces climbed within a few years to unbelievably high levels. Through this, a chain reaction occurred. It was something that even the best villagers couldn't stop anymore.

Divorced women had to find jobs instead of being housewives and mothers. And children shoved between the parents of those broken marriages roamed the streets till late in the night, brutalizing, stealing, and damaging everyone's properties. The village had lost more than all the armies of the world could physically steal to it. It had lost its inner beauty. It had lost its soul. For Eric, now sixteen years old, the world had opened up. He explored to the fullest what life had to offer a young man like himself.

Eric was also changing. His quick and inquisitive mind questioned everything, from girls to religion. He was slowly growing into manhood. Religion was something he could sit and dream about for hours. All his young life, it had been poured into him, first by his parents, then the schoolteacher, and then Mr. Pastor. Now he was questioning much of that information. Even as a youngster, he had questioned Mr. Pastor many times during catechism lessons but never really got satisfying answers.

He had questioned Mr. Pastor's teachings that when a baby was still born or died before it could be baptized, it would not go to heaven but would go somewhere in between heaven and hell or when a person takes his own life, he also could not go to heaven and so both would be buried at a special pace outside the blessed grounds of the cemetery. If our God was so full of love for his people, why then did he let these babies be born without a chance to go to heaven? And who knew what happened to the brain of a person who took his own life? But Mr. Pastor, annoyed with the constant questions from Eric, pulled him from his seat slapped him on his head and, with a kick on his behind, sent him home. This was the last time Eric went to catechism.

Without question, he accepted that there was an almighty God, and he talked to him many times, man to man. Eric would honor him constantly by appreciating the beauty of his creation. Everything was of interest to Eric, from the insects crawling through the grass (ants were his favorites) to the skies and heavens above. When he was working in the fields with Willem or sitting on his chosen spot on top of the hill, he could talk to his God. That was his religion. His parents wanted him to go to church at least on Sundays, but it was very boring to Eric and just a waste of time. He couldn't talk to his God in there, even if he wanted to, not with the interference of babies crying, people moving, and ladies wearing colorful dresses and odd-looking hats. With all this distraction, he couldn't concentrate and talk to his God. If he was late and had to accept standing room only in the back of the church between the men of the village, it was really hopeless. With lowered voices, they would discuss the pigeons and the soccer game that afternoon throughout the whole sermon.

He really liked dropping into the church operated by monks in the nearby city on Saturday afternoons. It was a beautiful very old church with masterful hand-cut dark woodwork. The sunlight shining in through the huge stained-glass windows transformed the church into majestic holiness. With only a few elderly people present, Eric could sit on one of those big benches and let his thoughts go free.

Once in a while, a monk, who would seem to come out of the woodwork, because they seemed to move soundlessly through the church and come out from nowhere, would stop by and, in a whispering voice, would ask, "Can I help you with anything, my son?"

But Eric, grateful for the man's concern, would only answer, "No, Father. I'm just sitting here where it's very peaceful."

The loving, all-knowing God the Father he could respect, but Jesus Christ was another matter. Eric was not so sure about him. He had read in some of the books from the library that our solar system was only a small tiny spot on the Milky Way. Through the centuries, they had discovered that there were hundreds, maybe thousands, of solar systems similar to ours, and if that was true, it would be ridiculous to accept that life would only exist at this tiny spot of dirt called Earth in the heavens. And if other planets were inhabited by people, maybe not of the same physical configuration, would they then have their own Jesus Christ? Or would our Jesus Christ, who was born on this earth, just travel around to all these other planets?

As far as Eric knew, Jesus Christ started the Catholic Church on this Earth. Would he then have started a similar Catholic Church in these other planets? After all, as far as Eric knew, Jesus's words were only true words, and he surely wouldn't have changed his mind at the other planets. It would be very interesting if during Eric's lifetime, they would discover life on other planets. And if these creatures were of higher intelligence than humans on Earth and had different religions, who then would be right or wrong?

Eric also read the Bible, but even that didn't satisfy his inquisitive mind. For example, the story about Adam and Eve was very questionable, and it really puzzled him when Cain, who slew Able, ran away to a village and found a maiden. If Adam and Eve were the first people, then where did these people from this village come from?

Besides growing mentally, Eric was also rapidly changing physically. At least once a month, he had to shave now. Also, the young ladies of the village had become more interesting to him. Carefully, so as not to be detected, he would watch their figures with pleasure, and his blood would jump through his system if the wind would blow the skirt up when a lady was riding her bicycle. Sometimes her legs would be exposed all the way up.

After the war, a piece of Germany called Zelfkant was annexed to his province to straighten out the borderline. It was now no problem to visit some of the villages in the Zelfkant, which for years had been closed off from visiting by the border patrols. Eric, with some older boys from his neighborhood, invaded this new territory on their bicycles many times. One small bar in one of these villages became their hideout. He always had pocket money because besides getting a reasonable weekly allowance from his parents, he also made good money by doing electrical work in his spare time throughout the village. His only limitation was the drinking age. All his drinking buddies were over the age of eighteen, and since he was still only sixteen, he was not allowed to be served in a bar.

The owner of the bar, who was also a small farmer, had converted one of the rooms into a bar and would only serve people in the evenings after the chores were done. If the local policemen found Eric being served in this bar, they could close the place down. Therefore, the old owner, who was not at all interested in losing his license and the extra income from the rough young men, told Eric he could not be in the bar but that if he wanted to drink, he had to go across the hall into the living room. With the lights out, he could then drink as much as he wanted and then return to the bar again.

Katherine, the owner's eldest daughter, was in her late twenties and was strongly built from doing the heavy chores on the farm. She had many times looked at him and had given him encouraging smiles. On one of his visits, she had whispered to him, "Why don't you stay in that room? I'll serve you the beer."

When bringing the beer into the dark room, Eric heard that she locked the door behind her. She knew Eric was sitting on the couch, and she found her way through the darkness, put the glass of beer on the table in front of him, and sat down right beside him. For a while, they sat there, talking about how she had noticed him many times and that she really liked him. Then she started to kiss his earlobes and neck. Eric felt her hot lips, and his whole body felt pressurized. He started to kiss her cheek, and slowly their heads moved until their lips touched. Katherine forced her tongue into Eric's mouth, and although he had heard about a tongue kiss, he had never experienced one. For a moment, he didn't like it, but then he started to let their tongues play together. With her left hand, she opened the buttons of her blouse and pulled one of her breasts out of her bra. Then she took Eric's hand and guided it to her breast. Eric, feeling the soft, warm breast and hard nipple, nearly exploded. Nature's forces were so intense in his body that the pressure was nearly unbearable.

Eric, panting for air under the intense kissing, still hesitated. But when her hand opened his trousers and touched him, his resistance broke. For the first time in Eric's life, he made love. The new, sweet taste of lovemaking became such a force in Eric's young life that for many months, he would sneak out of the house in the evening and would visit Katherine even without his older friends. He was full of excuses and lied to the gills when his parents questioned the many evenings he left the house.

Katherine, a hot-blooded woman, had lost her boyfriend during the war, and without enough eligible young men in the neighborhood, she satisfied her aching body with young Eric. This love affair ended suddenly one day when she told Eric that an elderly businessman had proposed to her. Grabbing her chance, she accepted and was married in no time, leaving Eric heartbroken. It took him quite some time to get over this loss. But being young and healthy and now knowing the pleasure of lovemaking, he found enough willing young maidens to satisfy him in the next couple of years. All the loving was done in the fields, starting in the spring when the wheat and rye was (as the young people would say) "two asses tall."

Because he was strongly built and unafraid of hard work, Eric was asked by many larger farms in the neighborhood to assist during harvest time, and many of their daughters would fall for his charm and eager body. One of the large farmers had lost his wife and married a twenty-year-old woman from another town. He already had four daughters nearly as old as his new wife.

Eric was earning some extra money by working weekends at this farm during harvest. The farm was located too far to go home, so Eric was allowed to stay over for a few days. However, the farmer did not allow him to sleep in the farmhouse (he must have had his reasons), but he could use the hayloft above the cow stall. Everyone (except the wife) worked together during the hot days of harvesting. The wife was cooking all day. In the evening, being hot and dusty, Eric would take off his shirt and wash and cool down his upper body in a very large wooden basin, which was a drinking bucket for the cows. He noticed that at that time, the girls would watch him and would make some remarks about his body.

One night, while he was lying in the hay, he heard a small voice at the bottom of the ladder. "Hey, Eric, are you sleeping?" When Eric answered her, she asked, "Do you mind if I come up and join you for a while?"

"Sure, I would like you to come up," answered Eric. What a question.

When she arrived, Eric noticed that she was wearing only a light nightgown. Therefore, it did not take long before their two hot bodies met. After a while, exhausted, she climbed down the ladder, and Eric fell asleep. The ladies must have talked together, Eric thought, because the next evening, another sister climbed the ladder. Before the harvest was over, Eric had made love to all the girls, including the wife, who told him that her husband did not know her needs. It had been a wonderful experience, but also dangerous, because the old farmer was still very strong.

He had become very knowledgeable and loved his job in the electric central station belonging to the coal mine. The management of the electrical department had decided, after giving Eric some successful tests, to send him to a special college just for the coal mines. Eric felt honored and knew that a chance like that wouldn't come along every day. Two days a week, he would travel by bus to another city where the college was located; the college was to educate the chosen ones in electrical and mechanical engineering, special for the coal mines.

Martha and John were very pleased with Eric's new opportunity to succeed in life. It was not more than a year ago when they had decided in a family meeting that Johann, who was the better student of the two, could go to the university to study languages. John had explained to his two older sons that he couldn't afford to send both of them to college, and Eric, knowing the eagerness Johann possessed for higher studies, had given up his right.

Some university electrical engineering students (not employed by the coal mining world) worked for one practice year in an industry during their school years. A young man named Peter would work together with Eric for a few months. It was actually short-lived, however. One day, while testing with Peter for carbon particles in the oil of the large oil-cooled high-voltage disconnects in the ten-thousand-volt switching room, an explosion occurred. In this room, uninsulated copper bars ran lengthwise through the switching room about ten feet from the floor.

These bars carried the high electrical power produced by the generators through air-operated safety switches to long rows of oil-cooled large disconnects, from there to the fuses in the room below and to the large steel-covered cables in the basement and to their destinations. Each disconnect was protected from the next one by about six inches of concrete walls. There was not much room to work on each side between the wall and the disconnect. This testing was routine work and was performed by Eric and Arnold on a monthly basis.

Eric and Peter, a young man from a nearby village, became friends in no time. Peter was very smart, friendly, and easygoing, and the two hit it off right way. That day, after performing the necessary safety procedures, they tested disconnect number six. The air safety switch above their heads was in the open position and was prevented from accidently closing by lock and key. Still, for additional safety, they tied a short piece of cable from the disconnect to a grounding strip mounted in front of the concrete dividing wall. A tremendous explosion rocked the whole building. Within minutes, everything had passed. A ten-thousand-volt short had occurred between two of the three copper bars right above Peter. It was like a lightning bolt had hit them.

Later Eric remembered the noise and smoke. Eric was testing on the left side, between the disconnect and the wall, and Peter on the right side. The explosion happened above Peter's head. Eric jumped out sideways and crawled through the smoke and heat to the stairway. The rescue squad that arrived shortly after the explosion found Eric unconscious on the bottom of the steps and carried him on a stretcher into the switch operator's room. It was there that Eric slowly opened his eyes and saw the remnants of the totally burned body of his friend Peter beside him on another stretcher. They told Eric later that he screamed like a wild animal and then fainted again. Eric was taken to the hospital adjacent to the coal mine.

The next thing he remembered, someone was calling his name as if from afar. It took him a while to recognize the voice, and while slowly opening his eyes, he noticed it was Nico. At the same moment, an excruciating pain went through his body, which made him gasp for air. The whole left side of his face was burned, including his lips, and his left arm was in bad shape. It was completely burned from his fingertips to two or three inches above the elbow, where the rolled-up sleeves of his overall had stopped. His wrist was broken of the same arm during his fall down the steps.

When Nico heard about the accident and that Eric was involved in it, he had dropped what he was doing and ran to the emergency room in the hospital to be with his friend. Eric didn't remember much about this time in the emergency room. The next thing he remembered was lying in an ambulance with Nico beside him. His entire head was covered by bandages, and his left arm was tied to a board and covered with a thick protective layer of cotton.

"Peter is dead, isn't he?" uttered Eric through his painful, burned lips. Nico didn't answer but bent his head. "What really happened?" questioned Eric.

"I don't know. I really don't know," answered Nico. "The only thing I found out was that there was an explosion in the electric central station and that you were in it. Someone told me that you screamed very loud when you saw Peter after the explosion."

At that moment, Eric remembered the sight again and cried, "Oh my god!"

For some time, they didn't talk. Eric's mind was in shambles. He couldn't concentrate on anything but only heard the soft, soothing noise of the tires on the road.

"Where are we going?" Eric broke the stillness.

"Home. They are bringing you home," Nico replied. "The doctor said it really wasn't necessary for you to stay in a hospital."

"I wonder if Mom knows about it already," said Eric. "Dad is working day shift this week, and if this ambulance stops in front of our house and Mom realizes it's me in it, she will have a heart attack. Maybe it would be better if you go in first and explain to her what happened and that I'm all right."

"Yes, I guess that's better," Nico replied.

He wanted to stop the ambulance a short distance before home; however, when they turned into his street, Martha and Mr. Pastor were already outside, awaiting their arrival. There were only a few telephones in the village, and Mr. Pastor had received a call from the coal mine, who had brought him up to date on what had happed. Seeing her son in the ambulance covered with bandages, Martha brought her hands up to her mouth and started crying.

When the two ambulance attendants carried Eric inside the house, he said, "Oh, Mom, I guess with all these bandages, it looks worse than it really is. I am all right. You will see me up and running around again in no time." Then Eric turned to the two attendants. "You don't have to carry me in. I think I can walk."

"Maybe you can," answered one of the men, "but we are not allowed to let you do that. We will carry you to your bed, and what you do after we leave is entirely up to you. By the way, we will come back a couple of days from now to pick you up for a checkup on your injuries at the hospital." Then they left.

Mr. Pastor stayed for a while, but when he noticed that everything was under control, he left with "I will pray for you, Eric." Martha guided him to the front door and thanked him for his concern.

When Martha came back into the room, they heard someone shouting downstairs, "Where is he? What happened?" It was

Willem. He ran up the stairs and nearly fell into the bedroom, where he repeated, "What happened?" And then he noticed Eric in bed. "What the hell—excuse me Martha… What happened? I just heard about it a minute ago when I came home with a load of alfalfa."

After holding Eric's right hand for a moment and listening to the story, he went over to the window and sat down on the windowsill. He looked outside and then jumped up again while shouting, "Stop, stop! Get away from there, you big son of a bitch! Excuse me, Martha. I just came back home with a wagon full of alfalfa and that goddam horse of mine is walking with the wagon behind him through the garden, eating up all the vegetables." And then he left with "I'll see you later, Eric."

Slowly getting over the original shock, and while straightening Eric's pillow, Martha said, "You must be in a lot of pain. I wish I could do something for you."

"I don't think there is anyone who could do anything for him," Nico answered. "But wait a moment, there is that old lady on the edge of the village. I have heard she can take pain away."

Martha replied, "Yes, I heard that she can really do that."

"I don't believe in such nonsense," Eric interrupted the conversation.

"You maybe don't believe in these things," said Martha, "but I have heard about some people with strange capabilities. Nico, why don't you go and see if you can get her to come over here? I think her name is Betty, but that's all I know about her."

Betty was a very old and strange woman who lived in a small house all by herself for many years. She walked very slowly with two canes. With her bent back and long gray hair, she reminded Eric of an old witch every time he saw her.

About an hour later, Nico returned with Betty. He had knocked on the door of her small house, and she had listened to his request. Then she had, without saying a word, put a shawl around her head and shoulders and slowly followed Nico. Arriving at the house, she greeted Martha and followed her up the stairs to Eric's bedroom.

She looked at Eric but directed her questions to Martha. "He is your son, isn't he? I think I've seen him around some time or another. Yes, yes, he has a lot of pain. I feel it."

With half-closed eyes, not looking directly at her, Eric watched every move she made. She bent over him, and while whispering something no one could understand, she blew over Eric's face and over the length of his arm. Eric, even with all his pain, had a hard time not laughing, because without any teeth in her mouth, blowing and whispering, she really looked like a witch. After a few minutes, he saw a noticeably painful look on her face.

Again she started murmuring. "Oh what pain… What pain…" Then she said, while leaving the room, "But not for him anymore. The pain will be gone in no time."

Martha wanted to thank her and give her some money or cans of preserves, but she wouldn't hear of it. Leaning on Nico's arm as if under a heavy load, she was escorted home. Eric didn't know what to believe of all this. He thought the old lady meant well, and he should be grateful that she came all the way over. He was keenly aware that the pain hadn't changed a bit. But when Martha came back into the room after making herself a cup of coffee, she found Eric in a deep sleep, which lasted until the late evening. Even in the days that followed, though it was surely painful, the excruciating pain that he had before old Betty's visit was gone.

Many times he thought about Peter and could not accept that he was dead. When they came and picked up Eric for his first checkup at the hospital, he found out what happened from Arnold, who was waiting for him. Arnold was still shaking, and tears rolled down his cheek when he saw Eric with his head and arm all wrapped up in bandages. Among the rubbish left by the explosion in the area where Eric and Peter had been working, they found tiny pieces of the remains of a rat. Somehow, a rat had found its way from the cable cellar into the switching room and must have jumped from one copper bar to the next right above their heads; its front paws and tail must have made an electrical short between the two bars of the ten thousand volts. The immediate lightning flash, which seemed to have occurred directly above Peter, was so intense that he had no chance whatsoever. It was still a miracle that Eric, who was only a few feet away on the other side of the disconnect, had escaped with his life.

The doctor later explained to Eric that since he was only scorched by the heat and not by flames or liquids, his skin would return to normal after a while. Mentally, however, he had received such a shock that when he tried to go back to school again, he couldn't concentrate anymore. When he explained to the mine's psychologist that he couldn't remember or retain anything he was learning, it was decided that he should quit studying for a while, at least for a year.

For the first couple of weeks after the accident, Mr. Pastor became a constant visitor. The first few visits Eric didn't like at all. The gap between them was too wide, and it only kept expanding. Mr. Pastor was the leading figurehead of the village, but Eric accepted him only as long as he stayed on his side of the fence and didn't interfere with Eric's life. Not a single word had passed between them for two years. Even for confessions, Eric had gone to church in the city where no one knew him. He always thought it was ridiculous for the villagers to confess all their sins to someone who knew them all as well as Mr. Pastor did. Though he had gone to Mr. Pastor for many years as a child, he could no longer confess to him as a young adult. After all, what could he say to a man like Mr. Pastor? He couldn't talk to him about girls or his job because the priest wouldn't know what he was talking about. Nor did he feel like talking about his wild engagements with the farm girls in the hay barns or in the fields. He had confessed them already and had been forgiven for his sins.

One afternoon, Eric was lying on top of his bed, reading a book, when he heard his mother opening the door and welcoming Mr. Pastor again into the house. After some small conversation, he heard them coming up the steps. Quickly, Eric dropped the book he was reading and pretended to be asleep.

Entering the room, the priest said. "Hi, Eric. How are you today? Oh, I'm sorry, I didn't know you were sleeping."

Eric couldn't pretend any longer. He was angry with himself that the plan didn't work, and he might just as well go through with it. "Oh, I was just taking a nap," he lied, "but please sit down."

It had been raining all day, and while sitting down, Mr. Pastor took a white handkerchief out of his pocket and cleaned the drops of water from the rather small glasses he had on, which were tied to the bridge of his nose with spring clips. Eric noticed the deep marks that the clips had left over the years on each side of his nose.

He watched for a while and then asked, "Mr. Pastor, doesn't that hurt?" Mr. Pastor looked at Eric, not knowing what he was talking about. Eric explained, "I mean, the imprints from your glasses seem to be rather deep."

"No, I don't feel them, at least not after wearing them for thirty years. I used to wear regular glasses before these, but I didn't like them. I constantly had to adjust them, or they would fall off while I was playing soccer. I broke more glasses at the soccer field than you can imagine."

"Soccer?" Eric questioned. "You played soccer?" He could not believe what he had just heard.

"Sure, I played soccer. And I was pretty good at it too. In my late teens, I even played in the first-class division of the KVV Club, you know." Noticing the look of disbelief on Eric's face, Mr. Pastor started laughing. "I see you don't believe me. It was many years ago, but I still have some newspaper clippings with pictures of me playing soccer stacked away somewhere. Next time I come over, I'll show them to you. I wasn't born a priest, you know," he said, still laughing. "Actually, in my teens, I was the rowdiest young man in my neighborhood. I was constantly in trouble, and I had girlfriends all over the place."

By now, Eric was sitting straight up in his bed. His mouth dropped open, and his eyes must have carried the encouragement for the priest to continue.

"Do you think that priests are just born? You may be destined to become a priest, but you don't know that when you're young."

Eric had to swallow for a moment, because this was news to him. For that matter, he had never really thought about it but had accepted the fact that priests had been religious all throughout their whole lives.

"I may even have been rowdier than you are when I was your age. I didn't even like going to church, and when I needed to go to confession, I would go to another place exactly like you do," Mr. Pastor continued.

"How—" But before Eric could say anything more, he was cut short.

"How do I know about all this? Very simple. Once in a while, you may come to communion, but I never see you coming to confession. You need only to add these things together to get the answer. You aren't the only person who does this, you know. Just come into the church on a Saturday afternoon when I'm holding confessions and see for yourself how many boys and girls your age there are from other villages."

Eric now had to laugh. "Well then, you don't hold it against me either," he said, now feeling for this gray-haired man.

"Not at all, my boy," he answered. "Really, it doesn't matter where you go as long as you keep going. I would prefer, however, that you come and see me. Even if you don't believe it, I know you better than anybody else."

"If all that is true and I have to believe you, then if you were so rowdy and had girlfriends when you were young, what happened to make you become a priest?" Eric questioned.

Smiling, Mr. Pastor answered, "The way you asked that question made it sound as if you think I did a bad thing by becoming a priest. But to answer you honestly, I don't know. I guess it was a chain of events. The Lord must have called me, because over a period of time, everything I had previously regarded highly became unimportant to me. Then one day I shocked not only my parents but also the whole village we lived in by announcing that I was going to study for the priesthood."

The deep gap between Mr. Pastor and Eric was closing, and for more than two hours, Eric, now sitting on the edge of the bed, talked with Mr. Pastor about his life and Mr. Pastor's, who was once called Jan Kuiper before he became a priest. When Eric heard about Mr. Pastor's real name, he had to laugh. He couldn't visualize himself calling Mr. Pastor Jan Kuiper.

Before he left, Mr. Pastor said, "I'm quite busy tomorrow. You see, Thursday I visit the villagers who are hospitalized in the city. But do you mind if I come back Friday afternoon?"

"Please do, Mr. Pastor," Eric answered. "I will be looking forward to it." And this time, he meant it.

About a year later, on a Saturday afternoon, Eric went with Nico to an old city close by. All Eric's injuries had nicely healed by now. It was a beautiful spring day, and both watched the young ladies parading in their new spring dresses. While the two were walking over the marketplace, a group of four ladies walked by, arm in arm, having a good time.

When they saw Eric and Nico, one of the ladies stopped and said to Nico, "Hey, Nico, how is your sister, Tina, doing? I haven't seen her for a long time."

"Oh" Nico answered, "she went to our aunt in another city for a while to help her because she is very sick. Nico's sister was his only sibling; she was two years older and was a nice but quiet girl.

One of the four girls was a slim and very beautiful girl. She had black hair and very dark eyes. With a smile on her face, she asked her friend, who had stopped talking to Nico, "Who is the other gentleman?" She pointed at Eric.

"I am very sorry," Nico answered. "This is my friend Eric. Can we walk with you girls for a while?"

"Sure, come along," the black-haired girl answered and moved closer to Eric.

From that moment, when the two met, something changed in Eric. He name was Lisa, and she was different from all the ladies he'd met before. He could not keep his eyes off her. It seemed as if they were the only two people in the world with an empty space around them. Sometime later, she told Eric that she had the same feeling when she met him. She was very different, and when he looked into her big black eyes, it seemed like they had known each other for a long time. Without asking, he took her arm. She looked at him for a moment but did not resist. Together they walked with the group, but it was as if they didn't even notice them.

He found out that the four girls worked together for a sewing-machine manufacturer. Lisa's job was to test out new machines before they would go into storage. They had all walked together for about two hours when one of the girls remembered that it was time to go home. Eric asked Lisa if he could meet her again soon.

"Oh, please," she answered. "I work from 9:00 a.m. to 5:00 p.m., and you know where the factory is located."

"I am sorry," Eric answered, "but I also work until 5:00 p.m., and it would be at least 6:00 p.m. before I could be here."

She thought for a moment and answered, "On Monday, Wednesday, and Friday evening, I go right from work to my aunt's. She and her husband have no children, and they have a fruit-and-vegetable store. I go there to help fill the bins. You can go there, and together we can bicycle home. However, my parents are old-fashioned and don't want me to have a boyfriend. I am too young. I am only sixteen years old. How old are you, Eric?"

"I am seventeen," he answered. "Then we have to see each other in secret for a while."

So every Monday, Wednesday, and Friday evening, Eric waited for her on his bicycle about a block away from the store. They would bicycle together for about three miles to her home. They chose a lonely road through the fields, so they could stop and kiss without being seen. However, if for some reason she did not go to her aunt's, Eric would be waiting for nearly two hours before going home. She had no way to contact him because except for some wealthy people, nobody had a telephone. Cell phones were not yet invented.

This secrecy went on for nearly one and a half years until finally her parents relented and Eric was allowed to bring her home. Lisa's parents didn't like Eric too much, because of his open nature, he guessed. And if they wanted to see a movie, they had to see the early show on Saturdays or Sunday because her parents wanted their daughter home before 9:00 p.m.

Lisa's parents had been married for nearly ten years, but her mother could not get pregnant for many years. One of her sisters gave birth to a son and died shortly thereafter. Her husband took the baby to Lisa's parents because he could not take care of him. When they had that baby for about two years, something happened with Lisa's mother. Now she had gotten pregnant and, over a period of ten years, had five children of her own. The first child was a daughter, followed by three sons, and then the last child was Lisa. It was a strange family for Eric.

Eric had taken Lisa from the beginning to meet his parents. Martha and John really liked her, and she quickly felt right at home. Both Lisa and Eric fell deeply in love and had a beautiful time together.

Eric mentioned to her that from the time he met the Americans, he promised himself to emigrate to America when he grew up. However, Lisa wanted nothing of it.

"Sorry, Eric. I would never leave my family and friends for another country."

This was the only thing they did not agree on, but Eric thought that it was still a long time to go and maybe she would change her mind.

CHAPTER 4

Most of the coal mines located in the southern part of Holland were owned by the Dutch government. Eric, now eighteen years old, had to make a decision—working underground in one of the coal mines or going into the Dutch Armed Forces. Since there was always a shortage of coal miners, the Dutch government decided that every young man who was willing to work underground had dispensation from the armed forces, which was mandatory at that time. Eric did not want to go into the forces because he would be away from Lisa; they had such good time together.

After quite a lot of discussion, Eric and Nico, by now full-fledged electricians, decided to work underground in the electrical department. After their preliminary checkup, the two joined a group of other young men for a two-week training session to learn the basic techniques in coal mining before joining the underground electrical department.

First, they received their coal miners outfits, consisting of a black helmet, two sets of black sweatshirts and gray cover shirts, heavy brownish trousers, jacket, thick woolen socks, one pair of heavy high shoes with steel noses and thick leather padding overlaying the laces, a pair of leather gloves, and two leather belts. One belt was for the trousers, and one was to hang the flat battery on, which was located on the right hip from where a cable would lead underneath the right arm to the headlamp loosely connected to the helmet.

First on the agenda was the clothing exchange and shower hall. By now, each young man had received his copper pennies showing his miner number. Eric's number was 1296, and Nico's number was 1354. This number would be their name, passport, clothing hanger number, etc. The clothing exchange hall was a very large room with all the miners' numbers on the walls. A long thin chain was connected to each number with hooks and a soap dish attached. After the exchange of clothing, it would be pulled up to the high ceiling. Connected to this hall was another large room with hundreds of shower heads hanging from the ceiling.

Eric and Nico started laughing when they changed into their new miners' uniforms. With the helmets on their heads and the big padded boots, they looked like real coal miners.

"You really look dumb in that outfit," Eric said jokingly.

"You don't look so cute yourself," replied Nico as they followed the group to the training center.

All the rocks that came out of this huge coal mine had been transported from the main shafts in large buckets on overhead cables to this location for over fifty years, resulting into a huge mountain. Long concrete hallways and rooms for training were made inside this mountain of rock. Everyone had to go through this training course before entering the mine and had to learn all about the hazards and safety precautions of deep coal mining.

When the two weeks had passed, Eric and Nico each were assigned to a first-class electrician to be their assistants for a while, and they would teach Eric and Nico all the phases of the electrical system of the mine. It was disappointing when they heard that both had to start on the nightshift and also that for a while, Eric and Nico would be in different sections. The manager of the electrical department, however, promised them that after their training programs with the first-class electrician had ended, they would become first-class electricians themselves and could work together again.

One Monday evening in the fall of 1952, both young men pedaled on their bicycles to one of the largest coal mines at that time in western Europe, called the Mauritz. It was about 8:00 p.m., and both were excited about their first trip down into the mine. Both knew about mining since they grew up between coal mines, but to actually go down was a new experience for them. They had to be earlier today because they still had to receive their sets of electrician's tools and the leather tool bag that would hang on their shoulders and distinguish them as an electrician, a highly respected trade in comparison to a man working on the coal. After exchanging their clothes and receiving their tools and their battery light set, they waited for their first-class electrician in their specific division indicated with name boards of every section in the mine. Nico waited in section C-1 for the 458-meter depth, and Eric went to B-2 for the 660-meter depth.

A deep coal mine was laid out as follows: First, two shafts were bored down each about thirty feet in diameter. By now approximately fifty years later, these two shafts had extended their depths to 810 meters and were continuing to 1200 meters (approximately 3600 feet). One shaft was the fresh air intake, and the other with its huge ventilators was the air exhaust shaft. To direct the flow of air through the entire mine and to prevent shorts between the intake and exhaust air, two thick shut-off doors at least a train length apart were installed in connecting hallways. At five depths (391, 458, 550, 660, and 810) meters were huge loading and unloading facilities. The open spaces around these facilities were enormous, with concrete walls that were two to three feet thick and ceilings that were twenty feet high. The huge halls were used as train stations to transport thousands of people and tons of equipment through the main hallways in all four directions and to receive trainload after trainload of coal and rock to be transported to the top again. From the four main hallways (north, south, east, and west), which were several miles long, side halls were made to reach the coal layers. The many sections where coal was removed (called pylers) were named for Pyler A. (Anton); Pyler B. (Betty), etc. A coal miner who was assigned to, for instance, Betty 1 (there could be a Betty 2 or 3) at the 660 meters knew that he had to find his comrades in the long hallway on top of the mine under the sign B-1 660. He would then go down with this group of workers to the waiting train at the 660-meter depth to the sign B-1 to be transported to Pyler Betty 1.

When miners on dayshift were loaded on top of the mine in the elevators consisting of four sections high, each batch of twelve persons, for a total of forty-eight persons, to go down to, for instance, the 660 meter depth, at the same time at this depth forty-eight persons who had finished their nightshift were loaded to come back up again. The whole traffic of thousands of miners was so organized that the first group to go down at the beginning of the shift were also the first to come up again at the end of the shift, and all took place in about an hour.

The coal mine operated in four shifts from Mondays through Saturdays. Dayshift was from 6:00 a.m. to 2:00 p.m. Afternoon shift was from 2:00 p.m. to 10:00 p.m. Night shift was from 10:00 p.m. to 6:00 a.m. the next day. And the special shift was from 8:00 a.m. to 4:00 p.m., which was only for a special group, such as scholars, shaft maintenance people, and management personnel. Saturdays had only three-quarter shifts, and the hours were from 6:00 a.m. to 12:00 noon for the dayshift. The afternoon shift was from 12:00 noon to 6:00 p.m. The night shift was from 6:00 p.m. to 12:00 midnight.

The afternoon shift was bad enough for a young man since they lost most of the evenings throughout the week, but at least they could go out on Saturday evenings. The night shift, however, was a real disaster. Not only were the weekday evenings shot but also the nicest evening of the week, Saturday.

After some harassment and some snippy remarks from other miners about his brand-new outfit, Eric found his section and the electrician named Math Voorschot. Math seemed to be a nice middle-aged man with a friendly smile who, after sixteen years, knew this mine like the back of his hand.

"This is your first day down. You must be very nervous," Math said, starting the conversation after the two introduced themselves.

"Yes, I am," replied Eric truthfully. All his young life, he had lived among coal miners, and he'd heard a lot about coal mining, but it still made him nervous.

Friendly, but teasingly, some of the miners would pull on his jacket, testing the new material, and pull on his pants to see if his belt was tight enough. Another one offered him some chewing tobacco while spitting out a stream of the black stuff.

Math smiled. "Don't let it bother you, Eric. They are just teasing. It is their way of accepting you as a kompel."

The word *kompel* meant "comrade," and it is only used in the coal mines of Holland and Germany. Constantly the greeting between kompels, "Gluck Auf, Kompel!" is used underground when miners and managers alike passed one another. "Gluck Auf, Kompel" actually is a short form of saying, "I wish you a safe return to the top, comrade."

Deep coal miners are a rare breed. They are pale-faced, enormously strong, rough, and generally uneducated, but are good down-to-earth people. Underground they needed one another and are truly dependent on one another. Unwritten heroisms are performed sometimes at the loss of their lives to rescue a kompel. They are comrades in danger. Besides sleeping to give their tortured bodies a well-earned rest, they worked in their vegetable garden, having the dust from their throats cleaned with the beer at the local pub and discussing loudly the latest news. Weather permitting, they would be sitting on a wooden kitchen chair, leaning backward against the front wall of a house, bringing up memories with other kompels about the good old times when horses instead of locomotives were used underground to pull the wagons. ("Horses who could actually count and who would not move if they heard the sound of one more wagon link than they were supposed to pull," they said.)

On Sundays, after church, they would visit their favorite pub (there were several in the village) for a couple of pints of beer or shots of Dutch gin. After dinner at noon, they would go to the local soccer game. The rest of the generally short time of their existence was, from generation to generation, concentrated around the coal mine.

The sparingly lit, dust-covered hallway before either of the elevator to go down in the mines was filled with the sound of heavy spiked shoes when the first stream of miners who had finished their afternoon shift walked by on the other side of the hallway. Tired, dirty people, some covered with grayish mud that distinguished them as hallway and shaft workers from the totally black workers of the coal front. The white of their eyes and teeth made a sharp contrast with the rest of their coal dust-covered body.

One of them shouted while passing, "Hi, Eric! I didn't know that you were one of us now."

Eric smiled and waved at him but didn't recognize him. A few weeks later, while walking through the village, he discovered it had been one of his own villagers.

Finally, the light on the sign of the group where Eric stood started to blink, indicating that it was their turn to go to the shaft. Eric followed quietly behind Math. The air in the hallway was now thickened with coal dust from the returning miners, which made Eric sneeze a few times.

"Don't let it bother you. After a few days, your whole breathing system will be used to the dust," said Math, and after giving their numbered pennies to the operator, the two went into one section of the elevator named kooi. Twelve people went into each kooi. The elevator operator closed the steel doors behind them and pulled twice on the signal bell to move the whole section down about eight feet to fill up the next kooi. When the section consisting of four koois was filled with a total of forty-eight people, the operator signaled the tower to let this section go down to its destination.

Eric's heart humped when it started to move. He could only see part of the trousers and shoes of his companions, for each one had their headlamp hanging over their shoulders, pointing downward to the floor. The rest was dark.

Will I get sick? he wondered. Sometimes if he used the elevator in a large store, he would feel the pit of his stomach, but nothing like that happened here. He could only feel some trembling of the kooi, which started to move very slow, and once in a while, he could hear some sharp whistling sounds of the whole section that was by then gliding at an enormous speed. The full speed of the elevator transporting people in this coal mine was twenty-seven feet per second, but no one noticed this speed because everything was in darkness. Only small flickers of light were visible when they passed other depths. It seemed like only seconds when the speed slowed down and finally stopped at the 660-meter depth.

The door swung open on one side, and Eric, still amazed by the speedy transport, walked out of the kooi, which was immediately filled up by miners who had finished the afternoon shift, walking from the opposite side. If he wasn't amazed already, he now really stood perplexed. By far, he could never have dreamed what his eyes was witnessing. The space around the shaft was so large and high, and it looked completely white as it was brightly lit with large florescent lights that dazzled him. It was completely different from what he had visualized.

Math had to laugh when he saw Eric's face. "I bet that you had a completely different idea about all this, but come on, or we will miss the train if we hang around here too long. We will come back with an earlier train at the end of this shift, then we will have some time to look around here," Math carried on.

"But why are the walls and ceilings so white?" questioned Eric. "I expected them to be black."

"You see," said Math, "with high pressure air guns, they blast these walls around the shafts with a thick white powder. I believe it is calcium. You will find all throughout the mine boards hanging on crossbars against the ceilings of hallways piled high with that stuff. There is a lot of mine gas that constantly has to be removed by the air flow through the mine, but if there would be an explosion, all that powdery stuff would come loose. It would mix with the air and dampen the fire."

The 550- and 660-meter depths had fresh incoming air. The deeper the coal mine, the more modern it was because every depth was a later addition. The 660 was dry and clean. At least the areas around the shaft and the main hallways were approximately twelve feet wide by eight feet high and well lit, and all through his years at the coal mine, it would be his favorite depth.

Eric followed Math and the rest of the group to the waiting train. The railroads through the mines were of the smaller track, not be confused with the larger railroads he was used to. Therefore, the enclosed wagons to transport miners to their destinations were also small, approximately ten feet long by four feet wide by five feet high with steel hanging doors. In the middle, the operator would remove the doors before the miners arrived. The wagons were high enough to walk in bent position and not wide enough to have two people sit across from each other. The sitting benches inside were staggered and mounted to the sides lengthwise in the wagon. After all the people had entered the wagons, the train conductor walked along the train to hang the doors back on again. The whistle of the train conductor blew, and the engineer moved the handle to start the high air pressure-operated locomotive.

On the fresh-air intake side of the mine were air pressure locomotives, and on the air exhaust side of the mine were diesel engines, which were stronger and could pull more wagons. Therefore, the air on the intake side was dry and fresh, at least in the main hallways, but would be very cold in wintertime. The side with the outgoing air was warm and moist but had the dingy smell of the diesel fuel.

It was not a smooth ride. The wagon wavered back and forth sideways at the speed of about ten miles per hour. Eric sat there listening to every sound and thought it was cozy. The puffing of the locomotive and the quietness of the half-sleeping people in the wagon made him feel warm inside. Now he really was a man; he was a coal miner.

"Hey, kompel, turn that damn headlight off!" shouted one of the miners.

"Yeah, Eric, turn it off," said Math. "Everyone likes to take a little nap in these wagons."

"Sorry," replied Eric, and he did as he was told.

The slowing down and the abrupt stopping of the train woke Eric up as he had also fallen asleep.

"Betty One [B-1]," called the conductor while walking along the train. One of the kompels moved to the door, removed it from the inside, and stepped out.

Eric wanted to do likewise, but Math told him, "Sit down. We have one more stop to go. I will let you know when we have to get out."

The man beside him mumbled "You are a new one, huh" and fell asleep again.

Finally, they reached their destination. The train had stopped after about a thirty-minute ride. Many miners got out and started walking into this sparsely lit hallway. Math stopped Eric and told him to wait, to have the miners go first. It looked quite different than the hallways around the main shaft. It was by far not as clean, and the big heavy steel studs made of railroad track along the sides and above were bent and twisted under the enormous pressures of the forever-moving earth. In one of the sites was a small cave. A piece of rough wood with a hole and cover on it on top of a barrel was neatly fitted between heavy studs. Beside it was another barrel filled with yellowish powder. It was an "outhouse" with no door in front of it.

"I see no paper. How can you—"

"That is why you never throw away the paper sandwich bag," Math said, shortening Eric's question. "After you use this, you can throw a handful of the yellow powder in it to diminish the smell."

Heavy steel wound electric cables hung on metal hooks along the studs. Math watched them with his headlight to see that no hooks were broken or cables damaged. After about a five-minute walk, the two stopped at an electrical station built into the side of the hallway. It was about five feet wide by fifteen feet long by five feet high and was neatly closed off by a fence with a door and lock. It was filled with heavy explosive-proof electrical equipment, and everything was kept fairly clean.

Math opened the lock and said, "Let's go in. Sit down and have a sandwich. We have to wait anyhow for the miners to go first into the pyler."

Eric's throat was dry and, before sitting down, took his one-liter flask filled with still-lukewarm coffee out of his inside jacket pocket and gulped the liquid down in large swallows.

"Hey, hold it. Don't drink that much at once. You have a whole shift to go yet," warned Math. "Let that be your first lesson. Always take only a little swallow at a time so you distribute the coffee the length of the shift. There is no drinking water here, so watch it."

After explaining the electrical equipment and the telephone systems in this coal mine, Math went on to explain the system of coal removal. "Let's take one pyler, for instance. Millions of years ago, all earth layers in western Europe moved and were crushed against a huge basalt block in Siberia thousands of miles long and miles thick. That's why all earth layers here are at angles, including the coal layers. Shine your light across the hall, and you will see the layers. The coal layers in between rock range from 1 inch thick to 7 or 8 feet thick and run on an angle from, let's say, the east side far away from the main shaft at the 390-meter depth through the next system of hallways at the 458-meter depth, then through the main shafts to the 540-meter depth, then to the 660-meter depth, and on. So a section of coal, let's say, Betty Two (B-2), where we are going to work in, runs all the way from the 390-meter depth to this depth 660 meters under an angle. This section of coal front is called a pyler. Miners are transported to this pyler at 540-meter depth, for example, and other miners are going to the 660-meter depth."

While telling Eric all this, Math drew a picture of the mine on the dusty front cover of one of the electrical boxes. Two vertical stripes represented the main shafts, four horizontal lines were the four depths, one small horizontal line at the bottom portrayed the 810-meter depth under construction, and then other lines at an angle from the top right to the bottom left through the shafts and depths showed the coal layers. He did such a beautiful job of it that Eric had to congratulate him on a job well done.

Math smiled and carried on, "The day and afternoon shifts are the coal-producing shifts. Starting with the day shift against the coal front are studs underneath steel crossbeams against the ceiling with small wooden boards in between to keep smaller loose rock from falling down. Next to the steel studs, which are telescoping and can be adjusted to the proper height, are conveyer belts as long as the pyler is. Then the next stud hold up the other end of the steel crossbeam. Another one is connected to this crossbeam with again studs underneath it. Sometimes instead of conveyor belts, they use steel sheets called shuttles. These shuttles are long steel trays that slide by air cylinders individually and quickly up and down to transfer the coal down the pyler."

"In the morning, the 'shuttle boss'—his actual title is foreman—crawls down the empty conveyor or shuttle. The miners follow him and mark with a piece of chalk four or five studs along the coal for each man so each miner has his own section. The miner uses his air hammer with a sharp pointed chisel and makes himself a niche in the coal while working over the moving conveyor belt. When the niche is large enough, he crawls over the conveyor belt into the niche and makes it larger. When he has gone deep enough into the coal, he connects one ceiling crossbeam to the one that was already on the coal front and installs a stud under the end in the niche. Now he hammers the coal loose and shovels it into the conveyor or shuttle with short-handle shovels until he has done his four or five studs one stud at the time."

"How does he get the studs and wooden boards he needs?" Eric interrupted Math.

"Some of the materials are transported from the top down on the conveyor belt, and he takes off whatever he needs. To get the studs, he has to crawl over the conveyor again to where the night-shift left them in the crawling space. The afternoon shift most times finishes the sections of coal the dayshift leaves behind, so at the end of the two shifts, a strip of coal about four feet deep all along the whole length of the pyler is removed. All this coal is transported over sometimes miles of conveyors to the train loaders in one of the larger hallways."

"What if something goes wrong in the pyler? What happens then?" Eric questioned.

"The electrical lights over the whole length of the conveyor have push buttons," Math answered. "When someone pushes the button once, all the lights will go out once, and the conveyor operator will shut down. As soon as the problem is cleared up, he will push the button two times to signal the operator he can start the conveyor again. Four times blinking the lights means break time, which is only ten minutes before the conveyor starts up again. Also, a thin steel cable is installed above and along the whole length of the conveyor. When this cable is pulled, the conveyor stops immediately. To start the conveyor again, the miner will push the light button twice to signal the operator to start up again.

"Most of the night shift people supply and store equipment, lengthen or shorten conveyors and hallways, and dismantle and move the conveyor or shuttle along the coal front again over the whole length of the pyler. Except for miners who work in hallways or shafts and maintenance personnel, the remaining and largest amount of the miners get everything ready for the dayshift again.

"Our job as electricians is to disconnect all sections of the light cables and hang them along the new coal front again, also to lengthen or shorten the cables to large motors of the conveyors and general overhaul. In other words, we will see to it that the electrical system is ready again for the day shift. If you are friendly with the miners and once in a while help them when they run into a problem, they will help you by moving the light section because they are working over the whole length of the pyler anyway. But if they don't like you, then you will work your butt off at night for sure if you have also some electrical problems elsewhere."

Far off in the distance, someone was flickering his headlight on and off. Seeing it, Math said, "Come on, Eric. They are signaling us that they have a problem. They know I am here. We have to hurry." Both men swung their leather tool bags over their shoulders again and rushed to the signaling man.

"Conveyor number 5 stopped, and they can't get it going again," complained the kompel.

"Okay, we'll take a look at it," Math answered.

They crawled up a small steel ladder into a smaller hallway where a three-foot-wide conveyor was running in the direction of the pyler to supply materials.

"We'll jump on it. Then we won't have to walk all the way. Watch me," Math said. He first threw his tool bag on the conveyor and then jumped on it. Eric did likewise.

"Is that allowed?" Eric asked.

"Sure," replied Math. "Everyone uses it. Do you see that red light in the far distance? That's where we have to jump off. That's the end of this conveyor and the beginning of conveyor number 2. In the daytime, this conveyor will run in the opposite direction to transport the coal to the train loader. Rollers under the conveyor with two on the outside at an angle upward and one in the center make it look like a moving cradle."

Lying flat on his stomach, Eric felt like getting a massage while passing over the rollers. It was very still in this hallway except for the soft sound of the turning rollers; once in a while, there was the noise of a bad bearing in the roller coming from afar to pass by and then into the distance again. Eric enjoyed all he had witnessed so far, and he really liked Math.

What a helluva guy! Eric thought. He couldn't have found a better man and teacher. *What would Nico be doing at this moment?* He hoped that he also had a companion like Math.

"Hey, don't fall asleep!" Math's voice echoed through the hallway.

"No, Math, I wasn't asleep. I was only thinking," replied Eric, wondering if he actually did fall asleep.

"Come on, don't overdo it now," answered Math jokingly.

In the meantime, the noise of an electrical motor and a red light came near, and Math got ready to jump off. They both jumped off at the same time. A miner who was cleaning up at the intersection of the two conveyors greeted both men with a "Gluck Auf" as they walked by.

After jumping on the next conveyor, Eric questioned, "If this is only the second conveyor and we still have three to go, how long is this hallway?"

"Oh, I guess at least a mile," replied Math. "This pyler, Betty 1, is an old one, and this hallway just follows the coal front. The farther they follow and remove this coal layer, the longer the hallway will be."

Finally, they reached their destination and walked along conveyor number five, which was not running, to the waiting miners, who had already cleaned up around the electric motor in case this motor was defective.

"It is about time you fellows got here," moaned one of the men. "We have to transport some equipment back through the loader, and we are running later."

"I hope that it is not the motor," replied Math.

"We have a spare one, but it is lying beside conveyor number 2, and it would be quite a job to get that one here."

"How are the lights coming along in the pyler?" questioned Math.

"I think it's going all right, but we have trouble in one section."

"I think there is a cut in the cable," answered another miner.

"While we are fixing this motor here, would you please call for a spare light section to be transported down from the top of the pyler?" Math asked the man.

While the miner cranked the handle of the telephone to call his counterpart on top of the pyler, Eric noticed how heavy and explosive-proof the telephone was.

The thing must weigh at least ten pounds! Eric thought.

"Eric, will you check the cable from the starter to the motor and see if it is pinched or damaged between the studs? I'll open the starter and see if the problem lies here," said Math.

Eric followed the heavy armored cable, which hung neatly on chains rolled up against the side wall to give added length for the following conveyor with the extended coal front. But Eric couldn't find anything wrong here. In the meantime, Math had loosened all the bolts and removed the half-inch-thick explosive-proof cover of the motor starter. Within minutes, he found the problem. One of the small wires had come loose, and in no time, the conveyor was running again.

"Sometimes we are lucky," said Math while wiping the sweat from his forehead. "Now let's go into the pyler and replace the light section." He hung his jacket on a cable hook. Eric did likewise and followed him but not after first taking some swallows of his coffee.

It was the first time Eric saw a pyler. This one was not more than three feet high. It was dimly lit, and the air was very dusty from the miners working on the conveyor and filled with steel studs like trees in a forest. The crawlspace between the studs, which were neatly in line, was about three feet wide, but it was filled with studs, ceiling crossbars, and people. For the first time, Eric was scared. As long as he could stand up, it had not bothered him, but now crawling on his knees, he felt a panicky feeling and the dangers of coal mining. Eric crawled on, pushing the tool bag in front of him. The helmet on his head constantly hit the crossbeams. His shoulders and arms scraped against the studs, and his knees and shins were bruised and scraped from the hard and sometimes sharp bottom and from crawling over what seemed like hundreds of studs and crossbars. At some places, the bottom was smooth like glass, and Eric would glide back a few feet, pulling himself forward again on the studs. Even his battery, which before hung loosely on his right hip, had been moved as he was crawling. It was now under his belly and was hitting him against his thighs. He felt the sweat dripping off the tip of his nose.

What a way of living, he thought. No, this was not for him. This would be the first and last day for him in any coal mine.

The sound of something like three or four pistol shots scared the living daylights out of him. "What was that?" was all he could get out.

Math stopped and, while lying on his side, looked at Eric. "Oh, that's nothing. You don't have to be scared of that," he replied, smiling as he saw Eric's panic-stricken face. "The night shift people also remove with hand-operated wenches and long steel cables the last row of studs and ceiling crossbars about twenty feet from the coal front and let that path slowly cave in. Those are the studs and crossbars lying in our way. The dayshift will use them again. At some spots, the ceiling without studs doesn't break up for a couple of days but slowly kind of bends down before breaking. When it bends down, these telescoping studs still standing give a little, a half inch or so at a time. Most of the time, this contracting of the studs, instead of gliding easily together, will jump and will give these sounds. You will hear that so many times it won't bother you anymore."

"Boy, it really scared me," confessed Eric. "I thought the whole thing was going to come down on us."

"I believe you. There will be many happenings that will scare you, but after a while, you will know the difference between the dangerous and the nondangerous sounds of a coal mine."

"Math, let's stop here for a moment. I'm exhausted," Eric asked while rubbing his sore knees.

"No, not yet. We first have to install that new light section so the miners can signal the conveyor operators again. I think we are nearly there." Math went on, and Eric struggled along.

A man shouted, "Hey, Math, is that you? Here it is. There is a cut right here in the cable where I am working." When they both arrived, the man showed them the infraction.

"Why did you do that?" said Math jokingly. "Now tell me, why did you cut the cable?"

The kompel smiled and answered, "If I didn't do that, you electricians would have nothing to do at all, and you would get way too fat to work the pyler."

"Look who's talking," said Math while pointing to the man's stomach. Matt was right. This man was huge—not really fat, but was tremendous muscular build.

He had taken his sweatshirt off, and his sweating body, which was covered with black coal dust, showed his muscular upper torso like that of Hercules.

"So that's your new assistant?" he said, looking at Eric. "He doesn't look so peppy. Here, have a piece of chewing tobacco. That will get your blood going again."

"No, thank you," said Eric. "I can't even stand the smell of that stuff, not to mention putting it into my mouth."

"You will learn," answered the man while biting a couple of inches off the twisted, rolled-up black chewing tobacco. "Nearly every coal miner chews. It keeps our mouth full of moisture so you don't have to drink as much." He offered his tobacco to Math.

Math accepted this gift but bit off only a small piece, which he then guided with his tongue between the cheek and gum of his upper teeth. Math, noticing the questioning look on Eric's face, answered him, "Yes, Eric, I chew too, but on me, it isn't noticeable. I guess it's because I only take a little bit at a time so I don't have to spit all over the place. Do you want to try just a little piece?"

"No, thank you, Math. I don't think my stomach could handle it."

"By the way, Math, your new section light is lying over there. I pulled it off the conveyor when it arrived here," the man said, changing the subject. "Do you need a hand putting it in?"

"No, thank you," replied Math. "You helped us already quite enough. Eric and I will have it done in no time." Math removed the ropes on the bundle of cable and lights and handed the plug of one end of the cable to Eric. "Never throw these pieces of rope away because we need them again to bundle up the defective light section,"

Math explained. "Now go down about thirty feet and unplug the defective section and plug in the new one. I will do the other end the same farther up."

Math pulled on his end. In no time, the light section was replaced, and both men took a well-deserved rest. They rolled up the defective section, tied it together with the pieces of rope, and left it with the miner, who would throw it on the conveyor once that was running again to be transported to the electrical repair shop on top of the mine.

While they were lying beside each other, Math congratulated Eric on a job well done. "You didn't do bad at all for your first day." Math started the conversation. "Most men that come down for the first time complain all day long and practically do nothing."

"Don't kid yourself," said Eric. "When we were crawling up this pyler, I promised myself that this was not for me. However, my mind is changing in the meantime."

"I know what you went through. No one can tell me that it isn't hard on you. Your whole body will be sore for days as it isn't used to crawling on hands and knees for hours, not even talking about the cuts and bruises you will receive all the time. After a while, when your body is used to it, you will move through these pylers like a cat without hurting yourself at all. You will also come to the conclusion that crawling down a pyler is just as bad as crawling up, because you will constantly glide down on the slippery spots into the studs and crossbars. Since most of the conveyor has already been put into place along the coal front again, not running yet, we can easily crawl down on top of it. If nothing else goes wrong, we will go down after a while, take a break, and go slowly back to the loading place. On the way back, we can inspect the electrical cables and see if we have to replace a few cable hooks. Normally, I crawl up to the top of this pyler to see if everything is still in good shape, but I was there last Saturday evening, and I don't think anything has changed since."

After some rest, Eric didn't feel as tired anymore, but his whole body ached. Like Math had explained, the trip down over the not-yet-in-operation conveyor belt was easier, and in no time at all, they crawled out at the bottom of the pyler into the hallway. Eric moaned from the sharp pain in his back when he finally could stand up straight again. He stretched a few times and felt pain shooting through his body. It seemed as if all his muscles were sore. His young and healthy body adjusted quickly, and after a couple of big swallows of his cold coffee, he put on his jacket, swung his tool bag over his left shoulder, and followed Math on the way back alongside conveyor number 5.

"Let's walk on for a while, maybe to conveyor number 3, where it is nice and quiet to sit down and take a break," said Math while adjusting the electrical cables where necessary on the way.

Once in a while, when a cable hook had stretched out under the heavy weight of the cable, Math would bend them back again. With his left hand, he would push the cables up, and by guiding the hole in the handle of a twelve-inch adjustable wrench over the hook, he would bend it back again with his right hand. Eric noticed how neat Math kept his domain and praised him for it.

"When you get your own section, Eric, keep it the same way, and you will have less problems," Math replied.

Coming closer to the exchange between conveyor number 5 and conveyor number 4, Math stopped abruptly. "Eric, quickly get the light off your helmet and shine it to the floor," he said in a soft voice. "Do you see that light on the floor right at the conveyor exchange? I'll bet you that is the old man sitting there with his headlight upside down in the dust and he has fallen asleep. Let's play a joke on him and give him a good scare. You know that it is against the rules to fall asleep in a coal mine, and it is reason for immediate dismissal if someone finds you this way. The reason is safety. If you are asleep, you don't know about any occurring dangers. It is unsafe for yourself, but more so, you can't warn anyone else of any danger."

Slowly and carefully, so as not to make any noise, the two walked up to the sleeping man. He was sitting on an old wooden toolbox with his back against two pieces of wood. One hand was holding the sandwich bag on his lap, and the other arm hung lifeless along his side. A half-eaten sandwich was underneath his hand. He was in a deep sleep, his head hanging forward against his chest, breathing heavily.

"Now, watch it," whispered Math. "I'm going to bring my head-lamp to within a couple of inches from his face and turn the light on. That will scare the living daylights out of him."

What they both expected didn't happen at all. They expected the old man to jump up as if a bee had stung his behind, but nothing like that happened. For a few seconds, nothing moved; his head or any muscle didn't twitch at all. Slowly, with his head still bent forward, he raised his hand and pushed Math's light sideways.

"You should be ashamed of yourself," he uttered without showing any shock or emotion and completely in control of his senses. "Can I not even have an uninterrupted prayer before I eat my sandwich?"

For a moment, Math and Eric looked at each other, not believing what just happened. Then they started to laugh until tears rolled down their cheeks. The old man had outfoxed them.

"Oh, Math, it's you. You surely gave me a scare," said the man while moving to one end of the box. "Come on, sit down, you two, and have a sandwich with me."

It took Math and Eric quite some time before finally calming down to sit beside him on that toolbox. "Never in all my years in this mine have I ever seen anything like this," said Math, still gasping for air.

"Well," said the man, "you're still a kid here compared to me. I have been in the mine for almost thirty-nine years, and if I hadn't learned anything by now, I would never learn."

While eating their remaining sandwiches, Math and the old man exchanged memories of their lives in the mine, memories of their hard and dangerous occupation.

"Sixteen years old I was," the old man carried on while neatly cutting off a piece of juicy chewing tobacco with a small pocket-knife. He then offered it to Math and Eric. Math accepted, while Eric shook his head. "Sixteen years old when I followed my father down into the pit. That was not in this mine. That was the Willem II. Mining was completely different at that time. It was by far not as safe as it is now. Horses instead of locomotives were used, and man and horse were dependent on each other. I must say the horses were better taken care of than the people. It would take them a while to get used to the darkness. In that time, lights were only used sparingly. But the horses adjusted quickly, and man and beast became one. If they would be transported back to the top again after some time in the mine, they had to be blindfolded because the daylight would hurt their eyes.

"The first two years, I had a job as stall boy at one of the depths, taking care of the horses. I can tell you quite some stories about them. Some of them were like pals and very smart. Other ones were bastards and would kick and bite you whenever you gave them a chance. One of them really got me." He opened his shirt to show the deep scars on his left shoulder.

He continued, "This one named Blackie was a big strong horse. Everyone had warned me about him, but after months of looking after him, I didn't think that he was all that mean. One day, however, when I was leading him into the stall, he got ahold of my shoulder, and the son of a bitch didn't let go. The sharp pain of tearing flesh made me scream so loud that it echoed through the hallways. I was lucky that one of the kompels in the hallway heard my screams and got me free from this devil. Otherwise, he would have taken off my arm. It took sixty-two stiches to sew everything together again, but my left arm has never been the same. This was Blackie's last deed, however, because that same day he was sent to the slaughter. After months of healing, I went down again but this time to work the coal front. I don't know where all these years have gone. Four more months and I will retire. It seems like yesterday I went down for the first time."

"Is your dad still living?" questioned Math.

"No, he died years ago at a cave-in at Willem II, and my younger brother died here in this mine while deepening one of the shafts. I have two sons, and I'm happy that neither one is even connected to a coal mine. The oldest one is married to a farmer's daughter and has taken over the farm, and my youngest son is a foreman at the shipyards in Rotterdam."

Eric could have listened for hours to the old man's stories, but Math thought it was time to move on. After wishing him "Gluck Auf," the two went on their way.

"I hope that he has many years to live and enjoy his retirement pension," remarked Eric.

"I hope so too," replied Math. "But as you well know, most coal miners after they retire at the age of fifty-five, are worn out and old for their age. Most of them die within ten years or so. It is a shame the only thing they knew all their lives was hard work in sometimes unbelievable conditions and once they earn their pension and for the first time in their lives can take it easy, they die. There must be a special section in heaven for coal miners where the sun shines all day and beer is in abundance."

The two walked on, passing one conveyor after another, adjusting the cables and hooks when necessary. The hallway seemed to go on forever, and Eric was getting tired.

"Math, the red light is broken at the loading section," mentioned one of the miners when the two finally reached the end of the hallway.

"Were there any calls for me?" Math questioned the man.

"No, Math. You are lucky today. Everything is running smoothly," the kompel answered.

Math and Eric replaced the light bulb in the red warning light and walked back down the hallway to the electrical station they had started from at the beginning of the shift.

"Should we take an earlier train back so I can show you the main electrical station around the main shaft?" Math asked.

"No, Math, if you don't mind, not today. I had enough for one day or, better, for one night. Now sitting here, I really feel how tired I am."

"You are right," Math replied. "This night was not too bad, but beside this kind of work, you also have to get use to the night shift."

For some time, they sat there. Then in the far distance, the dancing of small lights came toward them.

"The shift has ended. Those are the kompels returning from the pyler," Math said while closing the lock on the door of the electrical station.

They waited for the miners, and together they walked to the beginning of the hallway, where they would wait for the train, which would take them back to the main shaft again. Eric slept all the way back in the train. The sharp lights surrounding the main shaft hurt his eyes, and the cool morning air entering the mine made his body shiver. The whole group of Betty 2 stood there waiting until finally it was their turn. A man who was in charge of traffic control opened the box on the wall of the numbered pennies, which was brought down from the top of the shaft during the shift. The pennies were neatly hung in order so that any pennies left behind after every shift was immediately questioned by a telephone call made by the traffic controller with the proper authorities for their legality. If there was no reason for one of the pennies not being removed, an immediate search was made for this missing person.

In no time, the men from Betty 2 were loaded and brought up to the surface again. This time, they were passing in the hallway the clean-faced miners, who were waiting in their section to start the dayshift again. Math stopped for a moment on the sign of Betty 2 to discuss with his counterpart, the dayshift electrician, the happenings of that night. After leaving their light and batteries in the "battery-loading booth" and returning the tool bags in their lockers, both men walked on to the clothing exchange room and the showers.

"I will wait for you upstairs at the office of the electrical department to show you how to report," said Math when both men parted to find their own clothing hanger.

Here, for the first time while looking into a mirror, Eric saw how black he really was. The white eyeballs and his teeth made a sharp contrast with the rest of his face. Quickly he took off his shoes, dropped his miner's clothing on the floor, and walked into the huge steamed-up shower room. He felt strange when he saw hundreds of naked men standing under the showers, talking to one another. As a child, he had gone swimming naked in creeks with the other boys of the village, but never had he been between naked men. He didn't dare to look at their bodies or watch them washing their organs. While standing there, looking for an open shower, his eyes must have given away his shyness because one of the kompels threw a chunk of soft lava soap, which was in buckets along the walls, against his belly. Then three or four kompels started laughing.

"He must be a new one," shouted one of them.

"Here, you can have this shower. I'm finished."

Not knowing what to say, Eric mumbled "Thank you" while blushing all over.

"Don't let it bother you," said another miner with a smile on his face. "This is your baptizing. All of us went through this once, and you will do this to others too."

Eric smiled at the man and stepped under the shower. The massage of the streaming water over his body felt good. He could have stayed there for hours. He must have stood there for some time, dreaming.

The friendly man beside him put his hand on Eric's shoulder. "Come on, fella, you have to get going. Other kompels are waiting. Come here. I will wash your back."

Eric felt the hard calloused-covered hands of the man washing his back. It was not the soft hands he remembered of his mother when he was a youngster but the hard hands of a coal miner. When the man finished, Eric turned around. He wanted to wash his back, but he saw that another kompel was already doing that. Another one was washing that man's back, and a fourth one was washing the third man's back too, all in a row.

"Go to the last man, and wash his back," said the man who had washed Eric's back, noticing the look on Eric's face.

Eric walked over to the last man in the row. "Can I wash your back?" he asked politely.

"You don't ask, kompel. You just do it," said the man.

He also learned how to wash the coal dust from the eyelids between the lashes. This was hard to remove. The only way to remove it was by pushing and lightly rubbing one eye at a time against the soft wet flesh of the upper arm. This way, it left a black ring of coal dust behind on the arm like prints of the eyelashes. Trying to get it off with soap was impossible and would only irritate the eyes.

Fresh and clean again, Eric walked up the big stairway to the electrical offices where Math was sitting on a bench, waiting for him. Together they went to one of the small windows and waited until the foreman could see them.

"Morning, Eric," greeted the foreman while opening the small window. "How was your first shift?"

"All right," answered Eric. "It was not as bad as I thought it would be."

The foreman smiled and said, "You must have had a good night." Then turning to Math, he asked him if he needed anything for his section.

"Not now," Math answered. "But in the next two weeks, we need some more cable. I am running out, and the pyler is advancing rapidly."

"Okay, Math. I'll see to it."

When the two parted from the foreman, Math explained to Eric, "Since we will work together for a while, you don't have to report. I will do that for the two of us, but once you have your own section, you will have to come here before and after the shift."

"Okay, Math. You are a helluva guy to work with, and I will see you tonight in the Betty 2 section," replied Eric. Then he walked away to look for Nico.

After about a ten-minute wait in the large entrance hall, the two met. Nico also had a fairly easy shift, and both young men discussed their experiences of the night while walking together. After throwing their numbered pennies in a box in the exit hall, they went to the bicycle building. It was a rainy morning, and after putting their raincoats on, they pedaled their bicycles home. The whole trip back, they didn't talk much. Both were tired and cold from the early morning rain.

When they parted, Eric said, "Have a good sleep, Nico. I will walk over to your place around three this afternoon."

"Okay, kompel, and Gluck Auf," answered Nico. Both looked at each other and smiled. Their first shift as a coal miner had ended.

Eric put his bicycle under the porch and went into the kitchen, where his mother was putting breakfast on the stove. It smelled good, a mixture of fried eggs and strong coffee. Johann and Paul were sitting at the kitchen table, waiting for breakfast, and he heard Elly moving around in her bedroom upstairs. Elly, Eric's only sister and twelve years younger than him, was Martha's pride and joy. His father had already left for the dayshift.

"Well, good morning," greeted his mother. "You must be cold. Get your raincoat off, and first drink a cup of hot coffee. Then tell us how it was underground."

When most questions had been answered and he'd had his breakfast, Eric really felt exhausted. After wishing everybody a "good night," which seemed odd since it was about eight in the morning, he tiredly walked up the stairs to his bedroom, closed the curtains, crawled into bed, and fell asleep.

When Eric woke up early in the afternoon, his body ached so much he had to slowly roll out of bed. Every muscle in his body had stiffened, and he needed all his willpower to stretch them again. Painfully he dressed, but putting his socks on was real hell.

The rain had stopped. The dark-gray clouds had moved on, and the fall sun warmed the earth again, promising a beautiful sky. Sitting on a chair in the kitchen, he saw his mother feeding some leftover pieces of bread to the chickens in the meadow. He must have inherited his feeling for nature and its animals from his mother, he realized as he watched her. Standing there with all the chickens around her, it seemed that they knew her and she knew them. While talking to them, she slowly bent over and picked up one of them, who with her wings slightly spread had expected Martha to do so. Also, some trained neighborhood pigeons flew in, and one landed on her left shoulder. It was a beautiful sight to see—his mother standing there with one chicken in her arms and a pigeon on her shoulder. Eric watched this trio for a while with warmth in his heart for his mother.

When she walked out of the meadow, he went outside to greet her. "Hi, Mom. Isn't this weather gorgeous for this time of the year?"

"Oh, hi, Eric. Yes, it is. Take one of these chairs and move it into the sun. While you sit there, I will make you something to eat. By the way, Nico was here a few minutes ago. He will be back shortly. He just went to the store to get some cigarettes."

A few minutes later Nico walked in. "Hi, Eric. Is your body as wrecked as mine is?" he said while falling into another chair next to Eric. "When I woke up, I had the feeling my whole body was aflame and stiff as a board."

"Me too," replied Eric. "I felt terrible, but this sun feels good."

"Nico, would you like something to eat too?" called Eric's mother from the kitchen. "I am preparing sandwiches and some fried eggs."

"No, thank you, Mom. I have eaten already," Nico answered. "But I'll take a cup of coffee."

Both Eric and Nico had called each other's parents Mom and Dad since they were little.

The abuse on Eric's body lasted for about two weeks before the pain finally subsided. For another month, he worked together with Math and observed not only his ways of working habits but also the tricks of the trade. The most important lesson he learned was to never rush into a situation or break down regardless of the swearing or cursing of the pyler manager, who during the breakdowns would become inhuman. He should always observe, ask, and analyze a situation first, and only then could he work as fast and effectively as possible to correct the trouble.

Eric was well liked by the miners and, in no time, was known as a hard worker and a very good electrician. Eric's manager, who observed him closely, was very pleased and, within two months, promoted him to first-class electrician. He now had his own pyler to maintain, Kate Two (K-2) at the 458-meter depth. It was a small pyler, and the electrical installations were in chaos. The previous electrician who'd had this pyler for years had now retired and left everything in a complete mess.

The miners who had worked together with the old man for years missed him very much, and they regarded Eric as an intruder. Eric felt this resistance, but his friendly nature and helpful hand soon bridged this gap. His cleanliness and hard work changed the whole electrical system within a few weeks to an organized installation. He rolled up some of the heavy armored cables that lay on the floor in the hallways in everybody's way and hung them neatly on the walls with heavy chains and hooks. Also, he found a place to store spare motors and other electrical equipment that were lying all over the place.

He did such a good job that the manager of this pyler, a rough and tough man who through years of hard work had climbed the ladder from miner to manager, one day mentioned to him, "You did a terrific job, young man. I never saw this pyler that organized. I'll notify your management of a job well done."

One thing Eric still had to learn was how to divide his supply of coffee over the shift. This pyler was farther away from the main shaft than the one he had been in with Math, and the air was a lot warmer. Also, it was connected to the air exhaust shaft, so the air had a heavier smell. Every time, while crawling into the pyler, he would take his coffee flask with him so when he came down on break time, his flask was empty. The older kompels gladly gave him some of their coffee but told him that he had to learn to chew tobacco. If he chewed, he wouldn't need to drink all the time. But Eric didn't give in. He couldn't even stand the smell of the chew. He had finally agreed to leaving his flask in his jacket at the bottom in the hallway instead of taking it with him.

One day, however, they were going to teach him to chew, and without even thinking of the drastic results, some kompels dropped a whole roll of the black juicy stuff in his flask while Eric went into the pyler. When break time came along, Eric crawled down the pyler as fast as he could. He was completely dried out, his stomach felt like leather, and his throat was full of dust. Arriving at the bottom, he took the flask and gulped the coffee down his throat. When he stopped to catch his breath, however, he realized what had happened to his coffee, and without warning, his stomach pushed the liquid out of his mouth like a fountain. The remaining of the shift, he was so sick to his stomach that he couldn't do anything. The kompels, realizing what they had done, felt so sorry that they wanted to do anything to comfort him, but Eric was too sick and too angry to accept their gestures at that time.

"What the hell is the matter with you people? You bastards nearly killed me!" Eric snapped at them between the cramps in his stomach.

"We are very sorry, Eric. We didn't know that you would drink all that coffee at once. Most of us first take a small swallow to clean the dust out of our mouth and then spit it out before we drink," explained one of the kompels. "We had no idea. We really are very sorry, and we want to make it up to you." And they did. As long as Eric worked in that pyler, they assisted him whenever possible.

A few weeks later, he finally tried a tiny piece of chewing tobacco. "Put it between your cheek and gum of your upper teeth," explained one of the kompels. "There is not as much saliva. Just let it sit there, and don't suck on it."

Eric tried it and noticed right away the development of saliva in his mouth. A couple of times, he spit the saliva. Soon his stomach got used to it, and he could swallow small amounts. He rather liked it and, after a while, asked another kompel for some more. The next day, he bought a small roll that came in a small metal box, and Eric became a tobacco chewer like the rest of the miners. It completely changed his drinking habits. It was not only about the chewing; the giving or accepting of a piece of chewing tobacco was also an acceptance of friendship between coal miners.

Eric converted Nico, who also by now had a pyler to maintain in the same area, to chewing. They chewed underground but never on top of the mine. After a half year of having their own division to maintain, both young men became known by the management as top-rated electricians. They were relieved of their jobs in the pyler and trained as trouble-shooting electricians, the elite group in the electrical department. From night shift, they went to the three shifts and traveled many times together through the whole mine. The trouble shooting included all underground main electrical systems, telephone network, large electrical stations surrounding the shaft, and the electrical systems for mechanical pylers where the coal was removed by metal scrapers pulled by five-hundred-horsepower motors and steel cables three inches in diameter instead of miners because the layer of coal was only two feet high, too small for people to work.

Traveling through the whole mine, Eric witnessed and enjoyed all that deep coal mining had to offer. He studied the different-colored layers of rock and the beauty of some of the quartz crystals, which were dazzling when the light from his headlamp fell upon them. At the desk in his bedroom, he had already quite a collection of pieces of rocks covered with fossils of small clams and ferns, and the quartz crystals converted his bedroom into an amazing place; they changed colors when the sunlight was reflected off them.

During his early coal mine years, Eric fell deeply in love with Lisa. She was younger than Eric but matched him in wisdom and the feeling for God's beautiful nature. Together they would walk for hours through the fields and woods surrounding them for miles and enjoy the closeness of each other in this wonderful environment. Except for Lisa's parents, who still didn't agree at all with Eric's free-minded thinking about life, the lives of these two young people were full of discoveries, the way it should be for young people in love. They could talk for hours about their future together. Emigrating to America was forgotten.

While walking through the woods, they would rest on a layer of cool fresh fern leaves, the sun caressing them with its warm rays as if it was blessing two of its children. They would lie there with love-bursting bodies into nature's highest glory and most powerful force, the force of unification. After the storm and the lightning in their bodies had quieted down into a tranquility of calm and tenderness, they would lie beside each other and only then could feel the sun and hear the singing of the birds. Both knew that their love for each other would reach eternity.

Lisa was different than the other girls he knew. While she was from another village, she had heard all about Eric's wild drinking brawls and his numerous short love affairs, but that didn't bother her. She knew he was hers and hers alone, and that was all there was to it. Eric knew he was changing. Was it the chain of events that had occurred the last couple of years, or was it just growing up? He didn't know. Had it been the accident in the electrical central station; his many talks with Mr. Pastor, whom he now visited regularly and worked his garden into a colorful flower garden with fountains and small waterfalls; or Lisa, who patiently over a period of time had curbed his wildness into love for her? Even the times Eric and Nico, besides traveling to and from the coal mine if they had the same shifts and having their usual glass of beer after church on Sunday in their favorite pub, spent together was more sporadic. Nico also had a steady girlfriend now, and the two young couples would spend some evenings together, though most of the time they went their own way.

On a rare occasion, weather permitting, Eric and Nico would walk through the fields and end up at their still-secret spot on the hill. They could sit there and talk for hours about their loves and feelings while lying in stillness on their stomachs in the soft grass, looking over the valley or staring into nowhere, each in his own thoughts.

At the age of twenty, Eric was now a full-fledged, experienced coal miner and was again chosen by the management to join an elite group of young men to be schooled to become electrical engineers. This new arrangement changed his whole lifestyle. They had no more shift work. These students had a special shift from 8:00 a.m. to 4:00 p.m., which was more to Eric's liking. Mondays, Wednesdays, and Fridays, he could dress up to go to classes for coal mine electrical engineering. The only difference between this schooling and the one he previously had attended, which had a disastrous ending, was that this one was more specialized in the underground aspect of the mine.

Tuesdays and Thursdays, he would work underground from 8:00 a.m. to 4:00 p.m. Saturdays, he had the normal dayshift, from 6:00 a.m. to12:00 noon. The trouble was that Eric and Nico were not only split up in shifts but also working together. Once in a while, when Nico had the day shift, they would meet underground, which was a happy occasion. Nico, who was not one of the chosen ones, would tease Eric of being a big shot; Eric had his insignia on his helmet; it showed two crossed hammers, indicating that he was a scholar. Besides working only three days a week, the workload of these students was also changed by the management. Instead of the unbelievably hard work, the students would get easier jobs, like inspecting, traffic controlling, etc., to learn all the phases of this specialized industry called deep coal mining.

Eric was assigned to the "Electrical Inspection Group". He was to inspect all sections of the mine where the removal of coal had stopped to look for still-useable electrical equipment. He reported his findings at the end of his shift to his manager, who in turn had the nightshift manager and his men disconnect and remove these items marked with chalk by Eric. He enjoyed this job. All alone he walked through these old hallways and witnessed the tremendous power of the forever-working, moaning, and shifting earth. Steel studs made of railroad track could be twisted a full turn or could snap like a sound of a cannon, which rolled like thunder through the deserted hallways. The sound of cracking and falling rock and a train rolling by at a far distance was music to Eric's ears. He knew these sounds and instinctively knew the difference between the usual and the more dangerous ones.

Most people not connected to coal miners or deep coal mines believed that one must be crazy to work underground fifteen hundred to two thousand feet deep, having the weight of millions of tons of earth above them. This was actually not so. For example, if one took a big rock or concrete building block and drilled a hole in it, one on the top and one on the bottom, after many years, the hole on the bottom with more weight on it and then the hole on the top would still be the same. Only the air and the moisture in the air would loosen small particles and slowly close the hole. This would be similar to deep coal mining, except for the dangers of the forever-working and moaning earth.

Some hallways made in very hard rock could exist for decades without any maintenance to speak of. However, in some sections where the surrounding rock was broken while shifting into close-by sections where the coal was removed, the danger of cave-ins was high. Even an experienced miner like Eric, who practically had been in every section of this mine while trouble shooting electrical equipment, would proceed with the utmost caution in sections like this, his trained mind observing and calculating every sound and signal. Eric never had been afraid in this mine and accepted everything around as part of a coal miner's job.

One day, however, the luck of the Irish turned against him. He was inspecting one of the older sections of the mine, nearly fifty years old, at the first 391 depth. This old section was wet. The hallway he walked into was dripping with the constant drain, and the slippery mud at the bottom made walking difficult. The air was filled with the smell of rotten wood used in old times as studs and boards in between the studs. All over, small cave-ins had occurred. He proceeded with the utmost care. After about a half-hour walk and while straining his eyes to their limits, he found the old electrical station he was looking for.

All the old motor starters and transformers should have been removed a long time ago, he thought.

The constant dripping of the dirty water covered all electrical units with a thick, slimy mess. Eric thought about the electricians who would receive these units in the electrical shop on top of the mine. They would really appreciate this, but then they were used to receiving all kinds of electrical units completely covered with mud or whatever. After writing down all the requested information, Eric sat down on a wet rock. It didn't make any difference anymore if the rock was wet or not. By then, he was soaked to the skin anyhow. He took a good swallow of coffee out of his flask and stuck a fresh plug of chewing tobacco in his mouth.

In the not-too-far distance, he could hear the reciprocating pump operating, pushing the water in gushes through the pipe over-head. He was sitting there, kind of dreaming, when at once it seemed as if the sound of rolling thunder was coming closer and closer. Instinctively, Eric jumped up and moved between two massive steel studs used on the electrical station. He knew these dangerous sounds; this was the sound of huge slow-moving rock. Within seconds, all hell broke loose. The whole earth seemed to be vibrating, studs were breaking, and pieces rocks were falling and gliding off one another into the open space that once was the hallway.

Everything around him kept on caving in. The shockwaves and vibrations of the very heavy pieces of rock, some three or four feet across, made Eric push even closer between the studs, which seemed to hold at least for now. It all happened in seconds, but for Eric, it could have been hours. He stood there frozen for some time after the vibration and the moving sounds stopped. Through the heavy dust cloud that surrounded him, the light beam of his helmet's light fell against a wall of huge rocks to the left of him, covering the complete hallway. His return path to the main hallway was blocked off. How could he get out?

To his right, the hallway was still partly open. However, it was covered with some fallen rock. He didn't know where that way would end, but it didn't matter, as long as he could get out of here. As fast as possible, he moved in that direction, constantly watching the ceiling above him while crawling over and around slippery rocks. At some places, the hole created in the ceiling looked very dangerous and went up as high as a house. On these openings, he stopped before making the dash over and between the rocks. With his pounding heart in his throat, which was dried up from the heavy breathing in the thick dust cloud, he studied for a few seconds the danger of passing underneath it.

He passed the water pump, which was completely demolished by a big rock. Finally, he made it. The section of the hallway he came into held up and was in fairly good shape. He took a minute's rest to catch up with the still-difficult breathing. Only now did he feel the pain of his bruised body from falling constantly over the sharp, slippery rocks. Carefully but in haste, he carried on. It was still dangerous around him, and it would be dangerous to stay around this area any longer than necessary. He walked for a couple of minutes. Then the light beam from his head lamp discovered something that made him stop in his tracks. His heart stopped beating. Walking closer, he discovered that he was in a dead-end hallway. There had been a hallway to the right, but that had been closed off with rocks years ago. He was trapped.

When Eric realized this, his nerves, which had been on edge for so long, gave way. His whole body started shaking, and he couldn't concentrate anymore. He felt like a wild animal trapped in a cage. His legs were shaking so much that he had to sit down. He didn't know how long he sat there. Slowly his mind came to order again, and he started to analyze the position he was in.

He started to talk to himself. "I am still alive and still breathing. There must be a way out."

He knew that if at the end of his shift, his tag in the control box by the elevator by the main shaft of this depth had not been removed, they would look for him and would find the cave-in. As long as he had air to breathe, he could just wait it out. At that moment, however, he noticed that the air that was brought in by a one-foot diameter tube to the end of the hallway was not blowing out anymore. Also, the pump was demolished, and soon the water level would start rising. This realization made Eric panic again. How long would he have air to breathe, and how long would it take for this hallway to fill up with water and for him to drown?

He had to get back to that electrical station. That was the closest from the main hallway, where they could start working to get him out. When it started to crack above him, he knew that it was the right decision. If that whole hallway had caved in and he had survived it, they would never find him that far away from safety. After crawling over the rocks, he made his way back to the electrical station. The steel studs and crossbeams had given way under the pressure of the cracked rock and were lying on top of the heavy transformer and starters, which made it the safest place, at least for now.

He arrived just in time. Again the earth started shaking, and he heard the remaining hallway where he had just been minutes before cave in. The studs and crossbeams above him were moaning and groaning again, and finally, the crossbeam cracked. Thankfully, it held. Eric also noticed that the studs under the heavy pressure were slowly driven into the floor and had left enough space for him to sit down on the step of this electrical station.

The water pipe was still connected to the studs, and quickly he took a hammer out of his tool bag that was till lying where he left it when he took off supposedly for safety. Eric knew that the sound of hammering on the pipe, if the pipe was still intact, would carry far and anyone hearing the hammer sounds would know that someone was in danger. Every coal miner who would hear someone knocking on a pipe would make a mark where he heard the hammering and then walk a distance in each direction from that mark to find out from what direction the sound came from. Once he found out the general direction, he would answer by also hitting against the pipe between intervals of the knocking of the person in danger and then hurry in that direction. This person would also be looking for a telephone so he could warn the authorities of the happenings.

Eric looked at his pocket watch and noticed that it was already 1:30 p.m., the busiest and noisiest time in the mine, because all the dayshift people would be returning from their sections to the main shaft. Trains loaded with coal miners would fill the main hallway, and it could very well be that no one would hear his hammering. Farther down the hallway, it caved in more and more, and Eric was glad he had come back to this side. He couldn't have waited any longer. He started to hit on the water pipe—two times, four hits, pause, and then again two times, four hits. It was the sign of danger.

He couldn't remember how long he had been hitting when finally, his heart jumped. Was it true? Did someone answer? He put his ear against the pipe and heard the most beautiful music a person who was trapped could hear—the sound of someone answering. It seemed very far away, but someone had heard his cries for help and answered. Eric started crying; it felt good. After all he went through that morning, his super-tense nerves finally gave way. Someone had heard him and would set everything in motion to get him out of here. He kept on hammering for a while, and the answers came in very clear now but were still far away. Finally, the answers stopped, but this didn't worry him, because he knew that the person was contacting the authorities.

This good news made him think clearly again. He couldn't do anything except wait. He spit out the tobacco plug and replaced it with a new one, took a good swallow of his coffee, and sat down. He had no idea how long it would take before the rescue team would start working on the other end, but one thing he knew was that he had to save his battery. He switched off his light so he could use it sparingly.

Sitting in the dark, his thoughts floated from Lisa to his parents then to Nico and back again to the situation he was in. Would he really die here? Was this the place where his dreams about the future would end? The falling of rock close by woke him up. He had dozed off. His mind and body had released him for a short duration of the tension it had withstood for such a long time. He felt better, but he also knew the dangers of falling asleep. He had to force himself to stay awake to be ready to act at once at any further sign of danger.

For a moment, he switched on his light and immediately noticed the water level. Before, his shoes had been in the mud, but there was water now; it was nearly up to his shoelaces. He had forgotten all about the water. How long would it take to fill up this end of the hallway, and how long would he have air to breathe? Still there was no sound at the other end of the cave-in. How long would it take to get everything in motion to get him out of here?

The air around him was getting warmer without any fresh supply. Before switching his light off again, he took a quick glance at his pocket watch. It was around 4:30 p.m.

Where are they? What's taking them so long? He was getting angry now. If it had been one of the big bosses instead of him, they would have been working like the devil to get him out by now. But since he was only a peon, who would care? It wasn't fair. He had given so much to this mine, and he could do a lot more if they only gave him a chance. He was now getting scared, dead scared. It practically made him senseless.

At once, he heard the knocking on the pipe again. Yes, there it was! They were trying to find out if he was still alive. Excited, Eric hammered back, and for a while, the hammering went back and forth. His excitement dropped, however, when he heard the dim sound of air hammers of the men working at the other end. It was too far away. If the whole length of this hallway had caved in up to the crossing of the main hallway, it would take days, maybe a week, before they could get to him.

The adrenaline flow his body had released dropped quickly and replaced his anger and happiness with sadness and loneness. He started to cry and just let go. Louder and louder, his cries echoed through the still-open spaces. His body jerked, and he couldn't stop it.

"God!" he cried. "Why am I left alone here to die? What am I being punished for? What did I do to deserve this?" And what about his parents, his brothers and sister, Nico, Lisa, and Willem, the farmer? All these people would be anguished by his death. "If you let me die here, you must be a cruel God."

He really shouldn't think this way because soon he would be standing in front of God. How would he die—by slow suffocation, drowning, or cave-in?

He started to pray loudly now. "Our Father, who art in heaven…" He was tired. It was impossible to stay awake. He had gone through so much. Eric fell asleep.

He didn't know how long he slept, but when he woke up, he thought for a moment that it all had been a dream. Then again, the reality jumped like lightning through his head, and he discovered he was sitting in water—lukewarm water. How long had he been sleeping? What had happened in the meantime? He heard the rescuers working feverishly from still too far away. They were hitting the pipe again. How long did he sleep and not answer them? Maybe they thought he was already dead. For a while, he couldn't find his hammer in the water. After answering a few times, he dropped the hammer. It was no use.

He took another look at his watch, but it had stopped at six fifteen. Was it six fifteen in the afternoon, or was it the next morning? Eric took the last swallow of his coffee out of his flask and dropped it into the water. He watched it for a while to see if the flask would float in either direction, indicating that the water was running away. The flask didn't move. It was getting unbearable to breathe. He had to inhale faster and faster now. His battery was fading, and his light was slowly dimming now. He couldn't concentrate anymore, and he fainted.

When he woke up, he had no light left, and the water level was now up to his chest. "God, please help me." He started praying again. Then it seemed a last burst of energy went through his exhausted body, and thought flashed through his mind. *I cannot keep sitting here to drown. I have to get on top of one of those rocks.*

He knew he was weak, very weak. With his last thoughts and efforts, Eric crawled through the dark and the water and found a rock. It took all his remaining strength to get on top of it. His arms were lame, and his concentration was gone, but with his last ounce of strength, he found a still-intact crossbeam. He connected the battery belt, which was of no use to him anymore, and his trouser belt together. Then he tied the belts over the crossbeam and under his arms. Then he blacked out.

The rescuers on the other end were making good headway but had given up all hope to find Eric alive since he hadn't answered for a long time. Four sets of rescue teams had worked around the clock for two full days before the water broke through and then another day and a half for the remaining obstacles. They had given up all hope of finding Eric alive. They nearly stopped searching when in the early morning hours of the fourth day, one of the men broke through and saw the belts on the beam and found Eric hanging in his belts. With a knife, he cut the belts, and Eric fell lifelessly into his arms.

Quickly he checked Eric's heartbeat and then shouted in a jubilant voice, "He is alive! He is still alive! Quickly send the oxygen through the hole."

Eric, who had been in the dungeon for three days and one night, survived. Later he found out that the water had risen within two inches of his mouth and he would have drowned if it the rescue team had taken a few hours longer to break the water. Within minutes, these unsung heroes of the coal mines, who put their lives in danger anytime they were called upon, moved Eric through the hole and emergency tunnel they had built to the waiting train and doctors.

Hours later, in the emergency room on top of the coal mine, Eric slowly woke up. He heard voices, which seemed to come from far away. He opened his eyes but closed them immediately again when the sharp lights reflected against the white surrounding walls hurt his eyes. Where was he? What had happened? Finally, the voices became clearer now, and he noticed that his whole mouth was dry.

With the utmost difficulty, he uttered, "Water... Give me some water."

Someone held him up and gave him some water to drink. Only after he drank the water did he open his eyes a little bit and focused on a worried but smiling face of the man completely in white and had white hair, the one who had assisted him. Had he died and gone to heaven?

"You made it, kid. You..."

Eric didn't hear the rest. At that moment, a flash of memory came back, and he knew he was alive and safe. With a weak smile on his face, he dropped back into the dreamless darkness of unconsciousness.

Eric's parents, who had gone through grueling days, were standing beside his bed in the hospital when he opened his eyes again. He felt still very tired and weak, but his mind was clearing up.

He softly said, "Hi, Mom. Hi, Dad."

He felt the warm tears of his mother on his face when she bent over him and kissed his cheeks. He also saw his father crying.

With a choked throat, his father asked, "How are you, my boy? How are you feeling?"

"Tired, Dad. Very tired. How long was I down there?"

"Nearly four full days," his father answered. "Everyone had given up all hope of finding you alive except your mother and me."

At that moment, the doctor came into the room and asked his parents in a very friendly voice to leave. "He is safe now, and he needs all the rest he can get." The doctor guided his exhausted but happy parents out of the room, but not before his mother kissed him again.

In the early evening, the whole bunch came to visit him—his parents, Lisa (who had been waiting two hours in the waiting room before visitors were allowed to see him again), Johann and Paul (his brothers), and Nico. He felt sorry for Lisa, who couldn't stop crying and was completely exhausted.

After two days in the hospital, his whole body started blistering from the chemicals and the warm water he had been exposed to for such a long time. The itching was unbearable, and the nurses had to tie his hands on the side of the bed so he couldn't scratch the skin off his body. For another two or three days, the nurses washed his body every hour with some liquid to keep him from going out of his mind. Eric got stronger and stronger, and after two weeks, with new rosy skin and in the presence of Lisa, he left the hospital.

When he arrived home, the house was filled with flowers from the villagers, and his mother had made a huge cake with "Welcome home!" and three and a half candles on it. That evening, after he had kissed Lisa good night and all the well-wishers had gone home, he crawled into his bed and thanked the Lord for watching over him. He wasn't that cruel, after all.

The management had given him two months' leave. He enjoyed the time he was free but couldn't understand the manager's decision for such a long leave. He wouldn't mind going back to resume his daily normal life again. It had been a bad experience, and surely he wouldn't like to go through that again, but afraid to go back? No, he wasn't. Really, when he thought about it, physically he wasn't harmed at all, and mentally he was very alert and could even keep up his studies as much as possible. But if they wanted to give him two months off, that was their decision, and Eric considered it like a vacation.

If he only wasn't that tired all the time... He could sleep from early evening to midmorning, and still around three o'clock in the afternoon, he was tired again and would take another nap for an hour or so. And then there was the nightmares night after night. Some were worse than others, and many nights he would wake up drenched with perspiration. Most of these dreams he couldn't remember when he woke up. But one of the dreams seemed to constantly repeat itself.

In these dreams, it was the three of them who were involved—himself, Lisa, and Nico. Again, it was in the coal mine, and all three were walking in a hallway. That Lisa was in the mine, wearing a dress, he never questioned. They kept on walking until the next second, Lisa was gone. He and Nico looked back into the dark hallway but couldn't find her. They called and called her name, but no one answered.

"Let's walk back and find her," said Nico. "Maybe she got lost somewhere."

When the two hurried back, they found Lisa lying on the floor of the hallway, her foot stuck between two huge rocks. All at once, water started to rise very rapidly in the hallway. They tried to push and pull on the heavy rocks, but they didn't give way.

Lisa started screaming, "You have to get me out of here!"

They tried everything, but it was impossible to free her. The water kept rising and rising. "The only way we can get her out," said Nico, "is to cut her leg off." He said this while looking for his cable knife in the tool bag. Eric was there and not there. He seemed to witness it all, but was like a bystander. At the moment Nico's knife made contact with the flesh of her leg, Lisa gave a scream that echoed through the hallway.

It was then that Eric would wake up.

Or he would dream that while doing some electrical repair on the main shaft, he slipped and fell into the shaft. While he was falling and falling, the lights of hundreds of depths would go by, and he kept on falling into infinity, with all the horrors related to it.

Also, for quite some time, he was very sensitive. For no reason at all, he would become furious but within minutes again would become so sentimental that he would cry. Lisa, noticing these changes in him more than he did himself, knew that he needed her more than ever. She patiently, with great love, endured all this. Many times, he would actually be cruel to her, and she would leave him and go home with tears in her eyes. But she'd be back the next day, all smiling and full of love, not mentioning a word of what had happened the day before.

Then there were the times when walking or lying beside each other in the woods, he would be so sentimental that for practically no reason at all, he would start crying. Lisa would put her arms around him and hold him close to her body and, while gently caressing him, would say, "Just cry, my darling. Just let it all come out, and you will feel a lot better."

He had all this love around him from Martha, Lisa, Nico, and even John. He showed his affection by not demanding any work from Eric around the house. Even when he did ask, he would follow the question with "But you don't have to do it, you know."

Eric returned to his normal self in no time. Only Lisa noticed the difference in him. For the first time, he started to talk about emigrating again, but Lisa wouldn't hear of it.

"That was at that time, but we live here now, and I like it here. Why can't we just stay here and get married and have children? That's all I want."

"It's getting too small for me here," Eric carried on. "Holland is overcrowded, and there are practically no chances to reach something in life. I really don't want to work the rest of my life in that coal mine, even if I become a manager."

Lisa didn't answer. She had made her point, and it was left at that.

Months went by, and everything returned to normal again. Eric went back to working in the mine, and as he had expected, he wasn't scared. But he was more jumpy, and his ears were more sensitive to the sounds around him more than ever before. His love for Lisa was blooming, and he started talking about marriage. He still felt like a stranger whenever he visited her home. By now, they had accepted him, but that was all. Eric didn't let it bother him because within a year or so, he would be married to her anyhow. He wouldn't have to go to her home anymore if he didn't feel like it. On the other side, Martha really liked Lisa and accepted her like her own daughter. They could talk for hours while Eric worked with his father in the garden.

CHAPTER 5

✠

Eric still remembered his father's hand on his shoulder and could hear him saying, "Come on, boy. Let's go home."

Slowly he turned around and walked away from Nico's grave. No tears were in his eyes anymore, and he felt nothing but emptiness inside. His father put a raincoat on his shoulders, but it didn't matter. He was wet to the bone but didn't notice it. It was Sunday, and it had been raining all day. The energy he used to have in his steps were gone, and his shoulders were now slightly bent forward as if carrying a tremendous load. In the time span of a year and a half after his own accident, Nico and Lisa had died. He was now nearly twenty-one years old but looked ten years older. Lisa had died first. Lisa was buried in her village, and many times a week, he would visit both graves.

One Saturday evening, Eric and Lisa visited one of the many pubs in Eric's village. It was a very old bar, and both enjoyed listening to the miners and old farmers. Lisa was very much in love with Eric, but she also was very jealous. Eric had been, for several years, a goalie in the soccer club in the close-by city and was a hero when they won a game, but if they lost, he was shunned by the fanatic fans. They had played that afternoon and won 4 to 3. Sitting on the bar, Eric was naturally honored and received many glasses of beer. Across the bar were a couple of ladies looking and smiling at him.

Lisa didn't like that and, after some time, said to Eric, "Please, let's go home. I have a headache."

Eric, thinking it was her jealousy, got upset and answered, "Lisa, you know that I love you only. These ladies across the bar don't mean anything to me."

But Lisa replied, "I do have a terrible headache."

Eric didn't believe her, but he took her home. This supposedly nice evening was shot, and after a quick kiss, he went home.

Sometime during the morning, the bell rang on the front door. When John opened the door, he saw one of Lisa's brothers. He, on his bicycle, had raced to Eric's home. He informed them that something had happened to Lisa.

"She complained about a headache and, a little later, fell on the floor unconscious," he said. There was no telephone, so her older brother had jumped on his bicycle and drove to the hospital, which was located approximately five miles from their home to get an ambulance for Lisa. Then he drove to Eric's home to inform him. Eric thanked him, and he rushed up the stairs to quickly get dressed. Eric didn't hear the last word from his father. By that time, he was already outside the door and was racing to her home. Even though he made the distance in record time, for him, it seemed three times as far.

"My God," he prayed, "you can do with me what you want, but please not her, not Lisa." Arriving he threw the bicycle against the private hedge surrounding her home and ran through the back kitchen door into the living room. "Where is she? What happened to her?" he screamed upon seeing only her older sister and the two brothers sitting at the table, crying and praying at the same time.

"She's gone, Eric. The ambulance came and picked her up just minutes ago. Father and Mother have gone with her to the hospital."

"What happened?" Eric asked, feeling the blood draining out of his face and his chest tightening up.

"Well, this morning, when I woke her up to go with Mother and me to the marketplace, she complained that she didn't feel so well and had a headache. She didn't want to go with us, so we let her go back to sleep again. When we returned, we noticed that she was still sleeping. When I went to wake her up, she didn't move at all," her sister continued and started to cry again. "The ambulance arrived and took her to the hospital."

Now in shock, Eric ran outside. One of the neighbors called him and asked him something, but Eric didn't have the time for her. When Eric arrived at the hospital, he found Lisa's parents in the waiting room of the emergency section. At the same time he rushed into that room, a doctor entered through the swinging doors from the other side and asked Lisa's parents in a subdued but friendly voice to follow him. When Eric wanted to follow them also, the doctor asked him if he was from the immediate family.

When Eric said no, and before he could explain to the doctor that he was her boyfriend, the doctor rudely remarked, "Sorry, but you wait here."

Minutes went by, which seemed like hours, as he hoped and prayed. He remembered that last night she had complained that she wasn't feeling too well while they were sitting in the pub in the village. He should have listened.

The door swung open, and the doctor confronted him, "Are you a friend of the family?" Before Eric could answer, the doctor continued, "Young man, they need all your strength now. Their daughter just died." And he left the room.

Eric went into the room and stood beside her crying parents to see Lisa for the last time. She lay there so peacefully.

It's not true. It can't be! Lisa dead? No, no, no... He couldn't accept it.

He couldn't talk to her parents, and he slowly walked out and went in the direction of home, forgetting all about his bicycle. He didn't wait for her parents. He couldn't. He just had to be by himself now. He didn't know how he had walked home, but at once he was in front of it.

Seeing his mother sitting at the kitchen table, a lit candle and a rosary in her hands, he broke down. "She is dead, Mother. Lisa is dead." That was all he could say.

He found no relief from his crying mother and walked into the garden to find his father, in shock and constantly repeating that Lisa was dead. He followed Eric into the kitchen. Eric couldn't stand it any longer. It seemed as if the whole kitchen had started to close in on him. He walked into the fields but didn't notice the once-so-beautiful surroundings. For hours, he walked, and the sun was already fading when he finally returned home again. Nico and his girlfriend had been waiting for hours at Eric's house.

Martha had asked Nico to also go into the fields to find him, but Nico replied, "No, Mom, I cannot help him now. He has to be by himself." When Eric finally returned home, Nico put his arms around him, and the two stood there crying like children.

For months, Eric was heartbroken. He missed her terribly. He knew how much he loved her but only realized after she was gone how much she was part of him. An autopsy had shown that she had died from a massive brain hemorrhage. Even Nico, who spent more time than usual with him, couldn't reduce his loss and sadness.

Eric's world really crumbled when, only four months later, Nico died in the coal mine. Many times, Eric and Nico worked together, troubleshooting electrical problems. That day, they went together to a mechanical pyler C4 (Charly 4), where they seemed to have some problem with the electrical starters for the big five-hundred-horse-power motor. Big steel cables would pull the metal scraper across the coal frame. At one intersection, Eric went one way and Nico the other to first check the electrical supply cables and see if they were damaged.

Eric was about five hundred yards in his hallway when he heard a tremendous noise close by. Immediately he moved between the wall studs and thought of his previous experience. Would it again cave in? When nothing further happened, he walked back to see where the noise came from. When he walked to the hallway where Nico had gone into, a big cloud of dust came from there. Slowly and carefully, Eric entered it. About two hundred yards inside, he saw a cave-in. A lot of steel studs had been ripped away. He shouted for Nico but received no answer. Then giving him a tremendous shock, he saw at the bottom of the pile of rocks a foot sticking out. When he slowly moved some rocks, he saw that it was Nico. He had been killed instantly. Later, Eric discovered that one of the big steel cables had broken lose from the scraper and the impact had pulled studs down, resulting in the cave-in that had killed Nico.

The loss of Lisa was a terrible hurt, but the loss of Nico, whom he had shared his entire life with, was impossible to bear. He couldn't cry anymore. There was nothing left. Constantly, the question why battered his mind. Why was he left alone here on this God-forsaken earth? Why didn't he have just a normal happy life? Why couldn't God have just let him die in that accident on top of the mine or later underground? Why was everyone he loved taken away from him? As a young boy, it had been his dog, Prince, then Peter, then Lisa, and now Nico. He also knew that Nico could never be replaced.

Someone who had not gone through similar situations in life could only faintly understand what Eric suffered in the months following Nico's death. It was like a thick fog surrounded him. Many times he stood at their graves, asking them to help him and give him some guidance. Everyone he knew felt sorry for him and wanted to be extra friendly, but little did they realize that their behavior kept Eric's wounds bleeding.

That day, standing by Nico's grave as he had done so many times before, he had poured out his sorrows to the remains underneath that pile of dirt, as if somehow Nico could answer him from there. The answer would come, but he didn't realize it at that time. Slowly but surely, his mind changed from the deepest point of sorrow and bewilderment a human could stand to a tremendous willpower and determination. He had always believed strongly in the laws of nature. When trees in the forest gave way under a heavy storm and finally tumbled, soon thereafter new shoots would sprout again and grow, replacing the fallen one. He had always believed that nature would take away with one hand and give with the other hand.

One day, while sitting on a fallen tree in the forest and deep in sorrow, his eyes rested on a huge oak tree in an open space, showing its beauty to the surrounding pine trees. Eric glanced at it for a while, not showing any particular interest. He looked in another direction, but as if by force, he was pulled back to that tree again. It was as if the big branches turned into arms to embrace him. When walking closer, he noticed that some huge branches had been ripped off by many storms and healthy new branches had already replaced them, but the scars of nature's forces were still clearly visible.

All at once, it dawned on him that this oak tree represented his life. Just like him, it stood there, lonely, and had bent and twisted under nature's forces. It showed a lot of scars but had not succumbed.

Instead it had bounced back and grew new branches bigger and stronger than the ones before.

He stood there for quite some time, looking at the oak, and it was as if this tree talked to him.

"Look at me. I was here way before you were born and possibly will be here after you are gone. I have had many battles many times, but I never gave in. For that matter, I grew stronger."

For some time, Eric hugged this tree.

When he walked out of the forest, the heavy load on his shoulders seemed to be slowly fading away to be replaced by new energy. It was going to change his life completely. By now he hated the coal mine and everything connected to it. He had to leave the coal mine or, for that matter, the whole area. There was nothing here for him anymore except many bad memories, and if he started a new life and wanted to succeed, it should be somewhere else.

The dream he once had about going to America came back in full force. For months, he gathered information not only about America but also Canada, Australia, and New Zealand. Martha and John witnessed the new life that had sprung into Eric. At first, they didn't like the idea of him leaving the country, but they had to admit that his chances of success were a lot higher in these countries than in the small overpopulated Holland.

"Martha, Eric, anybody home?" shouted Nico's mother through the tiny open window of the front door while keeping her finger on the doorbell. When seeing Martha and Eric entering the hallway, she continued, "Martha, Eric, we have a grandson! Last night, Tina gave birth to a baby boy."

Tina, Nico's only sister, who lived in a close-by city and had been married for quite some time, had after several miscarriages given birth to a son. Nico's mother was so happy and so excited that she kissed Eric and Martha on both cheeks and practically fell over the carpet while doing so. The baby was born at home, which was common practice at that time. Women only went to the hospital if the midwife suspected problems in the forthcoming birth. Three days later, Eric went by bicycle to visit the happy couple and to see the newborn. Congratulating the father, Eric entered their small home.

"We are happy to see you," said the father, shaking Eric's hands. "We don't see you that often here anymore. It has been months. It is about time that you visited us again. Let's first go into the living room and have a good stiff drink to celebrate. Then we'll go upstairs and see Tina and the baby."

When they finished the drink and the happy father wanted to refill the glasses, Eric said, "No, not now. Let's first go and see Tina and the baby. You've kept me too long in suspense here. When we come down, we can have some more of that good stuff."

The bedroom was filled with flowers, and Tina was happy to see Eric. He bent over, congratulating and kissing her at the same time, and then he walked over to the crib in the corner of the room to look at the welcome newcomer. When Eric stuck his finger in the palm of the baby's hand, he closed his little fingers around Eric's finger.

"Is he ever strong! He doesn't want to let go of me," said Eric while slightly pulling on the baby's hand. "He is already strong enough to work in the coal mines." He laughed.

But Tina replied, "Never. My son will never go down the pit. I guarantee you that. By the way, I heard from Mother that you are planning to emigrate. Is that true?"

"Yes, I think so," Eric replied. "At least I'm looking into all the possibilities."

They sat there talking for some time. Then the doorbell rang.

"That must be the midwife. She told me she would come by today," said Tina. Then she looked at her husband. "Why don't you go down and let her in? She is very nice." She looked at Eric. "I'll bet you'll like her."

When the midwife entered the room, she said, "Hi, Tina. How are you today?" Then noticing Eric, she gave him a smile and asked, "Are you a friend of the family?"

Eric couldn't believe his eyes. Tina had said she was nice, but this young woman was absolutely gorgeous. In her nurse's uniform—with her blond hair protruding from her brown cap and veil on top of her head, which distinguished her being a midwife—she looked very beautiful. He didn't answer, but just stared at her.

Tina answered for him, "Yes, that's Eric. He's a very, very close friend of the family. Actually, we grew up together. We were neighbors for many years."

The midwife looked at Eric again and said, "I am Maria. It's nice meeting you."

"You really took me by surprise," Eric said. "You sure don't look like a midwife to me."

"Why?" she questioned. "What is wrong with me being a midwife?"

"No, no," replied Eric. "There's nothing wrong with you. It's just that you are so young and beautiful for being a midwife. All the midwifes I have seen are elderly ladies."

"Well, thank you for the compliment. I needed that today. I've had a very hard day. Now, gentlemen, would you please leave the room? I'd like to have some time with the mother alone."

On that note, both men left the room and went downstairs to have some more of that good Dutch gin.

The two men were having a ball and were really celebrating when the midwife came into the living room.

She said, "Gentlemen, please keep it down. I don't mind you two celebrating, but the mother and baby need their rest now. So please keep it down."

"Where are you from?" Eric asked her.

She mentioned the village where she grew up but said that she now lived in a big house with eight or ten other midwives about a mile down the road. "I'm going home now," she continued. "It has been a long day."

"Do you mind if I walk you home?" Eric asked. "I have to go in that direction anyhow."

To Eric's surprise and happiness, she answered, "No, not at all. Please do. I don't mind."

Walking to her home, they talked about her profession, and Eric was very surprised to hear about how much schooling she had to have before she could become a midwife. When stopping at the front steps of the big house where she lived, Eric asked her if he could take her to the movies the next weekend.

"I don't know," she answered.

"Oh, I'm sorry," Eric said. "I didn't even ask if you have a boy-friend or not."

"No, that is not it," she said. "You see, I was free last weekend, and unless I can find one of the other girls to sit in for me next week-end, I have to work. Why don't you come by Sunday evening, around six thirty or seven? If I can arrange it, we can go out."

"It's a deal," Eric said and jumped on his bicycle, which he had been pushing beside him while he walked her home. "Goodnight, Maria."

"Goodnight, Eric, and thank you for walking me home," she said while closing the door behind her.

The following weekend, they went out together, and when he walked her home, he mentioned that he was planning to emigrate.

"Oh, I would love to emigrate," she replied.

After a courtship of only eight months, they married and had their papers ready for emigrating. Maria, who was one year and nine months older than Eric, was the perfect woman he needed to emi-grate with. In many ways, she was the same as Lisa, but she was more educated and could stand on her own two feet if necessary anywhere in the world.

She came out of a family of sixteen children. Her father, who had been a manager in another coal mine, had been married twice. He had five children with his first wife, and when she died and her sister came to the house to help out, he married her and had eleven children with her. Maria was the oldest daughter of the second mar-riage and had a hard life behind her. She had been her mother's right hand, and besides doing the chores until late at night, she had still found time to study.

Maria's mother was a tough woman. She had to be, because rais-ing five children from her husband's previous marriage to her sister and eleven of her own was an unbelievably hard job. Maria's father was hit by a car and died when he was crossing a street. When Eric met her mother for the first time, he noticed immediately that she was not pleased with Maria's choice.

A few days later, Eric mentioned that to Maria, and she explained, "Oh, don't mind her. She will come along. She would like that all her daughters would marry doctors or lawyers."

Eric and Maria visited her home sparingly because Maria worked every other weekend. At that time period, for sure in Catholic families, young lovers were not allowed to be by themselves alone in either home before marriage without the presence of at least one of the parents.

Eric questioned his mother about this. "If we are in the fields, we can do anything we like to do. Why not here?"

But Martha answered, "What you do outside this house I cannot control, but inside nothing will happen until you both are married."

Eric knew that his and Maria's mother would not deviate from that. Even after they were already married by law for a while, it was not allowed until after the church wedding. That was supposed to be the real marriage. Eric found that out the hard way. Maria went home for a long weekend. Eric would visit her on Sunday, a distance of approximately sixteen miles. He went by tram, which would stop two blocks from Maria's home.

One very nice fall day, the two walked for several miles through a beautiful area the south part of Holland was rich of. They were close to the wedding and emigrating, and Maria's mother had accepted Eric and was easier to get along with. At around eleven o'clock in the evening, Maria, who would stay to Monday, walked with Eric through the garden and on to the back of the house. On the small porch, they hugged and kissed each other for quite some time, and then Eric departed to the tram stop. He stood there for a while and could not understand why no tram had come by.

An elderly couple walked by and told Eric, "If you are waiting for a tram, you are too late. The last tram on Sunday evening is at eleven o'clock. You must have just missed it."

Eric walked back to Maria's home to stay overnight. But no matter how much Eric and Maria pleaded with her mother, he was not allowed into the house. While walking back, he was hoping that he could hitchhike his way home. However, only a few people owned an automobile, and with it being Sunday night, there was practically no traffic. Also, there were no outdoor telephones for him to get ahold of a taxi, if available. So Eric had to walk. The area was full of small hills and valleys. After a few hours, he was developing blisters on his feet. He took off his shoes, tied the laces together, and hung them around his neck. For a while, he walked on his socks. But even they gave way, and he had to walk barefoot. He had to stop many times to give himself and his very painful legs and feet a rest.

It was around four o'clock on Monday morning when he finally stumbled into the door of his home. The noise he made woke up his father, and when John came downstairs, he found Eric sitting on a chair in the kitchen, completely exhausted.

"What happened?" John asked. "Your feet are bleeding all over." While Eric told him the whole story, his father found some ointment and bandages to wind his feet. "What are you going to do? The bus to the mine will be here in less than two hours."

"I have to go," Eric answered. "We have a special division meeting today, which I cannot miss." Eric changed clothes, and after eating a sandwich, he very slowly walked to the bus stop. Johann watched him walking and shook his head. Luckily, the meeting lasted all day, and Eric did not have to walk much. When in the afternoon, he came home, Maria was waiting for him. Martha had told her all about it, and both women were very sorry and were worried when Eric very slowly walked into the house. They both listened to his side of the story. Hugging Eric and crying at the same time, Maria told him that she had a very long and angry conversation with her mother.

"You shouldn't have," answered Eric. "She only did what she thought was the right thing to do. It was not her fault that I forgot to ask when the last tram would be leaving. Mother would have done the same thing." He looking at her. Martha did not answer, but he knew he was right.

In the beginning, he just liked Maria, but soon he knew that he was falling in love with her and that this time they were going to make it.

They had decided to go to America, but when visiting the US immigration office, they discovered that there was a yearly quota for

Dutch people to emigrate to the USA and that it was booked full for nine years to come. The disappointment must have shown on their faces because the immigration office mentioned, "Why don't you go to the Canadian immigration office and go to Canada? It is easier to get into that country surely with the education both of you have."

The officer had been right. The quota for Canada for that year had just been filled, but to their surprise, they heard that if their physical checkup and papers were in order, they could emigrate to Canada within six months. They filed the papers in September 1957, and that meant that they could leave for Canada around February 1958. Time went fast now for the young couple. Buying only the most necessary items and saving money whenever possible, they looked forward to starting their own lives together in the new country.

To prepare themselves and to get to know more about Canada, they enrolled in an evening course for Canadian immigrants. There they learned the basics of the English language and all about Canada, including their different way of living. On one of those evenings, Eric and Maria were invited to the home of Theo and Ellen Rudolph, a couple in their midthirties with three children who also were planning to emigrate to Canada. During that visit, they seemed to enjoy one another's company and decided that they would emigrate together. The Rudolphs had stayed in contact with a family, Maasen, who were friends of theirs and had emigrated to Canada several years earlier.

The Maasen family owned a large two-story house. Mr. Maasen was the foreman of the maintenance department at a large factory in Toronto. He had promised the Rudolphs the second floor of his home and also a job as machinist in his department for Theo, which was the latter's trade. Eric and Maria had no specific place to go to in Canada, but they had decided on Toronto because it seemed to be a large industrial city, which would make it easier for Eric to find a job and because English was spoken there.

Theo had written a long letter to his friend in Canada where he explained the problem of the young couple he had met and asked if he could let them stay also in his home even if it was only for a few days after they arrived in Canada. Eric and Maria really jumped for joy when a few weeks later, Mr. Maasen wrote in his answering letter that he was very pleased to welcome the young couple in his home. He had already started to convert the attic of the house into living quarters consisting of a small kitchen, living room, and bedroom. He even would try to find a job for Eric in the electrical department of the factory. Eric and Maria were so overjoyed with this happy news that they wrote a long letter thanking them for their kindness. Now they really had nothing to worry about anymore and could enjoy the remaining months together.

Finally, after months of waiting, both couples received a notice that all papers were in order and that they were booked on a special airplane for immigrants leaving for Canada on April 5, 1958. Eric decided not to tell the management at the coal mine of his plans for emigrating until the last moment. The reason for this decision was not to red-flag the Dutch government any more than necessary since the mine was owned by them. He hoped he would be already in Canada before the Dutch Armed Forces would get to know about his plans. He only had dispensation from the forces as long as he was in the coal mine, but as soon as he left, he had to join the forces for a period of two years. He was hoping that the delay in red tape, which governments were known for, would be long enough that he would be in Canada before they discovered it.

Eric and Maria planned their church wedding for March 26 in the year 1958, which just happened to be Maria's birthday. They were married by law the previous November so they could save the extra tax money that year for being married in 1957. This marriage by law was only a formality. They didn't live together, however, until after the church wedding, as demanded in a very Catholic society.

CHAPTER 6

✠

"Hey, Eric, are you deaf? I have been calling you for a long time."

Eric realized that someone was calling him, and still in a daze, he looked around and noticed Maria at the bottom of the hill, waving at him. He had been sitting there in deep thought for so long that he completely lost track of time.

"Hi, sweetheart!" he shouted back and waved at her. "Don't come up. I will come down." He stood up, stretched his body, found his wooden shoes, put them on, and walked down the hill. The sun was already subsiding and converted with its last rays the landscape into a touch of gold. Walking down the slope of the hill, he looked at Maria, who was watching the sun slowly disappearing at the end of the horizon and thought how beautiful she really was. It was only three days ago when they finally married at the church in her village but had left after the wedding in the late evening hours to his home. For their wedding night, they had used his bedroom and had remained at his home for the last few days.

It had been a beautiful wedding. To keep the costs down and to save their money, only the immediate family members had been invited. But with such a large family as Maria's, the house was packed all day. Their wedding was quite unique in many ways. First of all, they had to have dispensation from the bishop to marry during Lent, which was given to them since they were emigrating. Also, they were married by Maria's older half brother, who was a bishop in Africa and just happened to be home for a long well-earned vacation. Also, one of her older half sisters was a Mother Superior in a convent in another part of Holland. For some reason, she couldn't attend the wedding; however, she promised to be at the airport in Amsterdam when they left for Canada. Theo and Ellen Rudolph were the only nonfamily members at the wedding, but considering the future of both couples, they were practically family.

When Eric arrived at the bottom of the hill close enough for her not to shout anymore, she said, "Darling, I have some bad news."

When Eric arrived, he hugged and kissed her and said, "I love you, you know," while holding her in his arms.

"I love you too, sweetheart," she said when he finally gave her a chance to talk. "By the way, what were you doing up there all alone? I saw you sitting from way back. You know I went this afternoon to say goodbye to all the other midwifes, and when I came back, your mother told me that you went for a walk. It was Johann who told me that you might possibly at this hill. But how did he know, Eric? Is there anything special about this hill?"

"I guess I never told you, Maria, but that spot there on top of the hill is very sacred to me. That spot is where Nico and I spent many hours together. Nobody has ever been up there with us. No one knows about this spot and what it means to me." He looked at her but didn't notice any jealousy or anger about him not sharing this spot with her. Instead he only found warmth and understanding in her eyes.

Without saying a word further about it, she put her arms around him and said, "Come on, sweetheart, let's go home. Your mother had dinner all ready when I left, so they all must be waiting for us."

When walking home, Eric questioned, "Hey, didn't you mention that you had bad news when you were calling me?"

"Oh yeah," Maria answered. "I completely forgot about it. We got a letter in the mail from the immigration office, and they informed us that the plane on April 5 is cancelled. It has been delayed until April 13."

"Well, that's not such bad news," replied Eric. "We have waited for so long that a couple of days won't make any difference."

"It could be," she answered, "if you've already forgotten about the Armed Forces. Every day here longer than necessary could put the whole trip in jeopardy and scramble our dreams."

"By God, you're right. I had forgotten all about that," Eric replied. "Let's hope that it doesn't make any difference. Wouldn't that be something if after all we were prevented from going to Canada? It would be funny if all our stuff that we shipped a couple of days ago would be arriving in Canada without anyone there to receive it," he said laughingly.

"That's nothing to laugh about—not even talking about our dreams, but that could cost us a lot of money. We now have a special tariff being immigrants for shipping our things to Canada, but if it is decided that we did not immigrate, we not only have to pay for the full freight but also for the return freight because we surely want to get our things back."

"I guess you're right. Let's not just think about it and spoil the evening and the days we have left here."

He quickly changed the subject, but he knew that her worries were justified because any day now the Dutch Military Police could come to get him. The remaining days, however, went by without incidents and were spent with the two families, relatives, and friends.

The first rays of sunlight shining through the small roof window into Eric's bedroom woke them up. The day had finally arrived for their departure to the new and mysterious destination, Canada. It was April 13, 1958, the day after Easter, and the promise was there that it would turn into a beautiful spring day. Maria was still in a peaceful sleep. Watching her, he thought about their future together. What would be in store for them? Whatever it would be, he knew that together they would make it.

She really was a gutsy lady, he thought. Within eight months after they met, she had married him and now would travel with him to the other end of the world to build a home in that strange land. They had spent the last two days with Maria's family, but yesterday after arriving in his village again, he had walked by himself once more around the village and shook hands with all the people he met who knew he was leaving shortly. He had also visited Nico's and Lisa's graves with Maria and told them that as long as he would live, he would never forget them. He had spent a little time with Tony, the village electrician, but had spent most of the time with his good old friend Willem.

After saying goodbye to the rest of his family, they walked together to the cow stall and sat down at the wooden feedbox that had become part of Eric's life. Many memories were connected to that wooden feedbox, and many hours had Eric and Willem spend sitting on it as far back as Eric could remember. Willem had been his second father, teacher, and guardian and had always found time to listen and discuss Eric's problems. It was very hard for both to shake hands and say goodbye, and both didn't know at that time that it would be their last farewell because they would never see each other again.

His eyes, now used to the sharp sunlight, glanced around the small bedroom. He knew every inch of it, and every spot brought memories. The piece of quartz, now reflecting the sunlight into brilliant colors, reminded him of the coal mine. It had been over two weeks now since he had made his last shift, and when he stood under the shower to wash the coal dust off his body for the last time, he was happy that he was finally leaving this godforsaken hole. He promised himself that whatever would happen in the future, he would never go back into a coal mine again.

He heard his mother quietly going down the steps so as to not wake Maria. He sneaked out of bed, got dressed, and followed his mother into the kitchen. There was no need to hurry because all the hand luggage had been packed the night before and they still had three or four hours left before they would leave the house. Johann and his father and two of Maria's brothers who would meet them at the train station would travel with them to the airport in Amsterdam, where they would meet the Rudolph family and their relatives. His mother quickly got the coffee going, and in no time, the kitchen was filled with the aroma of the fresh brew.

"What would you like for breakfast this morning?" she asked. "Should I fry you some eggs and bacon? I know it's your favorite breakfast."

"No, thank you, Mother. I appreciate it, but I have a nervous stomach this morning. Just coffee will do for now."

"Why don't you go outside and breathe some fresh air? That will do you a lot of good. When the coffee is ready, I will call you."

Going outside, he felt the chill of the night slowly being replaced by the warmth of the sun. He took a couple of deep breaths. It felt good. He walked to the barn and saw a pile of kindling he had made for his mother a week ago. He smiled. "I'll never have to do that again." Then he walked to the garden, where he had spent so many hours in his spare time with his father. How was he going to keep that up without him? This garden was way too large for one person. He should mention to his father to lease part of it to some other people.

It was really odd how many things he saw that he had just taken for granted all his life. He was getting chilly, so he walked back into the house again. When he walked into the front room to move the luggage from there and into the hallway, looking around the room, he thought of how strange it was that all those years this room was never used. The same furniture that had stood there like statues were never moved except for cleaning once in a while. The same large pictures of the heavy mustached forefathers and the meekly smiling grandmothers still stared at him from the walls, and their eyes still followed him, watching every move he made.

He smiled at them and then said, "Well, until next time, when-ever that will be."

"I was just coming to call you to come and drink your coffee before it cools down," his mother said when he returned into the kitchen.

"Good morning, Maria," he said while bending down to kiss her. "I didn't know you were up already."

Maria was sitting by the coal stove, which was glowing by now, sipping her coffee. She replied, "I got up a couple of minutes ago. I smelled Mom's coffee from downstairs. Are you nervous?"

"Just a little."

"Me too."

When the rest of the family arrived in the kitchen, they had their breakfast, and now the time had come for what they seemed to have been waiting for endlessly. Finally, the time had arrived. With tears in their eyes, they parted from his mother, who embraced them for quite some time and couldn't say a word, and from his brother

Paul and sister, Elly. His father and Johan would be traveling to the airport with them.

They entered the city bus, which stopped in front of the church to get to the train station. Mr. Pastor had been waiting for them and, while wishing the young couple the best in the future, gave both of them a rosary.

He said, "I blessed them for you. You never know when you'll need it."

Eric again shook hands with his old friend, and when the bus left the village, Mr. Pastor was the last of the familiar faces of his village he saw standing there in front of the church.

After a three-hour train trip, wherein not many words were spoken, they arrived at the airport in Amsterdam and joined the Rudolphs. They had arrived earlier by car. Moments later, two of Maria's half sisters, the Mother Superior and another one Eric never met before who lived in the north part of Holland, also arrived at the airport. Eric felt quite embarrassed when the nun, instead of shaking his hand, kissed him on both cheeks. He had never been kissed by a nun, and it felt quite odd.

Eric embraced Johan and his father, who at the last moment was overcome with emotion and constantly wiped the tears from his eyes. Then after a lot of kissing, hand shaking, and waving, they joined Theo, Ellen, and the children in the long line waiting to go through customs. It took quite a lot of time before this planeload of immigrants passed through customs. Finally, after too much time spent in the sparely ventilated waiting room between very tired people and crying children, they entered the waiting plane and were guided by the friendly and helpful flight attendant to their seats. Most people, including Eric and Maria, had never been in an airplane and were amazed by its space and beauty.

Smoothly, the airplane taxied down the runway. Eric sat by a window with Maria sitting beside him, holding his hand anxiously, awaiting takeoff. Both didn't know what to expect. They had heard many stories about motion sickness but most times from people who had gotten their knowledge from hearsay. The four propeller engines started roaring, and a shiver went through the plane as it gained speed down the runway. It seemed to take forever before it finally took off into the air, and Eric, who was scared that the plane wouldn't make it, pushed himself hard into the seat. He also felt Maria's hand grip tighter on his arm. Moments later, it seemed as if the earth was slowly dropping away, and everything unexpectedly had gone smoothly.

Moments later, Maria asked, "Are we still on the ground?"

Eric—with a combination of fear, excitement, and interest—had watched the whole takeoff. With his nose pressed against the window, he answered, "No, Maria. We are off. We are in the air already. Look how high we are!"

Slowly not knowing what to expect, she bent over, and together they watched the slow disappearance of the landscape underneath them, filled with small houses with red-clay-shingled roofs. Here and there were windmills and the tulip fields divided into sections by small canals of their beloved Holland. When watching the coastline slowly fading away, he felt weak, and again he questioned himself if leaving had been the right thing to do.

Then abruptly he shook his head. *There's was no use thinking back. It was too late now anyhow. Let's forget about the past and concentrate on the future.*

Within an hour, they landed in Shannon, Ireland, to refuel. They were allowed to leave the plane to stretch their legs, and after having a cup of coffee at the airport, they took off again in the direction of Montreal. From Montreal, they'd get to their final destination, Toronto, by train.

By now it was evening, and after dinner was served, the light in the cabin was dimmed. Most people, after such an exhausting day, fell asleep. Eric and Maria talked for a while, but then her eyes started getting heavy also, and slowly she dozed off. Eric tried to sleep, too, but he just couldn't. With his head against a pillow in the corner between the backrest of his seat and the wall of the plane, he watched the long blue and orange flames shooting out of the exhaust ducts of the engines. No matter how hard he tried to forget the past, it was no use. If Nico had been alive, he possibly would have emigrated with them. But then from the other side, it could have very well been that he still would be working in the coal mines.

He couldn't remember how long he sat there dreaming, or maybe he did fall asleep. For a while, he watched the starts, which were sprinkled around like shining diamonds in the sky, slowly fade away for the coming new day. Somewhere at the end of the horizon was Canada.

The youngest member of the Rudolph family, a little girl about a year old, woke up and started crying. Maria moaned a little bit, opened her eyes slowly, and looked at Eric. She asked, "Didn't you sleep at all?"

"Oh, I guess on and off."

"You should have. I feel a lot better." Then she turned around and asked Ellen to give her the child so she could take care of her, while Ellen attended to the other two children.

The lights came back on now, and soon the commotion started with children crying and people stretching their legs and walking through the hallways. In no time, there were lineups for the toilets. When breakfast was served, Eric was so hungry that besides his own, he ate half of Maria's and some of the leftover from the children.

Someone shouted, "I see land!"

Everyone watched, filled with their own emotions, as their new country appeared in the far distance. The wild and rough northeastern shoreline of Canada was an unbelievably beautiful sight to see from the air. The gorgeous mountain ranges of northern Quebec looked as though nature went wild and played games with the earth's crust. The airplane now slowly descended, following the shoreline, and soon they saw the first Canadian homes still covered with snow. The captain announced that within an hour, they would land in Montreal, and everyone started to get ready for the arrival.

The first thing Eric noticed about his new country when coming closer to Montreal was the different-colored roofs on the houses. He had been so used to all red roofs in Holland that it really took him by surprise. The weather in Holland had been beautiful when they left, but here it seemed to still be winter, and the whole landscape was still covered with snow.

Maybe his father had been right when he asked some time ago, "How can you go to Canada? Only Eskimos live there."

The flight from Holland to Canada had taken twelve hours before they finally set foot for the first time on Canadian ground. Again, it took hours before these exhausted people cleared customs and gathered their hand luggage, and it took an even longer time before special buses arrived to transport them to their different destinations.

Arriving at the train station in Montreal, Theo, who was more knowledgeable in the English language than Eric, bought tickets for both families for their first train ride to Toronto. Not knowing enough English, however, they took a stop train instead of a fast one, who would leave an hour later. The Canadian people in the train were very friendly and helpful, and to relieve the two couples of the tired and cranky children, they took many walks with them through the passageway of the train.

Eric and Maria, trying to converse with an elderly couple sitting across from them, using more hand and feet suggestions than their vocal cords, received each a silver dollar from these friendly people as a good luck piece. By now it was late in the afternoon, and they hadn't had anything to drink or eat since breakfast early that morning on the plane. For hours, they had been on the train, and when the conductor came by, Theo stopped him and showed him some Canadian dollars.

He said, "Food and milk for the children."

After trying his best to explain to Theo that there was no food or beverage on the train but without success, the conductor finally said, "No food, no milk."

When the conductor walked on, a gray-haired distinguished-looking gentleman stopped him and had a lengthy conversation with him wherein Theo and Eric could only grasp the words *food, children*, and *immigrants*. The gentleman kindly indicated to Theo to sit down again because he had an idea.

When the train stopped at the next small station, he hurriedly guided Theo and Eric off the train, and the threesome, under his guidance, ran over the station, down and up the steps, through a viaduct, and to a small self-service restaurant. Out of breath, the gentleman shouted something to the row of people standing in line, and everyone moved out of the way to let them buy sandwiches and milk. Quickly the purchased items were thrown into bags, and back they went to the waiting train. Running down the steps, however, Eric had the misfortune of having the bag he was carrying broke open and all the sandwiches and milk he carried rolled down the steps. He was lucky that the sandwiches were individually packed. In a rush, he got everything together and pushed them into his pockets and underneath his shirt. The friendly conductor had held up the train until all three fell exhausted back into their seats.

This train trip lasted an unbelievable six hours. Theo's friends, the Maasens, had indicated in one of their letters that they would not be home upon their arrival in Toronto. The parents of his wife had been visiting them from Holland for some time, and that same afternoon, they drove them back to the shipyards in Montreal for their return trip to Holland and would not be returning until the following evening. He had, however, contacted a relative who also lived in Toronto, and after explaining to them the situation, they had very willingly given their phone number to be contacted upon their arrival in Toronto. After calling them and another hour of waiting, their eighteen-year-old son, who knew a little Dutch, picked them up in his Chevy, which seemed to be a huge car compared to the ones they were used to in Holland, and the young man drove them without much conversation to the Maasens' home.

A letter of welcome lay underneath a vase filled with flowers on the living room table and gave them directions to their sleeping quarters and the food supply. Everything was detailed up to the operation of their electric kitchen stove, where the ready-to-heat coffee percolator was waiting. The cuckoo clock let them know it was now nine o'clock in the evening, and since leaving their home in Holland and considering the time difference, they had been traveling for over thirty hours.

When the young fellow, after helping with the luggage, left, and the children were put to bed, the adults couldn't keep their eyes open any longer. The coffee cups on the table were still partially filled when the last light went out and the house darkened. They slept until the next midmorning and possibly would have slept longer if one of the children had not gotten up and started running through the house.

While the two women were preparing breakfast, Theo and Eric inspected the house. The large basement had been divided into two bedrooms—one for him and his wife and one for their one-year-old daughter. At ground level was a well-equipped kitchen, living room, and dining room. The second floor had been converted from three large bedrooms into four rooms—a kitchen (where beside the stove and refrigerator were so many cabinets that there was enough storage room for three families), a living room, and two bedrooms. Also, the full and only bathroom in the house was located on this floor.

Up a winding staircase, Mr. Maasen had all by himself converted the attic into a small kitchen, living room, and bedroom. The kitchen also had a medium-size refrigerator and stove. He had obviously just finished painting it, as the paint smell was still noticeable. A window was built in the living room wall, overlooking the street in front of the house, and also there was a window in the bedroom overlooking the backyard. There was no window in the kitchen, and the two side walls were straight up to about four feet but then bent in a sharp upward angle due to the fact that it was right underneath the roof. Living directly under the roof proved to be unbearably hot in the summer and icy cold in the winter, but for Eric, it looked better than he had expected, and he was happy. For him and Maria, it would be their first nest together, and amazingly, it looked like a nest underneath that roof.

In the early afternoon, another Dutch family who were friends of the Maasens arrived to give a helping hand wherever necessary. Eric was desperate to get out of the house and wanted to see something of the neighborhood. Many times, he walked inside and outside the house and had watched with interest the big cars driving by and the large number of cars parked in front of the houses down the street. The twelve-year-old son of the visiting family gladly accepted the invitation to go with Eric for a walk around the block. Actually, they walked two blocks down the street and ended up on Bloor Street, one of Toronto's main streets.

Besides the advertising of the stores and the people conversing in the English language, he also noticed that the men in general were more colorfully dressed than he was used to seeing. What really surprised him was the multicolored and sometimes numbered jackets many of the men were wearing. If he had worn such a thing in Holland, he would have possibly been shot. To him, it looked like Amsterdam with all these streetcars rushing back and forth.

When walking by a large store called Loblaw's, he noticed bags of peanuts behind the window with a sign indicating that they were twenty-five cents per bag.

"Why don't you go in here and get me a couple of those bags?" he asked his young companion, who could still speak Dutch very well. "My wife likes these nuts, and she will really be surprised." He took a dollar from his wallet, and tried to give it to the young man.

He answered, "Why don't you go in yourself? I will wait for you here. Sooner or later, you have to learn to speak English, so you better start now."

Eric knew that by far he didn't know enough English, so he hesitated.

"Come on. Go on. You can do it," the young man carried on, noticing Eric's hesitation.

"I think I'll leave it to another time," Eric answered while trying to continue on his way.

But the young man was very persistent. Blocking his way, he said, "Don't be a chicken. You cannot have someone around you all the time who will translate for you."

A chicken? Him, a chicken? No way! That did it. Without saying anything further, Eric opened the door and went into the store. He knew that these nuts behind the window were only for advertising, so he walked up and down the aisles, looking for them, but without success.

Finally, one of the young store assistants who noticed Eric walked over to him and asked very politely, "Can I help you, sir?"

Eric searched his mind for the correct English answer and finally said while showing the young man two fingers, "Two bags of monkey nuts, please."

"Pardon me?"

Eric thought that he had spoken too softly, so he repeated, but more strongly, "Two bags of monkey nuts, please."

For a moment, the young man looked at Eric with disbelief in his eyes and then started an uncontrollable laugh so loud that passing customers stopped and looked at the two. Noticing the commotion he had produced, the young man finally calmed down and wiped the tears from his eyes. Eric stood there very embarrassed but really didn't know what had gone wrong. He only had translated the Dutch word *apen noten.*

Finally, a light went on in the young man's head, and he mentioned, "Peanuts. You want *peanuts.*" And still trying to control himself, he took Eric by the arm and showed him the location. Noticing Eric's embarrassment, he tried to apologize and assisted Eric to the cashier, but Eric, after receiving his change, hurried out of the door.

His young companion, noticing that something had gone wrong, asked, "What happened? Your whole face looks red."

When Eric explained what had happened and still didn't understand what had been wrong with his question, *this* young man also started laughing, and it took him quite some time to stop, being a twelve-year-old, and explain to a grown-up what he had asked for. When it finally dawned on Eric what he had said, he also started laughing himself. But he made one commitment; for quite a time, he would not go into that store again.

The next morning, it was Ellen's and Maria's turn for their encounter with the English language. Mary needed a night pot for the children. Andre Maasen, with his wife and daughter, had come home late the night before and had heard about Eric's incident.

He thought it was very funny but said, "That's the only way to do it. If you want to learn the English language in a hurry, you will make mistakes, but there is no other way out. Therefore, since you two need a night pot, you two should go by yourselves to the Woolworth's store, which is close to the store where Eric was yesterday. They have all that stuff. It will be good for the two of you to get out of the house and get some fresh air. We can take care of the children for a while."

Without any trouble, they found the store. But just like Eric the day before, they couldn't find what they were looking for. After searching the whole store, Maria said to Ellen, "Come on, let's go home. I don't think they have anything like that her."

But Ellen wasn't giving up that easy and said, "Do you think that after we walked all this way down here, we should just go home empty-handed?"

They didn't know the English word for *night pot*, and it was too embarrassing to explain. Finally, when everything seemed hopeless, Ellen, in sheer determination, walked over to an assistant and pulled him to the back of the store. Maria was watching the twosome and couldn't believe her eyes when Ellen, in front of the man, sat on her heels and moved one hand under her behind as if she was removing something underneath her while in the meantime making a sissing sound.

She said, "Baby. For the baby."

The man, used to immigrants, studied her for a moment and smilingly said, "I know what you need. You need a piss pot."

Ellen and Maria looked at the man and couldn't believe their ears. They had wasted all this time and showed all these motions for nothing. *Piss pot* was exactly the same word in Dutch. The two had a real ball walking home, and repeatedly they laughed about Ellen's actions in that store.

Andre and his wife, Agnes Maasen, were unbelievably good people. Nothing seemed to bother them, and without hesitation, they assisted the young couples whenever possible. Andre was the only licensed driver, and he owned an old Chevy. His spare time in the first two weeks was occupied by chauffeuring everyone around wherever they had to go. Patiently he would wait while they walked for hours through the large stores, like Eatons and Simpsons. Full of amazement, they enjoyed articles they had never seen before. The outrageously low prices kept most of their attention, even after calculating the Canadian dollar against the Dutch guilder.

The first items Eric and Maria bought from their leftover money, besides some pots and pans, was a kitchen set, consisting of one table and four chairs, and also a large queen-size bed. Andre had given them an old small radio he'd used in his garage.

Sometimes in the evening, they gathered all together in the Maasens' living room to watch television in black and white. Their favorite program was *Playhouse 90* on Thursday nights, which always showed good movies, but only with sporadic translation from Andre or Agnes could they follow the movie. Most of the time, however, they were making up their own stories. The Saturday afternoon professional wrestling program, a sport (if it could be called that), which Eric had never seen before, drove him out of his mind. The endurance of these people was beyond his comprehension, and the fact that their entire bodies could withstand this enormous abuse really puzzled him.

Theo could start working at his new job within two weeks, and no matter how hard Andre had tried to find a position for Eric in the electrical department, he was unsuccessful. He and Eric had to look elsewhere.

One afternoon, about two weeks after their arrival, Andre shouted on the stairway, "Eric, can you come down? There is a telephone call for you."

"For me?" Eric replied while running down the steps. "Who can that be? No one here knows me."

Nervous, he picked up the telephone and, for a while, couldn't understand the fast Dutch-speaking man on the other end of the line. Finally, he realized the call came from the Dutch consulate. This person was really upset and gave Eric a long sermon about him leaving the country without first going into the armed forces. He told Eric that he had not been allowed to leave the country and that he really was in trouble now.

Eric kept his cool, and when he finally could get a word in, he lied, "Sir, it has been more than four years ago since I got my dispensation papers for work in the coal mines. Since that time, I have completely forgotten about it. Furthermore, the Dutch government knew already for more than a half year ago that I was emigrating, but no one ever mentioned anything about the armed forces."

It really scared Eric when this man started to talk about sending him and Maria back to Holland. But then he ended up with "We will see what we can do for you."

For weeks, they waited anxiously for the results by telephone or letter of that conversation. But nothing happened. Several months later, he received notification in a large brown envelope from the Dutch consulate that he was free from joining the Dutch Armed Forces, and that only if he returned to Holland would he be liable again.

In the first letter received from his mother, she wrote that at four o'clock in the afternoon on the day Eric and Maria left, a military jeep stopped in front of the house. Two military policemen knocked so hard on the front door that it scared the living daylights out of her. When she opened the door, they told her that they had come to pick up her son for the forces. The hard knocking on the door and seeing these stern-looking MPs made her so nervous that before she could answer, they had already forced their way into the hallway.

When she overcame the original shock, she told the MPs, "Gentlemen, you can look through the whole house if you want, but he isn't here. His plane left for Canada two hours ago."

"Sorry, we are only doing our duty," apologized one of them, and then they left.

The Dutch immigrating office had told them that there was an abundance of jobs available in Canada and that with Eric's experience and knowledge, he wouldn't have any problems. They even told him not to take the first job that came along, that with so many jobs available, he could choose the right one. He quickly found out that it was far from the truth. They had forgotten to mention that though there were jobs available, everyone wanted Canadian experience. After eight weeks and through the influence of Andre Maasen, he finally netted a job as a machinist in a small machine shop in one of the suburbs of Toronto. Eric had to travel more than an hour to and from that job by bus and streetcar, but he had a job, and that was all that was important.

During his schooling, he had picked up a little bit of knowledge in machining and welding, but by far, it was not enough to call himself an experienced machinist. It took the foreman, who was a German immigrant, only two days to discover Eric's lack of knowledge. But noticing his strength, willingness to work, and eagerness to succeed, the foreman took Eric off the lathe and gave him all kinds of handyman jobs to do.

By now Eric understood a lot more English, and he was picking up new words every day, but being able to make complete sentences was another thing. His willingness and eagerness, however, made the older and experienced mechanics overlook his handicap, and they requested the foreman to send Eric along when they needed assistance on an outside job. His first take-home pay was $37.00 a week. It was not much, even at that time there, but Andre wouldn't hear of any payments for rent until they were doing better.

One man Eric liked to work with in particular was an older master mechanic named Frank. Frank was a fatherly type, and he very patiently pronounced his words slowly. He taught Eric the technical English used in their trade, from tools to materials, up to the names of machines. Eric noticed that the knowledge of words and the ability to understand the English language, to him, who was used to pronouncing every letter in every word, had no rhyme or reason to it. The conversational English, he gained in the first three months, but technically, English was another matter again. The names of simple items, like hammer, nail, screwdriver, he had to learn not only to remember but to pronounce right to be able to assist anyone. Frank was a man who patiently and, through repetition, showed Eric how to say the name of each tool and wasn't satisfied until Eric pronounced it correctly. Then when he really thought he was progressing slang names, like monkey wrench instead of adjustable wrench and many other ones, completely threw him for a loop. But with all these handicaps, Eric was blooming. He loved the new challenge in life. Every day opened new horizons for him. Full of excitement, Eric and Maria could discuss for hours their new discoveries of the day and would assist and correct each other in the English language, which they found difficult.

With their progress in knowledge of words, their shyness in using them went away, and quickly they learned to bypass the hard-to-pronounce or unknown words. Also, the realization of being part of this vast mixture of people who had come from all walks of life all over the world to this beautiful country with its arms spread wide open made them feel welcome. Sitting in streetcars or busses, he would listen to conversations in many different languages, and he knew he was one of them. Now he knew why Canada, and possibly the USA, were such prosperous countries. People like him with the same drive and for many different reasons but all searching to succeed had come for centuries to this part of the world and, with their strength and endurance, had converted a wilderness into the most progressive and peace-loving but powerful nation of the world.

Maria, who became pregnant in their second month of marriage, had taken a job in the kitchen of a restaurant. Some of their new friends thought it was a handicap and that they should have waited. But for Eric and Maria, it was very happy news, and one extra mouth to feed would be welcomed. The only drawback was that when her pregnancy progressed, the constant heavy smell in the kitchen where she worked made her so sick every day that they finally decided for her to stay home. Eric, who was constantly searching for more income, found a part-time job assisting a young starting contractor in installing electrical wiring in a new housing project.

From some leftover beautiful pieces of wood used for cabinet doors and ready-made table legs bought in a store, he made a table for the living room. Maria supplemented the table with two inexpensive rattan chairs. And when Eric bought, for their first Christmas present together, a hi-fi radio record player for forty-seven dollars, they were the proud possessors of living room furniture.

There were many times, however, that he was lonely. The people in the house and all the new gathered friends were more than helpful, but they were still strangers, and he would have given anything to be able to talk to Nico or his father.

To Eric's delight, it soon turned into a hot summer, a heat Eric had never witnessed before. But he loved the sun and his deeply tanned face were witness thereof. The hot air, however, rising from the two floors below up to their living quarters and multiplied by the roof that was their ceiling made living in their apartment sometimes unbearable. Even the light drop in temperature during the night made no difference, and many nights, even lying on top of the sheets, they perspired so much that the sheets and the mattress were completely drenched.

The only relief from this immense heat came when the fall weather arrived. The autumn colors in the woods surrounding Toronto were breathtaking, and anyone witnessing for the first time this wonderful mixture of colors would be awed by it. Even the difference in color between one maple tree and the next was a sight to behold, and it was no wonder that Canada showed the maple leaf in their flag—because of its abundance of these trees.

The first Canadian winter for any immigrant coming from a different climate was unbelievably hard. By the end of October, the temperatures started to drop rapidly, and by the beginning of December, the ground was covered already by a two- to three-foot layer of snow.

Their first Christmas and New Year's in the new country went by, and although each one tried to make it a happy holiday, the loneliness and thoughts of Holland was felt by each one. Maria was in her eighth month of pregnancy and was not at all up to feasting anyhow.

Just as they had suffered through the intense heat of the summer while living in that apartment, so too did they suffer through the intense cold of winter. It was very cold in their living quarters, but with multiple layers of clothing and heavy blankets, this temperature was easier to withstand than the summer heat waves.

In early February, the temperature dropped way below zero, and waiting for bus or streetcar to and from the job made this way of traveling sometimes sheer agony for Eric.

CHAPTER 7

✠

On February 24, 1959, around eleven o'clock in the morning, Maria called Eric at his job and told him that it was time for him to come home because the baby was coming.

"Are you positive now?" Eric asked. The baby was already two weeks overdue, and Maria had been through many false alarms.

"Yes," she answered. "Please come home. This time, it's for sure. The pains are still far apart, but knowing that it takes you an hour to get home, I called you already."

Quickly Eric changed out of his working clothes and headed for the bus stop a half a mile down the road. While walking, he felt the cold, but the mixture of excitement, happiness, and fear made him neglect the subzero temperature.

Arriving at the bus stop, he noticed that he had just missed the bus, for he saw it driving away in the far distance. The bus stop was in the open, and there was no building or house around to protect him from the cold wind. It would take another hour before the next bus would arrive. At first, he tried to hitchhike, but none of the sporadic cars passing by stopped. He didn't know how long he stood there with his back toward the wind, slightly bent forward.

He was shaking like a leaf when out of the blue, a car stopped beside him, and someone shouted, "Get in. You'll freeze to death out here."

It was an elderly couple going to the store for groceries, and they had felt sorry for him. "What happened?" the man questioned when Eric crawled into the backseat. "Did your car break down?"

"No," Eric said, still shivering heavily. "I haven't got a car, and my wife just called me at the job that the baby is due. I just missed the bus, but if you would be so good to give me a ride to the streetcar stop, I would really appreciate it."

"Where do you live?" the woman asked.

"We live close to Bloor Street on Westmoreland Avenue," Eric answered, "but if you only bring me to the next streetcar stop, then I can get home from there."

She looked at her husband for a moment and then said, "No way. We will drive you home. It will be far out of our way, but then again, we don't have much to do this afternoon."

Eric was overwhelmed by the friendliness of these two strangers. He didn't really want to accept their offer, but they wouldn't hear of it. They drove him straight home.

Arriving home, he thanked them gratefully and invited them in for a cup of coffee, but they wouldn't hear of it. "You will have your hands full this afternoon," the woman said. And after wishing him and Maria all the happiness in the world, they drove off.

Maria was really surprised when she saw him coming up the steps. "How did you get here so fast?" she asked, "I just called you."

"I got a ride all the way to here," he said and told her what happened. Maria poured him a cup of hot coffee, and Eric changed into his best suit. Noticing Maria holding herself on the kitchen table, bending over from pain, he got very nervous and said, "Are you ready to go to the hospital? I will go downstairs and call a taxi. Andre and Theo have left for the afternoon shift already, so there is no car available."

"No," Maria answered. "Don't be so nervous. Everything is all right, and we have time enough yet. I don't want to sit for hours in that hospital."

More than two hours they waited, during which time Eric didn't know what to do with himself. Her pains started coming now in shorter periods, and he felt very sorry for her, but he couldn't help her.

Watching the kitchen clock, she finally mentioned to Eric, "I think it is time now to call a taxi."

Within twenty minutes to a half hour, they arrived at a small privately owned hospital designated by their physician. It was operated by nuns, and a friendly-looking, rosy-cheeked nun guided him into a small office to fill out the necessary papers. Shortly thereafter, the doctor arrived and took Maria into another room. Minutes later, he returned and told Eric that it would still take hours given the way the baby was positioned and that it would be better for Eric to go home instead of waiting all that time. The doctor promised to call Eric when it was time to return to the hospital.

Maria agreed, and after kissing her and wishing her strength, Eric left the hospital, took a streetcar, and went home. It was around six o'clock when he arrived home, and after making himself a cup of coffee, he sat down and waited. He waited and waited, not knowing what to do with himself. He walked up and down the steps of the house, periodically watching television with Agnes and Ellen.

Finally, shortly after midnight, the phone rang, and before Agnes, who was waiting for her husband to return from the afternoon shift, could call him, he was already down the steps. It was the doctor, who then told him that Maria had given birth to a daughter but that it had been a difficult birth for mother and daughter. It had been a breech birth, and both had suffered quite a lot.

Eric heard all these words and, very scared, interrupted the doctor, "But how is my wife now? And how is the baby?"

"Oh, they're okay now. If you want to, you can come over, but your wife is still under heavy sedation, and she lost a lot of blood."

Eric mumbled a couple of words of thanks, hung up, told Agnes in haste what had happened, put his long winter coat on and a shawl around his neck, and ran out of the house and down the street in the direction of the streetcar stop.

Agnes shouted, "Wait, Eric! Andre and Theo will be arriving any moment. Andre will give you a ride to the hospital." But her voice was lost in the wind.

What a question from his doctor! "If you want to come over now…" Naturally, Eric would want to come over, and he felt very sorry that he had left the hospital that afternoon. Within minutes, he sat in the streetcar. He was happy that he had such good connection

165

but couldn't help being angry at any car blocking the traffic in front of the streetcar. Arriving at the hospital, he was welcomed and congratulated by one of the nuns for the birth of his daughter.

"Can I see my wife first?" Eric questioned.

But the nun answered, "No, it is better that you first see the baby. Your wife is still in the operating room, and the doctor who is with her doesn't want her moved until he is sure that all the bleeding has stopped. She is in deep sleep, and you cannot talk to her anyway." Walking with Eric through the hallways to the nursery, she told Eric that it was a tall and beautiful baby and that he shouldn't be scared when he noticed the bluish color of her skin. "You see, the length of time it took for this delivery produced a shortage of oxygen in the baby's blood. That's what gave her the bluish color. By tomorrow, it all will be gone."

"But are you sure that she is all right and that there will be no aftereffects?" Eric asked, very worried.

"Sure she is all right, and generally, there are no aftereffects. You don't have to be worried," she replied smilingly.

Arriving in the nursery, the nun knocked on a large glass window, and another nun inside the room showed Eric for the first time his daughter. Her face was all wrinkled, and she had long black hair covering her whole head. He also noticed the bluish tint of her skin, but it was not as bad as he had imagined. He didn't know what he felt. It was his baby all right because there were no other babies in this small one-room nursery. At that moment, it was a little human being, a stranger to him, and without being able to touch or hold her, he had mixed feelings. He knew, however, that he was going to love this baby with all his heart.

When the baby was put back in her crib, Eric, now worried and in a more demanding voice, told the nun, "I want to see my wife now."

The nun looked at him for a moment and then answered, "Let me first talk to the doctor and see what we can do."

When she left, Eric looked once more at his baby before he walked back to the reception hall and thought, *You know, little one, you are the first and only real Canadian in our family.*

Within minutes, the nun returned with the doctor. After shaking Eric's hand, the doctor said, "I guess there is no problem in seeing your wife for a few minutes. I still don't want to move her to a room. Let's give her wounds some more time to heal. By the way, could you do me a favor and deliver this tube of blood and a note to the Sick Children's Hospital? You know where that is located?"

When Eric nodded, the doctor continued, "You see, your blood is O, positive and your wife is O negative. This is a sample of your baby's blood, and I'd like to have it checked in their laboratory. We haven't got the proper facilities here in this hospital. I would have delivered it myself, but I have been called out on an emergency."

"No problem," replied Eric as he put the tube and the note from the doctor in his coat pocket.

Walking with Eric to the operating room, the nun explained that the bleeding hadn't stopped completely but was minor now. On the doctor's advice, they were not moving her to a room until the bleeding stopped completely. Arriving in the operating room, Eric noticed immediately the suffering Maria had gone though. Her hair was wet and glued against her head. Her pale lips, colorless face, dark shadows around her eyes were witness thereof. The white sheet covering her showed a big spot of coagulating blood, and the nun quickly covered it with another sheet. With the shock of sadness, helplines, and sorrow, combined with a deep love for her, he couldn't prevent the tears that rolled freely down his face.

Slowly he bent over and kissed her wet forehead. "I love you, sweetheart. I love you so much," he whispered.

A few moments later, she opened her eyes and noticed Eric standing beside her. She started to cry, and reaching out for him, she said, "Hold me, Eric. Just hold me."

Eric put his arms around her, and raising her a little, he let her cry on his shoulder.

Through her crying, she said, "It is a girl, Eric. Did you see her? It's a girl, and you wanted so much to have a boy…"

He loosened the grip and smiled at her. "It really doesn't make a difference. Yes, I have seen her, and she is beautiful. You just lie down now and go back to sleep. Everything is all right now. I will come back later on this afternoon." He gently lowered her on to the pillow, and after again kissing her, he left the room.

Coming outside, he remembered that he still had to go to the Sick Children's Hospital. It was now 1:30 a.m., and with the tube of his baby's blood clamped tightly in his fist in his coat packet to keep it from freezing, he went to that hospital, which was farther down the road by streetcar and bus. The doctor hadn't given it a thought that Eric didn't have his own transportation, but it didn't bother Eric, because it was the precious blood of his daughter. At that moment, he would have delivered it to the end of the world, if necessary.

The night receptionist at the hospital, seeing this young man in his long overcoat and a shawl around his head, opened the small window. Without expression on her face and with a harsh voice, she asked Eric, "What do you want?"

Eric noticed that she was reading a book, and he must have interrupted her. "I am delivering the blood," he started to explain while handing her the small tube and note from the doctor. But she rudely interrupted him, thanked him, and closed the window again. Eric felt the blood gushing into his face. At that moment, he could have broken that window and shaken the living daylights out of that nurse.

Bitch, he thought. *She's a real bitch.* That was his baby's blood she accepted. At least she could have been friendly.

The return trip seemed to be uneventful until the streetcar, which supposedly was to go straight down Bloor street, made a turn onto another street four blocks from Eric's stop. When he questioned the operator, he told him that after 2:00 a.m., at hourly intervals, only every other streetcar would go straight down Bloor Street. He got off. It had been nice and warm in the streetcar, but the subzero wind dissipated this heat in seconds. Quickly he wound the shawl around his entire head, leaving only his eyes visible; pulled the collar of his coat up high; and started walking.

Bloor Street, which was usually lively at night, was empty. It was cold, unbelievably cold. He kept close to the store windows; it gave him some protection from the wind, which seemed to go right through him. The shawl was of no use because the wind blew right through the knitting, and the wind was so cold that he was developing a splitting headache. The moisture in his breathe crystallized immediately and converted the part in front of his face into an ice pack. Some of the moisture crystallized on his eyebrows and eyelashes, and it had built up so heavily that having his eyes practically closed, protecting them from the wind, they would freeze together, and he couldn't open his eyes. Even his gloves were of no use, and with his hands practically frozen from holding the coat close around his neck, the other hand holding the bottom part from blowing open, he wiped the crystals off his eyelashes, which felt like rubbing sand out of his eyelids.

His feet had no feeling left, and his legs were getting so stiff that it became more and more difficult to bend the knee-and-ankle joints. He was getting very tired and wanted to rest in the entrance of a store, but he had read somewhere that people who froze to death slowly fell asleep. He was chilled to the bone and couldn't stop his body from wildly shivering. He had to keep on walking, he thought, and keep on moving his muscles so they would produce heat.

All the restaurants he passed by were closed. If he could only have one cup of hot coffee, just one cup of coffee and five minutes in a heated room… After what seemed like an endless struggle, he reached the crossing of Bloor Street with the street he lived on. The stores had partially protected him from the wind, but entering his street, the wind met him head on and was so fierce, as if giving him the final blow. He struggled on. He had to make it home. His entire body had no feeling anymore and was so stiff that he couldn't keep his balance anymore. He fell down several times, and only with great difficulty did he get up again.

Ellen woke up from the racket someone was making in the downstairs hallway. A glimpse at her alarm clock told her it was four o'clock in the morning. Still half asleep, she heard someone slowly coming up the steps, then a heavy bounce, then nothing.

Jumping out of bed, she woke up Theo. "Someone came into the house and fell on the steps," she said while rushing out of the bedroom. Moments later, her scream echoed through the house. "Oh, my god! It is Eric! Theo, Andre, Agnes, anyone… Please help. It is Eric. His is frozen!"

They found Eric unconscious, completely covered with ice crystals halfway up the steps. Quickly they carried him into the living room and, after undressing him, covered him with warm blankets. His whole face was snow white, and Theo noticed that the upper edge of his earlobes were frozen because they were filled with ice. Slowly Eric's consciousness returned. He heard familiar voices but couldn't make out what they were saying. Someone was rubbing his hands and another one his feet. He opened his eyes. Everything seemed to be blurred, but then his eyes regained their focus. Looking around, he saw the worried faces of his friends.

"Here, drink this," Ellen said, holding a glass containing a warm liquid to his mouth. He was still cold, and he started shaking heavily, which spilled half of the liquid all over his face. The brew—which Ellen had prepared from hot water, brandy, sugar, and a shot of lemon juice—entered his body, and he felt the heat penetrating all parts of his innards. When the warm blood entered his toes and fingers, it produced such an unbearable pain that Eric almost screamed. His whole body started glowing now. It gave him the feeling as if he was covered by a light sunburn. His face felt really hot, but his ears felt like they were aflame. After he drank his second glass, he felt a lot better, and he explained what had happened.

"The last thing I remember," he said, "was that I fell down halfway down the street and had trouble getting up. The rest is a complete blank."

Ellen told him what happened after he had entered the house. "The tremendous temperature difference when entering the house must have hit you, and given your exhaustion, you passed out."

Seeing that Eric was all right now and after listening to his story, Andre got angry. He said, "Why the hell didn't you call me? Or call a taxi? You nearly froze to death! You know, on my way home from work, the radio announced that the temperature had dropped to thirty-four degrees below zero and that the wind produced a wind chill of about fifty degrees below zero."

But Eric replied, "I really didn't think I had a problem. It only started when that streetcar turned into that street, and at that time, there was no way to contact you or anybody."

After telling them about Maria and the baby, he was tired, and after taking a couple of aspirins for his bouncing headache, he went to bed and fell immediately asleep.

It was around noon when Eric woke up. He still had a headache but not as severe anymore. Apart from the aching muscles through his entire body, he felt fairly good. Crawling out of bed, he thought about his ordeal. Only now did he realize how lucky he had been. Ellen, who heard him moving around upstairs, called him down for breakfast, and while eating bacon and eggs, she told him that she had called Maria that morning and had told her all about his return trip. Andre came up the stairs and told Eric that he had notified Eric's employer and that he didn't have to go back to the job until after the weekend.

"When you are through," he continued, "I will drive you to the Western Union office so you can send telegraphs to your family and Maria's family."

That afternoon, two telegrams were sent to Holland with the message "We have a daughter, born last night, twenty minutes before midnight. Letter will follow. Greetings, Eric, Maria, and Nicole."

More than a month ago, both Eric and Maria had already decided that if the baby was a boy, they would call him Nico, and if it was be a girl, they would call her Nicole.

Theo and Andre had taken the day off from work, and all five of them visited the hospital in the late afternoon, but this time in Andre's car. When they arrived at the nursery, a nun took Nicole out of her crib and showed her behind the glass divider to the visitors. The wrinkles were gone from her face, and she now had a beautiful rosy color. The nun had brushed her hair, and with jerking motions in her arms and legs and gripping with her tiny hands at nothing, Nicole tried to open her eyes against the sharp lights of the room.

"What a beautiful baby," Ellen said. "Look at her thick black hair and beautiful blue eyes, but then at this time the color of their eyes doesn't mean anything, because most babies are born with blue eyes, which will change color shortly thereafter."

When they all entered Maria's room, she saw Eric's still-red face and swollen lips with deep cuts in them. She looked very worried and asked him how he was doing.

"Me?" he answered. "I am all right. You know I am indestructible."

"You sure didn't look indestructible on the steps when we found you this morning," Ellen joked. Everyone laughed.

When Eric tried to do likewise, his lips split open, and he started bleeding again. Grasping for a napkin, he said, "Don't make me laugh. It hurts too much." But then he turned to Maria. "Let's forget about me. How are you? You're looking a lot better than early this morning."

She still was pale in the face, but she smiled and said, "I feel a lot better. The nuns here are very friendly, and they are taking good care of me. They even washed my hair early this afternoon." Then turning to Ellen and Agnes, she discussed the horrors she had gone through with this birth.

Mother and child remained for a week in the hospital. In the meantime, Eric had built a beautiful crib from a half-inch-thick plywood. All weekend long, he had been sawing and hammering on his kitchen table, which echoed through the house and drove the rest of the people out of their minds. But no one mentioned anything about it. It was a beautiful crib, with a large oval pointed backboard and rounded footboard, finished with a high bent steel rod mounted behind the backboard and covered with a beautiful veil made by Ellen from Mari's wedding gown. It covered the head end of the crib. It stood there in the corner of the bedroom, waiting for the arrival of Nicole.

CHAPTER 8

Two years had gone by, and Nicole grew up to be a beautiful, happy little girl. She was a joy not only to Eric and Maria but also to all the neighbors. If by chance the front door or the porch in the backyard was left open, she was gone and could be found on the lap of some of the neighbors, talking like crazy in a language no one could understand. She now had big brown eyes and dark-brown hair, which she inherited from Maria's father. Both Maria herself and Eric's family were all blond-haired with blue or hazel eyes. However, she also was very independent; nobody could play with her. She wanted to do everything her own way.

Even as a child, Eric often had troubles with his tonsils, but in the last couple years, he'd had tonsillitis so many times that it really started to bother him. He was already twenty-six years old and still had this problem. It was about time that he had them removed and get it over with. After visiting his family physician, the agreement was made that the following Tuesday night, he would enter a hospital in Toronto and have his tonsillectomy on Wednesday morning.

After three years in Canada, his knowledge of the English language was coming along far enough that he could follow a normal conversation, but whenever uncommon (or what he called "expensive" words) were used, he was lost. The necessary preliminaries, like blood samples and paperwork, were all new to him, and it took quite some patience from the admitting nurse not only to make him understand the questions but for them to understand his answers and finish the whole process.

Finally, he made it to his room, and after changing into his brand-new pajamas, which Maria had bought specially for this occasion, he laid down and watched television until late at night. It took quite some time before he fell asleep. He was all alone in this room. The footsteps and the soft-spoken voices of the nurses moving through the hallway gave him a kind of eerie feeling. He could even hear the rubbing sound of their starched uniforms. Lying there, slowly dozing off, his thoughts went to his own operation. The doctor had told him it was a minor operation but that his throat would be sore for about a week. Tomorrow, by this time, it would be all over.

A lot of people in this hospital wished they were as lucky as he was. Many of them would possibly be waiting anxiously for an answer after an exploratory operation; some were even lying there after a heart attack or open-heart surgery. For a moment, he felt sad. All these people in so many rooms on so many different floors—all had the same thing in common. They were hanging on to their precious life and wanting to get back as soon as possible to their loved ones and, if possible, back to their normal way of life. Eric was not an everyday praying religious man, but many times, he would talk to his God man to man. This night, he asked God to give all the sick people in this hospital and, for that matter, in hospitals all over the world, a peaceful sleep and a hopeful following day.

The voices of the busy nurses woke him up. It was about six on Wednesday morning, the day of his tonsillectomy. A small cute nurse came into the room and brightened Eric's day with a friendly smile on her face.

She said, "Good morning. Did you have a good sleep?" She looked like and maybe was a Hawaiian girl. She had beautiful black hair, friendly dark-brown eyes, and light-brown face. Wearing her white uniform, she looked like a movie star. While taking Eric's blood pressure, she asked in a very friendly manner if he'd had a bowel movement that morning.

Eric completely missed the question, and in shock, he answered, "No, no, not balls removed. I have my tonsils removed." Oh boy, there you have it. These nurses yesterday misunderstood him while filling out the paperwork and had put him in the wrong section!

The nurse, not believing her ears, looked surprised at Eric. His worried face made her drop the blood pressure band, and with one hand covering her mouth and eyes as big as golf balls, she ran out of the room and down the hallway, laughing all the way as hard as she could. For a moment, the laughing stopped when the nurse reached the nurses center in the middle of the hallway, but then all the nurses at that center broke out into hilarious laughter. Eric, still in shock, heard all this laughing and realized that something was wrong. But whatever it was, it had to be changed in a hurry. A big built elderly nurse came into the room, her eyes still with tears from laughing.

She must be the supervisor, Eric thought. Calmly, and trying hard not to burst out laughing again, she assured Eric in a slow spoken English that he was in the right section and that it only had been a language problem.

The operation was a success, but the remaining four or five days in the hospital were very painful for Eric. His pains were softened, however, by the constant attention of every nurse on the floor, who cared for him like a baby after that incident.

He was still working for the same company and had progressed quite a lot. He now brought home between sixty and eighty dollars a week, depending on the amount of overtime he could have. Also, his position was changed.

One day, a big radial drill press broke down at the time that they needed it the most. The foreman called an electrical company to come over and take a look at it. They waited for hours, but still no one showed up yet. Eric was unloading steel from a big truck outside the yard.

When he heard about the problem, he went inside and said to the foreman, "I can fix that machine. I used to be an electrician. Do you still have any electrical drawings on this machine?"

He did not really believe Eric but looked for the drawings in his office desk anyway. Finding them, he handed them to Eric and said, "Here they are. I hope you know what you are doing. But maybe you'll find out what's wrong with it and get that thing in operation again."

Eric studied the drawings for a while and then opened the large electrical control box of the machine. Within a half hour, he found the problem and corrected it. One of the control wires had broken off on its terminal. The foreman, pleased with Eric, mentioned it to the owner, and that same day, he became the maintenance electrician, which included a raise in pay.

One weekend, he wrote on every page of a notepad that he would clean out garages, repair, and install electrical equipment, and even do gardening for a dollar an hour. He deposited these pages in every mailbox in the neighborhood. As a result, on evenings and weekends, he was doing side jobs to enlarge his income. Aside from all the overtime he could get at his workplace, he also became well-known in his neighborhood as a man who could do and fix almost everything. Using the extra money, they bought more furniture and a television.

Most of the people appreciated Eric's work and even paid him extra. But there were always people who misused a trusting and innocent immigrant, and Eric, who was brought up in an environment where a handshake was more than a legalized contract, found out the hard way that he was misused.

One well-to-do family, who purchased a big house with a large property on the outskirts of Toronto and had heard about Eric's expertise in gardening, contacted him one day and offered him $1.50 an hour if he would landscape their large property for them. It was quite an undertaking, but Eric, knowing he could do it, accepted the job. He drew the layout and discussed it in detail with the owners. Nearly all summer and fall, he worked at it in his spare time, including weekends, converting this property into the most beautiful garden in that area.

At first, they told him they would pay him at the end of every week. Then they said at the end of each month. However, at the end of the first month, they invited him into the house for coffee and a piece of cake and told him how happy they were about his accomplishments. They even gave him the remains of the cake to take home to his wife and child. Then they told him it would be better for him if they would pay him a lump sum in the fall. He could really surprise his wife then with a nice Christmas present, and they even would give him a nice bonus if he could finish before the bad weather arrived.

Eric, still trusting these supposedly friendly people, thought that it was not such a bad idea and accepted this agreement. By early fall, when the job was finished, he had supposedly earned over $1,000. He had even bought some of the bushes and plants from his own pocket money. Every hour of work and every penny spent he had recorded on a piece of paper. When he handed it to the owner, they said they were really pleased and that the job was well done but that they would send him the check in the mail and include a large bonus they felt he had earned. When after one week he still didn't receive the check, he called them, and they explained to him that they only wrote out checks at the beginning of each month and that he had to wait a couple of weeks. He waited and waited and finally called again the second week of the following month.

The woman of the house told him that she couldn't talk to him and that her husband would call him back as soon as he came home. Eric felt a funny feeling in the pit of his stomach and knew that something was wrong. The husband didn't call back that day.

When Eric got him on the phone the next day, he answered in a rude voice, "What do you want?"

"What do you mean what do I want? You promised me more than a month ago that you would send me the check, but I haven't seen it yet."

"What check?" he hollered. "I have paid you every week in cash. You damn German Nazis are all alike. If you don't stop calling, I will call the police!" And then he hung up.

Eric stood there, the telephone still at his ear, and he couldn't believe what he had just heard. For the first time, his belief in human integrity and honesty was shattered. Eric knew that he would never receive that money, and since there was no contract, at least no *written* contract, he couldn't do anything about it. Not only had he lost all his beautiful evenings and weekends away from his family, but also instead of receiving what for him looked like a small fortune, he lost over $200 in expenses. For the first time, he realized that here in this new country, not all people had been reared the way he was and that many people would do anything for money. He also learned that friendliness and trustworthiness was a commodity to possess. To reach higher goals, he had to be tougher and harder. He had learned his lesson the hard way. But not all was lost, and this knowledge gained prepared him for the future.

Maria seemed to be as fruitful as her mother had been. In the same year Nicole was born, she had a miscarriage but gave birth to a healthy son the following year. They named him Steven and not Nico. Eric just couldn't do it. They had promised each other before they left Holland that if they could afford it, after three years, they would go back to Holland for a vacation.

Steven, their son, was ten days old when they moved to another location because their living quarters were too small now. They rented a second floor of a house owned by Italian people, which consisted of a large living room, two fair-sized bedrooms, and a kitchen. Also, the bathroom was on their floor but had to be used by both families. The monthly rent was low, and these people seemed to be friendly and helpful. There was one drawback, however, with living in this house. The predominant smell of garlic used in their food and the heavy smell of brewing their own wine, which filled the whole basement, made living there sometimes unbearable.

Overjoyed and while whistling a happy tune, Eric walked home. He had gone that morning to an interview on a job he had answered a few weeks ago in the newspaper. The interview had taken no more than an hour, and now he was accepted as maintenance electrician in a large dairy plant. It was located only a mile from his home in Toronto. He still couldn't believe it. After two weeks, he could start with practically doubled hourly pay and the fringe benefits that were grossly enlarged. He was so happy that he kicked an empty can so hard that it flew over a private fence into and someone's front garden. Someone yelled at him, and through the corner of his eye, he saw a heavyset lady standing behind an open window, raising her blood pressure about that empty can in her yard. But nothing and no one could harm Eric today. He didn't answer but hastened his step.

What a job! he thought. Since it was close by, he could walk to the job and would be home in no time instead of being in this day-in-and-day-out traveling by streetcar. I bet Maria will be happy when she hears this good news. I wonder. *Should I write her, or should I wait and really surprise her when she arrives with the children next week at the airport?*

He really looked forward to her return from Holland with the two children. Two months ago, they had gone to Holland as promised for their vacation and to show their children for the first time to their grandparents. Eric could only stay three weeks, but Maria and the children stayed on for another month and a half. He could only get, and afford, his two weeks' vacation and plus one week without pay. It seemed like nothing had changed in his village. The three years had gone by so fast that it looked like he had just left.

The village and the people were still the same. Only Eric and Maria had changed. They were not the village people that they used to be and were very quickly bored by the usual village small talk. At some time or another in the last three years, they had been homesick, mostly during the Christmas season or at the birth of their children. But being there, witnessing again the village and the disadvantages and jealousy that came with everyone knowing one another, they were glad that they had emigrated and were living their own life without interference.

The last five or six weeks since he was back in Canada, he had been very lonely, and he missed Maria and the children. He had looked forward to her letters, wherein she mentioned that she also missed him but that showing off the two little Canadians to her many family members, who were spread out all over Holland, was a real joy for her. He really missed her, but he also wanted her to have a good time because she'd earned it. It had not been easy for her the past three years.

He decided to wait until she came back before telling her about the new job. Tomorrow he had to give notice at his present job. He didn't look forward to that affair, because these people had been very good to him. There were a lot of opportunities in this country, and no one was going to stop him. The only one he was going to miss was

Frank, the master mechanic. He really was a nice guy, but Frank had told him many times that he should look for a better job.

The new job became quite a challenge for Eric. It was a huge dairy plant. Being the only electrician in a large plant like that with all its machinery, such as automatic bottle washers and bottle fillers and miles of conveyor belts, had its glory but also its drawbacks. He was respected for his knowledge and quick action when needed in case of emergencies, but the job also laid a heavy burden on him. He was completely responsible for all the electrical equipment, and aside from having the help of a few maintenance mechanics, kept the plant in operation day and night almost by himself.

Living within walking distance of the plant, he was called back many times during the evening or night hours for an emergency breakdown. Most of the time, he was called back to replace a fuse that had blown due to the heavy use of water by the cleanup personnel of the nightshift. It wasn't always pleasant to be called back during all kinds of weather and certainly not after he had gone to bed already. But then it was his job, and he never made a fuss about it. For the nightshift people, it was also quite a change. They had been used to an elderly electrician, who always showed up very angry or grouchy after they had to call him in for an emergency breakdown.

All the large vats, floors, and walls were steam-cleaned every night and could play real havoc with the electrical equipment. One day, Eric was called in for a breakdown around four o'clock in the morning. He got up, put on his work clothing, and still yawning, stepped outside in the fresh early morning air. It really didn't bother him that he was called in again. This was the third time this week. With all this overtime, he would get a fat check next week.

Arriving at the plant, he found the night shift foreman waiting for him.

"Morning, Eric. Sorry to get you up this early," he greeted.

"Morning, Jack. No problem. The walk in this beautiful morning felt good. What's the problem?"

"The electrical counter in the cold storage room broke down, the one that counts the milk cartons going to the loading docks, and

I have a whole bunch of trucks lined up, waiting to be loaded," Jack replied.

"Let me see what I can do for you, Jack," Eric answered. "While I get my tools out of my locker, could you get me a cup of coffee? I didn't take the time this morning."

"Okay," said Jack. "But hurry up. Every minute is important."

Eric quickly grasped his heavy jacket and tool bag out of his locker and rushed to the cold storage area. Working in a large refrigerated room early in the morning or, for that matter, anytime was no pleasure. Even with a heavy jacket on, he had to work fast because the cold slowly would chill him to the bone. Jack arrived with a steaming cup of coffee. Eric took a couple of good swallows then took the cover off the counter. Looking inside with his flashlight, he came to the conclusion that an electrical short had made the counter unrepairable. He knew there were some spare counters in the electrical storage room, but now when he needed one, he couldn't find it. Arriving back in the cold storage room, he found Jack still waiting.

"Jack, I cannot find one. We have to wait until tomorrow morning so I can have one picked up at an electrical supply company."

"Damn it, replied Jack. "Now I'm really stuck. I guess the only thing we can do then is put a man by this counter and hand-count them. I have to get these trucks loaded. The only problem is, I am already short of manpower this morning. Could you do me a favor and count these boxes for me so I can help loading the trucks on the platform?"

"Sure, Jack. I will get some paper and pencil and count them for you," answered Eric.

He put on extra heavy clothing for working in the storage room. Marking on his paper one stripe, two stripes, three stripes, four stripes, and a fifth stripe crossing the other four and over and over again, Eric sat there in that cold room, counting hundreds of boxes filled with milk cartons passing by him on that conveyor until the dayshift people arrived. Jack had left a note in the maintenance department, and soon Jim, one of the dayshift people, arrived at the scene.

"Eric, what in the world are you doing here? Some people are always getting the easiest jobs," he said jokingly.

Eric, not in the mood for this and getting very tired by now, answered, "Don't you see what I'm doing? Go and see if you can find a spare counter for me." When Jim kept on talking, he cut him short and said, "Please don't bother me, Jim. I'm constipating instead of concentrating. I have to constipate on these boxes."

Jim burst out in hilarious laughter, and within an hour, the word *constipate* had spread throughout the whole plant. Thereafter, every time Eric was in deep thought, they would jokingly make the remark, "Don't bother Eric. He is constipating."

Eric quickly exchanged the counter Jim had located for him and went home.

Then there was Big Joe. Actually, his name was John Clemmens, but except for this name being mentioned on his paycheck, everyone knew him as Big Joe. He had a towering height, and the width of his shoulders could cover two normal-sized people. His arms were as thick as Eric's thighs, and his hands and fingers were so huge that when you shook his hand, it would disappear completely into his. He looked like a huge gorilla when he walked slightly bent forward, his huge arms loosely hanging from the sides. Big Joe was a maintenance mechanic, and Eric believed that he was hired more for his strength than for his brains.

The old saying that heavy people were generally happy and friendly people sure didn't fit Big Joe. He had a nasty disposition. He seldom talked, and if he did, it was more like growling. Also, he used so many four-letter words with pride that it seemed as if he had invented them. There were two kinds of people in that plant— the ones that were abnormally friendly to him and the ones that stayed out of his way. Eric was neither one of them. They had to work together many times on breakdowns. Big Joe was a man who always knew everything better. Most of the time, it ended up in a very unfriendly situation, with one or the other finally walking away from the job.

Eric had respect for this man, but only for his strength. As long as Big Joe could use a hammer or chisel or move heavy equipment with a flare of demanding respect from the onlookers, Big Joe was in his glory, but when he had to use his brains on some of the machines, he was lost.

One day, a fully automatic bottle-filling machine broke down. Thinking it was a mechanical problem, the production foreman called for a maintenance mechanic. Moments later, Big Joe came walking up the metal steps, which bent under the heavy load. The tool bag hanging over his left shoulder looked like a lady's purse compared to his huge body. Every bystander moved out of the way when Big Joe arrived at the machine. Eric, exchanging a motor on a standby conveyor, was watching the happenings.

Big Joe shouted at everyone within hearing distance, "Get out of the way, and stay out!" He opened his bag and took some tools out. Looking up, he noticed Eric watching him, and the look in his eyes told Eric that this was also meant for him. Big Joe loosened and tightened bolts again and hammered all over with the only tool he knew something about for more than an hour, but without success. By now, the production was far behind, and some of the management people arrived, distressing Joe greatly. It seemed that most management people had a knack for asking dumb questions at the wrong time.

They asked these questions like "Why isn't it running yet?" and "Do you know what you are doing?"

These made the heavily perspiring Big Joe so nervous that he was completely lost. Once in a while, he glimpsed at Eric with a desperate look in his eyes. Eric felt sorry for him, but he also knew that Big Joe would never ask him for assistance. Eric put a couple of small tools in his pocket and slowly walked over in their direction.

As he arrived at the machine, Big Joe looked at him and said, "What the fuck do you want?" Eric didn't answer because he heard in the tone Big Joe used that he was really asking, "Please help me…"

Eric knew this machine like the back of his hand, and a quick glimpse over the machine told him that it was not a mechanical problem but that somewhere one of the many limit switches was defective. And he was right. Walking to the back of the machine he noticed one of the tiny limit switches hanging loose. Without drawing attention to what he was doing, Eric pulled the screwdriver out of his pocket and tied the limit switch back on its base again. No one had noticed it except Big Joe, who had watched every move Eric made. Eric blinked an eye and nodded his head to him, indicating that the machine would run now.

With a meek smile on his face, Big Joe called the operator, and looking at the management, he said with pride, "Start it up. It's fixed now." The operator pushed the button, and the machine was in production again.

One of the managers slapped big Joe on the shoulder and said, "Well done, Joe. You sure know what you are doing."

Eric didn't mind because he felt Joe had suffered enough and only for that reason should he receive the glory. Getting his tools together, which were spread all over the floor, Big Joe noticed Eric and said in a reduced voice so no one else could hear it, "You are bloody lucky, you know."

"I guess so," Eric replied, and together they walked down to the maintenance department to have their delayed lunch. "Joe, let me tell you a story. Do you know about the $10,000 service call?" When Joe didn't reply, Eric continued, "Well, there was that fully automatic German-built machine. In the US, the machine worked perfectly for more than a year, but one day, it broke down, and no one could fix it. The whole maintenance department, even an outside service firm, took a shot at it, but without success. Finally, after days of nonproduction, the management called the German company and requested a serviceman to come over. When the serviceman arrived, he walked around the machine and looked at everything for about ten minutes, then he took a little hammer out of his tool bag and hit one of the parts very slightly. He put the hammer back into his tool bag and said to the operator, 'You can start it now. It's fixed.'

"That same evening, he got on a plane back to Germany again. A month later, this company received a bill for that service call. When the manager received it on his desk, he was outraged. 'Ten thousand dollars! That is ridiculous!" he said, and he wrote a nasty letter to that German company. 'Please explain,' he wrote. 'Your serviceman arrived in the morning. He spent only fifteen minutes on the machine, hit only once with his hammer, and left again. We feel that a $2,000 charge, including travel, would be more than enough for this call; $10,000 is outrageous!' The German company answered, 'Travel cost is $975; hit with hammer is $25.00; knowledge to know where to hit with hammer is $9,000; total is $10,000."

When Eric was finished, Big Joe looked at him and said, "So?"

Eric replied, "Just think about it, Joe. That's all."

The whole incident with the machine and Eric's story were never mentioned again.

A few days later, the phone rang in the maintenance department, and Joe answered it. He listened for a moment and then answered, "No, that's not for me. I'll tell Eric about it. He is pretty smart about that stuff, and he will fix it for you," Then he looked at Eric. "They need you on the bottle-washing machine." And he hung up.

"Thank you, Joe." And Eric meant it. "I'll get my tools and go right away."

The moment the two men looked at each other, there was no real friendship in their eyes but a lot of understanding. For more than two years after that, they would work together, never really friends but respecting each other—Big Joe for his strength and Eric for his knowledge.

When Eric left this company, he shook hands with all the people he had worked with, except Joe. He looked all over but couldn't find him. At the moment he was about to leave the building, he heard someone calling his name at the far end of the hall.

"Eric, hold on for a moment!" The loud voice echoed through the hallway. With his big heavy jacket on and a brown knitted cap over his head, Eric thought Big Joe really looked like a grizzly bear. Coming closer, he said, "Sorry, Eric, I nearly missed you. I was working on a conveyor in the cold storage room."

Standing in front of him, Eric noticed again how huge this man was.

Big Joe wiped his dirty hands on his trousers and shook Eric's hand. "Eric, I wish you all the best. You are a good man, and I really learned a lot from you. I'm going to miss you." Before Eric could answer, Big Joe turned around abruptly and walked down the hall-way again without ever looking back.

Eric watched him for a moment. He wanted to call out to him, but then he whispered softly, "Good luck to you, too, Joe."

After several years of hard work, it was time for Eric's family to visit their relatives in Holland again. It was quite exciting for the children, who had not seen Maria's and Eric's families since they were little. Eric could only stay a few weeks, but Maria and the children stayed for two months. One of Maria's many brothers was waiting for them at Amsterdam airport. The children did not see much of the beautiful landscape while traveling from Amsterdam to the south part of Holland. Completely exhausted, they slept the two and a half hours in the car after nine hours of flying. A lot of family members were waiting for their Canadian cousins, but all, including Eric and Maria, were too exhausted and went early to sleep—but not before Eric and Maria walked into the garden and remembered the first time they visited her home about one year before they married about thirteen years ago.

They hugged each other, and Maria said, "A lot has happened during those years, but we did okay, didn't we?"

"You are right," Eric answered, "but I hope that the longest time is still to come."

After a few days of enjoying meeting Maria's family again, they went to Eric's home. Martha and John greeted them with open arms and hugged the children so hard that Steven cried out, "Dad, she is killing me!" A few hours later, this very good-looking young lady arrived and went straight for Eric, hugging him profusely. Eric was very surprised, and while being hugged, he looked over her shoulder to his mother with a question on his face: "Who is this?"

His mother laughed and said, "Think nothing of it. It is your sister, Elly."

Eric did not recognize her because the last time he saw her, she was still a very young girl. Now she was a grown woman.

The first thing Eric wanted to do was to visit his good old friend Willem (the farmer), with whom he had not been in contact for many years. However, he came to the shocking conclusion that

Willem and his two sisters (his parents had died) had moved to the north part of Holland, and no one knew the address. Eric felt very sad because that was a very important part of his trip—to see and talk with Willem about the good old times together.

Next, he went to his bar (one of the many in the village), which had been such a large part of his coal miner years. When Eric entered the bar, he felt like a stranger because he did not know most of them. However, the bartender recognized him and, without saying a word, turned around and looked at the many beer steins hanging on the old ceiling above him. He took off one of them, cleaned it, filled it with beer, and handed it to Eric.

He said, "Welcome home, Eric. I knew that sometime you would come back."

It was Eric's stein, which he had used many years ago. When he had emigrated to Canada, someone had put his name on it. Eric felt home again, and in no time at all, they started to recognize each other. The beer flowed easily, and it was not a steady walk at all when he went home. The only thing Maria said to him when he arrived was "I guess that you felt home again." The next Sunday afternoon, Eric went with his father to the game of the village soccer team. Like the old times, Eric yelled as loud as his father when the home team scored the winning goal.

Within a few days, Eric visited the graves of Nico, Lisa and the good old oak tree. It was still standing there, majestic and powerful. When Eric got close to it, he felt again the feeling he had so many years ago. Again, it was as if the very large bottom branches opened up, like spreading its arms to welcome him. The closer he came, the sadder he got, and his thoughts went back to Lisa and Nico. He put his arms around his friend and cried. However, it was a mixture of sadness and happiness—sadness for the two heavy branches he lost but also happiness and gratefulness for the new branches for Maria and the children. Before Eric left, he looked back at the tree. He felt that it was telling him that the future was still to come and not without branches to break off but also new ones to grow on. After two weeks of enjoying with the children the area Maria and Eric grew up, it was time for Eric to go back to Minneapolis, because he had only two weeks' vacation.

Two weeks after his return, he got an urgent telephone call from Maria. The day before, she had taken the children to a park that had a lot of items for children to play with. One of the items was for older children to use. It was a cable between two towers. On one side, the cable was higher than the other side. A roller on top of the cable had a handle on each side so the children while hanging on the handles could roll from one to the other side. For a moment, Maria had lost sight of Steven, and too late to stop him, she saw him go down the cable, showing off and yelling like Tarzan in the forest. He hung on only with one hand. Naturally, his one hand could not hold him, and immediately he fell off.

Maria said, "He screamed and then was unconscious. I was amazingly calm and right away asked some of the people that came running to me to get an ambulance. "Please," she had begged, "please help me."

Finally, someone got in contact with a local hospital, and within a half hour, the ambulance got Steven, with Maria and Nicole to the hospital. Maria had asked one of the nurses to telephone one of her sisters to pick up Nicole from the hospital. After the checkup in the emergency room, a doctor told Maria that Steven was in serious trouble. He had fallen on his left arm and broken it, but worse was that his spleen was torn, and he had internal bleeding. They had to operate immediately.

When Eric received this information, he was shocked, but it was already evening in Minneapolis, so he could not fly out until the next morning. However, Maria told him to stay close by the telephone and that she would keep him up to date. She had told the doctor that she would contact Eric to fly over, but the doctor answered, "Please wait until after the operation. Maybe it is not as bad as we think it is presently."

Eric sat in the living room all night, waiting, hoping for good news. *Is that what the oak tree tried to tell me, that there still will be branches to break off?*

"Oh please," said Eric. "Do not let it be this time."

At seven o'clock in the morning, Maria called Eric and told him the good news that the doctors had repaired the spleen and set his arm, and there was no internal bleeding anymore. Maria and Eric both decided that she would keep Eric informed day by day and if necessary, he would fly to Holland immediately. Steven was young and healthy, and within one week, he could leave the hospital. Later when he was home in Minneapolis again, he told Eric that it was stupid, what he did, but he was never more spoiled so much from each family until they returned home several weeks later.

During this time period, Eric got very interested in outer space—aliens, extraterrestrials, and spaceships. His mind really opened when he read Erich Von Daniken's first book, *Chariots of the Gods*, and the books that followed. He thought that it would be very strange that hundreds, maybe thousands, of people all over the world had witnessed flying saucers and that all those people were wrong most of the time. He would watch on the science channel on television the latest information and discoveries of the universe.

At one time, they mentioned that there are more stars and planets in space than there are sand (granules) on the whole earth. It could not be possible that life (intelligent life) could only have developed on this comparably tiny dust spot we call Earth. Eric figured that if life had started on one planet, only one million years before life started on Earth and their time of development were similar as mankind, they would by now be one million years ahead of us in all phases of our capabilities at the present. Therefore, if we can send manned missiles to the moon, it is only logical that life one million more advanced than us could have technologies we cannot even dream of. So some of these extraterrestrials could have traveled to Earth many thousands of years ago and assisted mankind in the development of our present technology.

We have ultraprecision telescopes traveling around the earth that could look far into space without the interference of Earth's atmosphere. Eric learned that they now could find galaxies with each thousands of stars and planets more than a million light years from Earth. Eric figured light travels at a speed of approximately 180,000 miles per second, that would be 648,000,000 miles per hour, again multiplied by 24, that would be 15,552,000,000 miles a day. Times 365, that would be 5,676,480,000,000 miles a year, or one light year.

It is mind boggling that the astrologers were mentioning galaxies they could see and that these were over one million light years away. Sometimes, on a clear night, Eric would lie down in his chair outside and watch the tiny spots of light in the sky. It could be a galaxy like our own, the Milky Way, with its millions of stars and planets. He figured that he could be looking back in time because this galaxy could have stopped, giving off visible light for thousands or even millions of years, but the light was still traveling. In later years, he read all the books written by Zecharia Sitchin covering the relationship between us and the gods from out space more in detail. His many years of studying and translating the Sumerian language, considered to be the oldest written language discovered this far, gave his writing an in-depth knowledge of the origin of mankind. After all he'd read and watched on television, Eric was sure that "we don't live alone." Eric believed that most governments in the world, including the Vatican, know much more about outer space and visits on Earth by extraterrestrials than they're showing.

This, Eric thought, *is very understandable*. If government would officially acknowledge their knowledge of this subject, the whole Earth would be in uproar because of the many different beliefs and religions. Many people questioned if these extraterrestrials would come down to Earth to harm us, but Eric did not believe that, because if they'd had that in mind, they could have done so many years ago.

CHAPTER 9

✠

Nothing and no one could stop Eric anymore. His eagerness and search for higher positions and better standard of living completely changed his outlook on life. For the first time in his life, Eric changed his working clothing for a suit with shirt and tie. It had been a long search, but finally, he had been awarded the position of electric design engineer for a large electrical company. He loved this job. For the first time, he finally reached the position he studied for in Holland. Also, for more than half a year, they had been Canadian citizens. There the children were Canadian by birth, both Eric and Maria had decided since Canada had been good to them, they would become Canadian citizens. It was the right thing to do, but standing there in front of the judge with a whole group of people to be sworn in, it felt strange to give up the country they loved so much and become a citizen of Canada.

Both knew, however, that it was only a formality because deep down they were still Dutchmen.

Also, Eric had moved his family again, this time to an apartment building where they both accepted the job of part-time live-in caretakers. For their services, they received from the owners, a friendly Jewish family, free living quarters plus a hundred dollars a month. It took them many evenings and weekends to get this rather older building in shape again because the previous caretaker had really neglected it.

It was a four-story building, and the once-beautiful parquet floor hallways were so dirty that it was impossible to clean them. Eric rented a floor sander, and dedicated many hours of hard work to clean it, wherein Maria did as much as possible. She was pregnant with their third child, and they sanded, sealed, and varnished all the hallway floors and returned it to its natural beauty. The owners were so pleased with these hardworking immigrants that the following Christmas, they delivered a box full of food supplies plus an extra bonus of $200.

Besides his new job (which took, including traveling by street-car and bus, ten to twelve hours a day), Eric spent most of his remaining free time in this building. Every day there was something he had to fix. After dinner, he made his rounds. Changing broken light bulbs, fixing water taps, opening clogged up sinks and toilets in bathrooms, he repaired appliances from the tenants in his small workshop in the basement. Thursday nights, he had to shovel ten to twelve garbage cans out of a large hopper in the basement at one end of the building and carry them up the winding steps to the ground floor and then to the sidewalk on the back lane for the next morning's garbage pickup.

In this section of the basement was also the coal-operated huge hot water furnace heater, which in the winter months supplied the heat throughout the building by hot water radiation. Between this furnace and the outside wall was an enormous coal bin, which had to be filled twice during the long winter months. In front of the furnace was a coal hopper, and between them was a screw conveyor, which carried the coal automatically when needed into the furnace. The only problem was that in the cold winter months, Eric had to fill this hopper by shovel around six o'clock in the morning before he left for his job and again in the evening around ten o'clock.

However, many nights this old furnace would break down sometimes at two or three o'clock in the morning. Receiving one telephone call after the other from the unhappy renters, Eric had to get out of his warm bed and go into the ice cold basement to fix it again. Sometimes he was lucky, and it was only a minor repair, but most of the time, the fireplace inside the furnace had caked up, and the shear pin would break on the screw conveyor. When that happened, he had to shovel the whole hopper empty and, with half frozen fingers, replace the shear pin again. After that was done, he had to open the furnace, hammer the caked coal loose, and start the conveyor again.

If he was lucky and the cake hadn't baked itself to the end of the conveyor, it would start up. and after replacing the hopper and filling it with coal again, he could go back to bed for an hour or so. If it didn't start up, he had to crawl inside the furnace to make the conveyor free again. Then he was so dirty before he was finished that he then had to take a shower before he could go back to bed, if there was still time left.

Eric loved tools. For all the money he could spare, he bought tools, and by now, they covered one wall of his workshop. Frank, the master mechanic, had told him some years ago that you always could tell a good tradesman by his tools and how he took care of them. Eric believed that and all tools were hanging up neatly row after row on that wall.

With two old telephones left in the building and a DC convertor put together from parts, he had made his own intercom system from the kitchen of their apartment on the first floor with wires along the outside walls of the building into his workshop so that Maria could call him every time she needed him.

Some of their neighbors down the street were Hungarian immigrants and had become close friends of Eric and Maria. They showed Eric how to make raisin wine. He started with a five-gallon clay pot in his workshop, and soon the fermenting started, with the workshop smelling like a saloon. When the brew was finished, he would fill the empty bottles by sucking the sweet high alcohol content out of the jar. For weeks, he had saved the empty bottles from the building garbage bin. Most of the liquid went in the clean bottles, but a small amount stayed in his mouth. He got so stupid drunk that by the time the bottles were filled, he couldn't stand up straight. Crawling on hands and knees, he made it up the stairs through the hallway and into his living room. Maria was furious but helped him up and into the bedroom, where he passed out on the bed.

The end of this wine industry, or whatever, came a couple of weeks later. On a Sunday afternoon dinner, Eric had the bright idea to have some wine with the dinner. When filling a glass for Maria and himself, Nicole and Steven——who was by now around two years old and, in contrast to the dark hair and brown eyes of Nicole, had curly light blond hair and blue eyes—also wanted some of the wine. Eric poured a small amount in each of the children's glasses. Maria was against the idea because the children were way too young, but Eric persuaded her by telling her that a tiny bit of wine in a glass wouldn't hurt them.

Before they were actually starting with the dinner and Maria was putting the potatoes in a bowl on the kitchen stove, Eric noticed the two had already finished their wine. Signaling the children not to tell their mother, he quickly put some more wine in their glasses. Nicole didn't say anything but just looked at him with her big brown eyes. Steven nodded his head and had a smile from ear to ear. When the dinner was finished and all the glasses were empty, Steven started acting very strangely.

When they asked Nicole if she liked her wine, they found out what had happened when she answered, "I didn't like it. Steven drank it all." Small wonder that he acted strangely.

Some hours later, when the children were in bed, and Eric and Maria had a quiet evening, watching television, they heard the children talking to each other in the other room. Maria was still angry at Eric for such foolishness, but she really raised the roof when moments later they heard a big bounce and ran into the bedroom. Steven was lying on the floor with a big smile on his face. Nicole told them that Steven had a lot of fun, hung over the side of the crib, and then fell on the floor. The big smile on his face, looking at them with wide-open eyes, told them that he wasn't hurt, but that was the end of wine-making. Within weeks, there was no bottle to be found anymore. Maria had seen to that.

Early in the morning on the first day of his new job, when Eric was taking a shower, Maria prepared a special breakfast for him. She had laid very careful his brand-new suit bought for this occasion and his shirt, tie, and socks on the bed. She was proud of him. Now that he was an engineer, she was an engineer's wife. Eric was full of excitement about this day.

Funny, he thought, *how life can change*. Even shaving, he had to do it every morning from now on. He wasn't afraid at all about this job, because he knew he could do it. His father had told him when he was a young boy that there was nothing in this world he couldn't do if he really wanted it. And he really wanted this job. He also knew that he would now be in contact with a different kind of people and if he played his cards right, new horizons would open up again. After his shower, he went into the bedroom and put on his new suit. Naturally, Maria had to adjust his tie.

She silently watched him. After he looked at himself in the mirror, he said, "Not bad, not bad at all."

She started laughing. "Yes, you really look handsome, but hurry up. Your breakfast is getting cold."

When Eric walked into the kitchen, he saw a breakfast fit for a king spread out on the kitchen table. He really didn't feel hungry this morning, but after all the work she had gone through, the least he could do was eat something.

"My god, is that all for me?"

"Yes," she said, "and you're worth it."

After breakfast and another cup of coffee together, it was time to leave. He took his raincoat out of the closet and headed for the door.

"One moment." Maria stopped him. "I have a surprise for you." And she went quietly into the bedroom as the children were still sleeping. Moments later, she returned with a beautiful new shining briefcase. Eric couldn't believe his eyes. "I bought this already over a week ago and hid it underneath the bed," she said. He wanted to say something, but she interrupted and said, "Now get going. Wouldn't it be something if you came too late the first day?" And she opened the door.

He kissed her and then walked down the hallway to the front door of the building. One of the tenants returning from his night shift looked very surprised at Eric and said, "What happened? Why are you all dressed up?" When Eric told him about the new job he was starting that day, the man congratulated him. Changing the tone of his voice, he said, "Does that mean you're going to leave us now?"

Eric laughed. "No, don't worry about that." But when he walked to the streetcar stop, he thought, *Soon now, I don't need that job as caretaker anymore and will move into a home.*

During his interview, he had met some of the people in the office, but as soon as he arrived, the chief engineer walked around and introduced him to the remaining ones. Depending how quickly he progressed, he would be an assistant to another engineer for a while. He was a little bit disappointed but then thought that he wouldn't be an assistant for very long. He really grew with pride, however, when they showed him his brand-new desk with a big drawing board at the side of it. When he noticed his own telephone on top of the desk, he really got excited. Not showing it, he watched how nonchalant some of his coworkers picked up the phone, and he started dialing it likewise.

The first call he made was to his home. "Maria," he said, "I'm calling from my own telephone, and I have a brand-new desk and chair." Maria heard the excitement in his voice, and then abruptly as if nothing had happened, he said, "Well, I have to get to work now. "I'll talk to you later." And he hung up.

He really felt important when two of the engineers took him out to lunch. They even asked him if he wanted a drink before the meal arrived. Eric wasn't sure to take one of not and hesitated. Then one of his companions said, "It's all right, Eric. We're going to have one too." So Eric ordered a glass of wine.

What a way of living, he thought. Sitting between all these businesspeople in that restaurant, he felt ten feet tall.

In the afternoon, the engineer, after showing him the drawers full of different sizes of drawing paper, gave Eric a sketch of a design he made and asked him to draw it on paper. The time went so fast that it was already five o'clock before he knew it.

"Aren't you going home?" the engineer questioned while putting his jacket on. "You don't have to finish that today, you know. You can do the rest tomorrow."

"Do you mind if I finish it today? I have only a little left, and I still have some time before my bus leaves," said Eric.

"Suit yourself," the man said. While walking to the door, he said to the chief engineer, "I think we have a good one this time."

Eric was now half a year at that job and had not only proven to be a good and hard worker but even more so that he was a sharp and knowledgeable engineer. After two months, he had been on his own already, and there was no design too difficult for him. Assisting everybody and asking thousands of questions, he was liked by everyone, and soon his name changed from Eric to Dutchman. It was Dutchman here and Dutchman there, but Eric didn't mind. He'd rather be called Dutchman than something else.

He was now nearly thirty years old, and Maria had given birth to another baby girl. They called her Michelle. Michelle was very tiny when she was born, and she cried day and night. When they questioned their physician, he told them that Michelle was born with an underdeveloped stomach. They had noticed it because Maria had breast-fed the other two children but this one couldn't even stand skim milk. For nearly six months, Michelle cried practically day and night and finally fell asleep from exhaustion. It was hard on Maria, but it drove Eric completely out of his mind. A hard day at the office then working late at night in the building and not being able to sleep was too much for him. Michelle cried so much that some tenants called the department of child abuse, because they felt the baby was being neglected.

On one Saturday morning, after another sleepless night, Eric called the obstetrician and told him that his nerves were so on edge that if he didn't do something about it, he couldn't be liable anymore for what might happen.

"Well," the doctor answered, "why don't we put her in the hospital for a while? It won't do much good for her because it takes time for her stomach to develop, but at least it will give you people a rest. Bring her in next Wednesday. I will make the necessary arrangements."

It was as though the little girl had heard the conversation because that same night, she slept all the way through till the next morning without crying once. When the next morning Maria fed her a mixture of regular milk and water, she drank it all and didn't heave like she used to. From that moment on, she slowly gained weight and turned into a very happy child.

Once in a while, his thoughts drifted back to Nico and Lisa, but it was so far in the past and so much had happened since that time that it seemed like ages ago. Even the visits of the Maasen and the Rudolphs (who had bought a house at the end of town) were more sporadic. They were still the closest of friends and, when needed, would help each other whenever possible. But for the rest of the time, each had their own future and family to think of.

One day, an electrical contractor just starting his own company came into the office and said to Eric, "Say, Dutchman, you haven't got a car yet. Would you like to buy my wife's? It's only six months old. She didn't use it that much, so it looks like brand-new. I'll make you a good deal on it. I need the money, so my wife and I decided to sell it. But I need the money in a hurry, like this week, to pay the bills."

Eric hesitated. "I don't know… I first have to talk to my wife about it." Eric and Maria had been talking about buying a car for quite some time now but hadn't made a firm decision yet.

"I'll pick you up tomorrow afternoon," the man continued, "if you are interested. Then you can see it, and we'll drive it to your home so your wife can also take a look at it. If you both like it, I'll make you a deal you can't refuse."

It was a beautiful shining gray Canadian Pontiac named Laurentian. Like the man had said, it looked brand new. The inside was also gray but had some blue in the weavings of the seats. For Eric, it was a gorgeous car, and when he told them it had automatic transmission, Eric was sold. Maria was waiting in the back lane of the building for the two to arrive, and when she saw the car driving into the lane, Eric noticed to his delight that she also was sold on the car if the price was right.

Together they walked across the street to their bank and had a talk with the bank manager. Eric and Maria had an outstanding credit, and after the manager checked the price the man had asked for, in one of the reference books lying on his desk, he whispered to Eric, "This guy is giving you a helluva deal. If you want this car, take it. You won't have any problems here." The deal was made, and the car ended up that afternoon in Eric's garage, which he had been using as storage space.

After he received his check from Eric, the man shook his hand, took a taxi, and went home. Now Eric had a beautiful car in the garage, but he was unable to drive it as he had no driver's license yet. For two weeks, the car stayed in the garage. Every day when Eric came home from his job, he opened the garage door, started the engine, and let it run for a while.

What a beautiful feeling, he thought. He owned a car now, his first car ever. And what a beauty!

In the next two weeks, he had five one-hour driving lessons from an instructor, and when he took his test, he passed the first time. When the instructor drove him home after he passed the test, he gathered his family together and drove for the first time his own car out of the garage to visit and surprise the family Rudolph.

Slowly he drove down the lane. The car handled nicely, and he felt very secure. At the end of the lane, he made a right turn into the street and drove one block before he had to stop on Sinclair Avenue, one of the busiest main streets at that time of the day. The traffic lights didn't work, and an officer did his best to direct the hundreds of cars to their destinations. Eric had to make a left turn, and he waited patiently for the signal of the officer to go ahead.

When he finally got the indication, he pushed on the gas pedal, and the car went ahead, but only ten feet and the engine died, right beside the officer, who then started shouting at Eric to get out of the way. It made him so nervous that he didn't know what he was doing anymore. When the engine sputtered but died again, he opened the window and, with a desperate look on his face, told the officer that the car wouldn't start.

A lot of cars were blowing their horns, which made the officer really furious. He shouted at Eric, "I don't care what you do, but get that damn thing out of here!" He then looked into the car. "You damn idiot! It's out of gas!"

The officer, outraged, called a couple of bystanders watching this incident, and together with the officer pushed the car to the side of the road. Having the engine running for the past fourteen days at night-time in this garage, Eric had completely forgotten to look at the fuel gauge and had used up all the available gas. He was lucky, however, that there was a gas station not more than fifty yards from that crossing.

As Eric got out of the car, leaving his family in an embarrassing situation, he couldn't help noticing the chaos he had caused and felt very sorry for the officer who tried his utmost to get out of this chaos. The noise of blowing horns by the now patientless drivers was over-whelming, and some of them continued while passing Eric with such an angry look in their eyes that they could have sentenced him to the firing squad. All the exciting feelings of driving his first car were gone by now, and he felt very nervous and stupid at the same time.

A young gas station attendant gave Eric a can with a few gallons of gas to get his car going again. Minutes later, he drove to that station and filled up. Before Eric could drive away, the young man, who had witnessed the happenings and noticing how nervous Eric was, had a smile on his face, "Don't let it bother you, sir. This can happen to the best of us." But when Eric smiled at him, he continued, "But to the most ignorant first." Eric's smile faded, and with a destructive glare in his eyes, he looked at the young man, who immediately stopped smiling. "Sorry, sir." And Eric drove on.

For some time, he drove without anyone saying a word. Even the children, who had been excited at the beginning of this trip, were abnormally quiet, noticing the nervous tension of their parents. This tension broke, however, when Maria broke the stillness and said, "What a driver." For a moment, Eric could have killed her, but then noticing that she was smiling, he started laughing. Everyone, including the children, felt the relief.

The Rudolphs, who had an old Chevy, marveled at this new Pontiac, but they couldn't help laughing and joking when they heard all about the experience that evening.

On departure, Theo shouted at Eric, "Are you sure now you have enough gas to make it home?"

Eric smiled. "Theo, you know what you can do?" And while stepping into the driver's seat, he continued, "Go to hell." They smiled at each other, and Eric started the car and drove off.

The company Eric worked for had received the contract for designing the complete electrical layout for a huge shopping plaza on the outskirts of Toronto. It was considered at that time the largest one in the world. With its huge hallways and approximately one hundred modern stores all under one roof, it turned out to be the most beautiful shopping center Eric had ever seen. The electrical layout was divided so that each engineer in the office had one section to design. One section of the specification of that building was designated to a large fountain and lights combination to be built in the center of the entrance hallway.

Eric, being more knowledgeable in hydraulics than his companions, received that section, and upon approval of the building architects, the design was completely left up to him. The only description the specification mentioned of the fountain was that it should be designed so that it would be not only eye-catching but also glorious and majestic as one of the main attractions of the building. Beautiful benches for the weary and tired customers, exotic flower sections, and even live palm trees would surround the fountain.

It took Eric weeks and multiple sketches before he finally decided on his design. The whole fountain complex consisted of six main fountain heads. Each main fountain head, which could push the water up to twenty feet high, was surrounded by three rings of smaller spouts, each directed at a different angle. The fountain heads, which were approximately six feet apart lengthwise, were surrounded by four different-color lights—blue, red, gold, and white. The inner basin, which included the fountain heads to be built out of natural rock, poured its water through eight waterfalls, three on each side plus one on either end, four feet down into the large outer basin. Each waterfall would have similar lights installed underneath them, the same as the fountain heads.

In the basement underneath this fountain complex, a huge pump plus stand-by pump, rows of electrically operated water valves, and large electrical panels with the controls for multiple combination of valves and lights would be installed. His final design ended up in twenty combinations of fountains and sixteen different light combinations. When he proposed it to the architects, they were thrilled with Eric's design and gave the okay that it should be built accordingly. During the construction, Eric visited the building many times, and when the final adjustments were made on some of the water flow control valves, the fountain complex was in operation.

A week before the opening to the public, the owners, architects, engineers, and some of the contractors were present when Eric showed for the first time his creation to them. Now with slightly dimmed lights in the hallways, they witnessed Eric's masterpiece in its full glory and brilliance. It took a full half hour to go through all its combinations. Then the cycle would start all over again. Everyone was amazed about the color combinations. At one time, it looked like the fountains were spitting out nuggets of gold while the next it was a brilliance of thousands of diamonds. Eric felt very proud of himself when all the people present surrounded and congratulated him.

One of the architects mentioned, "In our specs, we asked for an eye-catching fountain, but we never expected such beauty." With this design, Eric earned high respect from his coworkers and an increase in salary.

Many evenings, he visited this plaza all by himself or with Maria. Sitting on one of the benches between the visitors, he could listen with pleasure to young and old gratifying his design.

His car was his pride and joy. Every week, he would wash and polish it to keep the car shining and looking like new. He was a defensive and careful driver, and after that incident of running out of gas on his first drive, he didn't run into any more problems and enjoyed his new transportation in comparison to the streetcar rides of the past.

One day in October 1963, on his way home from the office, he passed a large hospital in the northwestern suburb of Toronto. His eyes caught the sight of a beautiful woman standing at the crossing ahead of him, awaiting for the traffic lights to turn green for her to cross the street. Her white nurse uniform and her small white cap covering part of her beautiful wavy blond hair, which covered her shoulders, made her look like a movie star. It had been a beautiful early spring day, and Eric, who had the window on the driver's side of the car rolled down and his left arm resting easy in the open window, enjoyed looking at this beautiful young woman while slowing down for the stoplight.

When the light turned green for her, she crossed the street in front of Eric's car. Her beautiful hair bounced with every step she took. Eric followed her movements until she was about halfway across the street. Then at that moment, he heard and, at the same time, felt the shock of a car crashing into him from behind. It all happened in an instant, and before he realized what had occurred, the driver of that car was standing beside him.

He asked with a worried look on his face, "Hey, I'm sorry. Are you hurt?"

Eric moved around in his seat for a moment and answered, stuttering, "No, I guess… I don't think so."

The man's worried face lit up, and then he said to Eric's surprise, "Did you see that gorgeous blonde? Wasn't she a real beauty!"

Eric couldn't believe his ears. This man, who later identified himself as being from Cleveland, Ohio, had crashed his beautiful Cadillac into the rear end of Eric's car while watching this woman. His first impulse was to be angry at him, but then he realized that he had completely disarmed him. Both cars were damaged but still drivable, and after exchanging driver's license numbers, the man from Ohio told Eric to find out and let him know what the damage was on his car and he would pay for it. He didn't want to go through insurances because he had already trouble enough with them the way it was. For a moment, Eric didn't know if he could trust such an arrangement, but then again, a man who had honored beauty above his Cadillac couldn't be all bad, and after shaking hands, they parted.

The bumper was completely bent out of shape, and one of the taillights of Eric's car was broken. The estimated cost for repairing it was around $200. Eric mailed a copy of the estimate to him, and a week later, he received a check for $400 and a small note that said, "The extra two hundred dollars are for your inconvenience. Thank you very much for your understanding."

He obtained a slight whiplash, but it didn't bother him because the inconvenience was so slight that it didn't interfere with his normal way of life. Two months later, however, he started to develop such headaches that in some instances he could hit his head against the wall. He blamed it on the car accident, and when large doses of aspirin had no effect anymore, he went to a doctor. It took weeks of tests and large doses of pills with no results before he was referred to a physician specializing in nose, throat, and ears. After a short examination, this physician diagnosed that the center bone of the nose was so enlarged on the left side that it completely closed off the drainage from the sinus cavity above the left eye. It had nothing to do with the accident at all.

A massive infection had developed in that sinus cavity, and only an immediate operation could prevent more serious consequences.

"You must have noticed the slow closing of that side of the nose for quite some time," said the physician, "and you waited too long before having someone look at it."

Eric didn't answer, but he knew the man was right. He had noticed it for quite some time, but it had never bothered him until the last few weeks. Within a week, he was in a hospital, and the next morning, he went through such unbearable pain during that operation that he nearly went out of his mind. He was seated in a sort of barber's chair and was tied down from head to toe. The nurses pulled the belt so tight over his forehead that he thought they were going to split his skull.

The surgeon tipped the chair backward and went to work. "I can only give you a local anesthetic," he explained. "Working on that bone structure in your nose will be uncomfortable, not painful, but opening that infection in your sinus cavity will be. I will be as careful as possible."

The reason for "only a local anesthetic" didn't register in Eric's mind was that the terrors that followed were so hellish that he thought he was in a torture chamber and tried to rip the tie down belts from the chair.

With an actual small hammer and chisel, the doctor started breaking part of the central bone structure away. The local anesthetic made the operation not that painful, at least in the beginning. But the hammer pounded an echo through his head as if a heavy sledgehammer was used, and the free-flowing warm blood running down over his left cheek made him sick to his stomach. When that part of the operation was completed, Eric thought that it was all over with. He didn't know, however, that it was just beginning. Another physician took over, and Eric screamed from intense pain when this doctor pushed a tube right through his nose and into the sinus cavity. The rest of the operation was so painful that Eric passed out several times before ending up unconscious in his room.

When Maria visited him late that afternoon, she didn't recognize him and thought for a moment she was in the wrong room. His whole face had swollen so big that he looked like a creature from another planet. From his upper lip to the top of his forehead, only the tip of his nose and small slits for the eyes were recognizable. Eric was still in a lot of pain, but at least it wasn't pounding anymore. The only thing he could do was watch television all day.

Three days after his operation, November 22, 1963, the show he was watching abruptly stopped, and with large letters, it said, "President John Fitzgerald Kennedy was shot in Dallas, Texas."

All programs showed this outrageous deed. Walter Cronkite, the famous news announcer, kept everyone up to date. A few hours later, with tears in his eyes, he announced that President Kennedy was dead. Eric was shocked. He liked this president very much. He had even watching the results of the voting till the early morning hours when it was decided that he would be the next president. President Kennedy was dead at such a young age. Unbelievable! All channels showed not only the funeral but the president's life over and over again for several days, which was very boring for Eric.

Within days, the swelling subsided, and the pain lessened. But the cotton that plugged up his nose openings was very uncomfortable, and Eric was overjoyed when a week later, it was removed. He could freely breathe through his nose again. He was happy it was all over with, but if he had known before what kind of operation it would develop into, he would have rather died than committing himself to such treatment.

CHAPTER 10

✠

Another division of the company Eric was employed by had developed a new kind of instrumentation for the metal machining industry. Many European companies were interested in this new development, and several groups of their management personnel made a trip to Toronto to study these instruments. As Eric was the only one in the organization who spoke several languages, and many of the visitors couldn't speak English, so the company asked Eric to be their guide and translator.

He actually welcomed this additional change of pace, and in no time, he mastered all the technical knowledge needed to satisfy the questions and answers of the visitors. Most of the visitors arrived in the later afternoon, and Eric who would welcome them at the Toronto airport, then drive them after they received their luggage, to one of the surrounding hotels. Several of the elderly people, tired from their long journey, went to sleep early, leaving Eric some time to relax in the bar of that hotel.

On one of those evenings, two gentlemen occupied the only two bar stools available to the right of him. The barstools were very close together. One of the new arrivals sitting beside him was smoking a pipe, which he held in his mouth at a sharp angle, and Eric had to move his head sideways every time the man looked in his direction. Listening intensely to his companion, he didn't notice the inconvenience he was causing Eric. For some time, Eric didn't say anything about it, but when the heavy smoking pipe ended up directly under Eric's nose, he interrupted their conversation.

He said, "Gentlemen, I don't want to bother you, but, sir, could you do me a favor and move your pipe to the other side of your mouth for a while? I know that you don't realize this, but you nearly burnt my face a couple of times."

The man apologized and quickly put his pipe in the ashtray in front of him. Then turning to Eric, he introduced himself as Jim Simmons. He was the sales manager of a large machinery manufacturer located in Minneapolis, Minnesota, USA. He also introduced his companion, John Clark, as a salesman from his Toronto base distributor. He was very interested in Eric's job and background and asked Eric if he would be interested in moving to Minneapolis because his company badly needed an engineer with Eric's experience.

"If you offer me a terrific job, naturally, I would be interested," Eric replied. "You know, since I was a young boy and became friends with many American soldiers in our village, I always wanted to go to the United States, but I ended up in Canada, though I also really like the job I have here."

After they exchanged calling cards and Eric wrote his home phone number on the back of his card, Mr. Simmons told him he would discuss Eric with his management as soon as he returned back to Minneapolis.

Coming home that evening, Eric told Maria about the people he had met but also told her that he had met many people in the last year or so who offered him a better job opportunity but that no one ever called. Three months went by, and this incident was long forgotten. Then on a Tuesday evening, during their dinner, the phone rang, and a person introducing themselves as Jack Konrad, vice president and chief engineer of a company in Minneapolis, inquired if Eric was still interested in changing jobs. When Eric answered that he was not interested at all, the caller apologized and hung up.

"That was a strange call," Eric said to Maria while resuming his dinner. "This man called all the way from Minneapolis, wherever that is, and inquired if I was still interested in changing jobs. I don't know anybody in that city, and I don't know where he got my name and telephone number from."

Later that evening, Maria called him into the bedroom and said, "I know where you got that call from. Here is a calling card from Minneapolis. I thought I remembered something that you mentioned some months ago." She had developed a habit of saving all calling cards she found in his suit jackets before taking them to the cleaners, and she put them all together in a small box in one of the drawers in the bedroom.

Looking at the card she handed him, a light went on in his head. If Jim Simmons had called, he would have remembered, but hearing this strange name, he realized he had completely forgotten the conversation he had at that hotel. The next day, he called Mr. Konrad from the office and explained what had happened.

When Eric apologized, he was interrupted, "No, don't apologize. It is my fault. I should have taken the time and explained the situation to you better. We are interested in meeting you. Is it possible for you to come to Minneapolis not this weekend but the weekend thereafter? We will send you the plane tickets."

Without hesitation, Eric accepted his offer and promised him he would arrive Friday evening of that weekend and, as Mr. Konrad had indicated, take a taxi from the airport to the North Star Inn hotel in Minneapolis, where he would meet him for breakfast on Saturday morning at eight o'clock sharp.

Eric had accepted it because even if he was not interested in the job and if they didn't offer him quite an increase in salary, nothing was lost. He would still end up with an all-expense-paid trip to Minneapolis. What could be wrong with that?

During the two weeks before Eric made this trip, he and Maria discussed the pros and cons of moving and immigration again and decided on going if the offer was to Eric's liking.

It was early fall 1965 when Eric arrived, after an uneventful smooth trip, to his hotel in Minneapolis. After putting his luggage in his room, he took a walk around the block. The city was buzzing with Friday evening traffic, and he was surprised to find out that there was practically no difference between walking though Toronto or Minneapolis on a Friday evening. Even the people seemed to be the same, and except for product prices behind store windows and the lack of different languages spoken, he could just as well had been walking through Toronto. He was a little bit disappointed and didn't know what to expect, but he surely had hoped for some difference.

The next morning, he was up early and was already drinking his second cup of coffee in the breakfast area of his hotel when Mr. Konrad arrived. For some time now, he had sat there, trying to visualize what he would look like. A few minutes before eight o'clock, a stocky man about Eric's height neatly dressed in a blue suit and a blue-and-red-striped tie walked in. Without hesitating, Eric stood up and waved at him when he saw that this man was glancing through the room. Many people had walked in for their breakfast, but somehow this man fit his imagination. Answering Eric with a smile, he walked towards him. Eric had seen paintings and a film of Napoleon Bonaparte, the French dictator who after the French Revolution had conquered most of Europe. Except for his friendly smile, Mr. Konrad could have been a reborn identical twin brother of that famous Frenchman.

After the initial handshake and introduction, Eric mentioned to him his amazing likeness of face and posture to the Frenchman who had crowned himself kaiser.

Mr. Konrad found it quite amusing, and he said, "Well, I never met the man, and I really don't think he was my father. My father's family came from Russia."

"Aha," Eric replied. "Now we have the answer. Napoleon himself had been in Russia where his armies were defeated. No one knows what could have happened on those cold winter nights over there."

Mr. Konrad had to laugh with that answer.

They had a nice informal breakfast, and not until they were on their way to the factory did they discuss business. It was close to ten o'clock in the morning when they arrived at the factory, where the president and owner, Mr. Dick Fletcher, was awaiting them in his office. Eric had never seen such a beautiful office; the walls and floors were covered with hunting trophies from small and large animals all over the world. He looked very distinguished with his slightly gray hair and his very slim but strongly built body, which made him look taller than he actually was.

"Come in, come in," he said, shaking Eric's hand. "I hope you had a nice trip to our beautiful city. Would you like coffee? There is nobody here today except us, so I made it myself. I don't know how good it is."

Eric accepted not because he needed another cup of coffee but more so out of respect for the trouble the man had gone through in making it. At first sight, Eric liked what he saw in both men. Both seemed to be friendly but down-to-earth businesspeople, a combination Eric highly regarded. Mr. Fletcher returned to his huge leather-covered chair behind his desk and sat down.

When all three were seated and Eric had taken a sip of his coffee, Mr. Fletcher said, "And?" He was looking at Eric with a question on his face.

Eric cleared his throat and answered, "First of all, I would like to know—"

"No," interrupted Mr. Fletcher. "The coffee. How do you like my coffee? I made it pretty strong because you Europeans appreciate coffee better than we do and like strong coffee. I guess you don't like this coffee at all, Jack, do you?"

"You're absolutely right, Dick. To me, it tastes like poison," answered Mr. Konrad.

"Oh, I like it," Eric lied, because the coffee was really bitter, but what else could he say?

"You see?" Mr. Fletcher said, turning to Mr. Konrad. "I was right. These Europeans have developed a real taste for coffee. I know, I was over there, and our coffee seems like dishwater to them."

For the next two hours, they discussed business. First, they told Eric what they would expect from him if he accepted the job as project engineer in charge of designing all control systems on their machines. Then they asked him what his expected salary was. He thought for a moment and then asked for quite an increase in salary, over what he was used to. To his surprise, they accepted. It was another matter, however, when he expected them to pay for all expenses necessary to immigrate and move him and his family to Minneapolis. Mr. Fletcher suggested to go halfway. He would pay originally all the costs involved but then deduct half of it from Eric's salary over a period of two years. Eric didn't agree with such an arrangement and mentioned that it was they who wanted him and he didn't feel it should be at any cost to him.

"Could you take a walk through the plant?" he said to Eric after thinking a moment. "I would like to have a private conversation with Mr. Fletcher. I will come and get you."

"Sure, no problem," Eric answered and walked out of the office, closing the door behind him.

He walked through row after row of machinery all neatly lined up and was amazed at the beauty of these machines. About half an hour later, he was called back into the office, and Mr. Fletcher now looked very serious at Eric.

He said, "Young man, I have to ask you one more question. If you were given the opportunity in this company to reach any goal or level, what would you like to become?"

Eric thought for a moment then looked him straight in the eyes and answered, "Mr. Fletcher, given the opportunity, in time I will be after your position and hopefully end up in that chair you are sitting in."

Mr. Fletcher and Mr. Konrad looked at each other for a moment after that answer, and Mr. Konrad nodded his head positively.

"Eric," Mr. Fletcher said, breaking the stillness, "you have the position if you want to, and we agree on paying all expenses."

"I accept," Eric replied, barely keeping from jumping in the air with enthusiasm.

After shaking hands on the deal, they discussed further details while having lunch at a nearby restaurant. Upon his return to Toronto, Eric would start all necessary paperwork and motions for immigration. They figured it would take a couple of months before he finally could start his new employment. They figured wrong, however; it took nearly one full year and several trips for Konrad to the US Department of Labor in Chicago, explaining Eric's capabilities necessary for this job, before the Department of Labor was satisfied and granted immigration papers. The company had to show, after advertising two times, that no one had the electrohydraulic education that Eric had.

At the international airport in Minneapolis, he called Maria and, stuttering from excitement, told her the results of his trip. Leaning back in his seat in the airplane, he closed his eyes, and his thoughts drifted back into the past when he was still in Holland. What a long way he had come, he thought, from small village boy and coal miner to this position in America. But this was only the beginning. He had now the taste of success and wouldn't stop until he reached higher and higher goals.

But why these goals? What was it in him that produced such high pressures to reach limitless heights? He had been very happy with his job in Toronto and had a reasonable income. Why couldn't he then just not be satisfied, or was he part of a tremendous force of nature that not only produced a balance in the wild kingdom of animals but also in human beings? Could it be that an unexplainable force destined human beings already by birth, forcing them into roles they had to play to prevent extinction after the human race? Was that the reason some people reached high levels of what was called success and other people were just perfectly happy in being a small farmer, coal miner, or tradesman?

Or even deeper, could it be that people like Hitler, Stalin, Napoleon, and many more before them all the way back to the beginning of mankind were born to destroy large masses of the world's population and, in doing so, control nature's balance with all these wars? Was it not always why the young healthy male population, who, for nature's sake, were the high producers of human life on this earth, were destroyed?

And it's also true that famine and all kinds of sicknesses all through the centuries had killed millions, maybe billions, of people; but always when such famine like smallpox had killed large masses of people and the balance became endangered, nature produced a person who was destined to discover some product that had been in nature already since the beginning of time in order to conquer this destruction. Then a more fierce and totally different epidemic starts decades or sometimes centuries later, and nature again would produce a person with the intelligence to discover an antidote and start the cycle all over again.

If everyone on this earth was really destined, that could be the reason and explanation for so many people having nervous breakdowns. Maybe they had chosen the wrong direction or occupation and had completely sidestepped their destination. Eric knew he was on the right path because every time he had reached a new level, he was not afraid of complications, but instead the success of conquering that new goal made him feel young and energetic. It seemed like all he had done before this time, all he had suffered and accomplished, had only been a learning period and that accepting this job was the second step to whatever he was destined for.

And what about Maria? had she been destined also to cross his path to be his companion in this long and difficult journey up till now. He had loved Lisa deeply, and she had given him part of her beauty and softness during the short relationship, but she would not have been the right personality for emigrating and enduring such a hard and struggling life. Maria was the opposite; she had a harder personality with an urge of discovery and conquering hardships. Where other people would break down, she could make the right decisions under enormous pressures. For an immigrant, she was cut out of the right wood.

Some of their combined natures showed itself already in Nicole. Already as young as she was, she showed determination and wisdom far for her age. A few years ago, when she was four years old, after Eric accompanied her only once by streetcar to the kindergarten, she insisted that she was capable of doing it all by herself. Eric, to satisfy himself, had on one day entered the streetcar one stop ahead and took a seat way in the back to witness Nicole entering at the next stop. As if there was nothing to it, she entered, deposited the ticket in the slot of the container mounted by the conductor, wished him a "good morning" with a friendly smile and sat down on a seat close to the entrance. The conductor seemed to know her already and, while smiling, said something that Eric couldn't understand. Her eyes just reaching the bottom of the window watched everything that passed by. It seemed that reaching a huge white house was for her the signal to stand up on the seat and pull the cord, which indicated to the conductor that someone wanted to get off at the next stop. Standing by the exit door, she waited until the streetcar came to a full stop, waved at the conductor, and then departed.

Eric also departed but through another door. Walking down the street, the streetcar passed her, and again she waved at the conductor. She then ran about half a block to the entrance of the kindergarten. Eric had watched this whole incident and was proud of his daughter. She had done everything so naturally as if she had done it for years; no doubt she had her parents' blood.

Steven was not as independent as Nicole but showed an unusual high interest of anything technical. When Eric was working on the motor of his car or repairing a toaster or a mixer from one of the tenants in his workshop, Steven was always around, driving Eric crazy with his questions, and had an unusual comprehension for Eric's answers. Michele had a very friendly nature and was loved by the whole neighbourhood when she visited them wearing small wooden shoes Eric had purchased for her in Holland.

It was November 12, 1966, when Eric left by car to Minneapolis, USA, he would travel through Winsor, Canada, and then enter the United States, crossing the border in Detroit. He'd have to make the long trip in a southwest direction over Chicago, along the bottom half of Lake Michigan, up to Minneapolis. First, he would find a place to live in or around Minneapolis before Maria and the children could join him. The evening before, he had said farewell to all his friends and neighbors, and now he was ready to depart. He should have been happy that finally the day had arrived. After several months of signing papers and endless medical examinations for the whole family and the hardship of leaving his job, which he had really enjoyed and where he was well liked by management and coworkers; but he was not happy. He left Canada and all it stood for. He loved its enormous mixture of people with all their struggles for happiness and their open-armed assistance to new immigrants.

Walking through the bedroom, he noticed the beautiful plague that was presented to him a couple of months ago by the Canadian Red Cross. He thought, *At least I leave with something behind in gratitude for all it has done for me.*

Since he was eighteen years old and was still in Holland, he had become a blood donor to the Red Cross and had religiously given a pint of blood every four to six months. He knew he was a healthy specimen as doctors would call him and he always felt good when he could so something for someone who was in need.

It was a beautiful plague with letters written in gold that said, "Presented to Eric Oosterbeek, who voluntarily gave at least twenty donations of blood. This is an example of generosity and self-sacrifice worthy of all praise and beyond all price. From such a magnificent gift will come new life for many of our fellow Canadians."

It made him feel a little better, but leaving Canada was hard. Also, this immigration was different than the previous one when they had left Holland. It had only been Maria and himself, but they had traveled with Theo and Ellen Rudolph and their children, and arriving in Canada, it had been Andre and Agnes Maasen who had taken care of them. But now they would immigrate to a different country all by themselves, knowing nobody when they arrived.

After a good breakfast, he hugged his children and Maria, promising them that they would soon be together again. Then he drove the car out of the garage and was on his way.

Only two pieces of luggage and his hunting and fishing equipment filled up the trunk of the car. The rest of the household would be shipped by moving van after Maria and the children arrived in Minneapolis. Mr. Konrad had mailed him a package of maps indicating the shortest and best route he should take. It was raining hard, and the long ride from Toronto to Detroit with an occasional pit stop became very difficult. He expected some trouble from the customs officers because of the hunting guns in the trunk, but no one seemed to be interested in it, and they didn't even look inside the car. Within minutes, all papers were approved, and Eric entered the United States.

The raining had stopped, and the clouds were breaking up. Driving through hours in the rain had tired him somewhat, but the sporadic patches of sunlight rejuvenated not only his stiffened body but also cleared his mind. He adjusted to an easier position, and the sound of the tires over the by now dry highway, interrupted by the rhythm of the evenly placed sections of concrete, made him sing an old Dutch song. He reduced his speed; it was no use chasing over this highway because he had enough time. He only had to report to the factory on Monday morning. The city of Detroit was now far behind him, and he enjoyed passing through the greenish-brown flowing landscape of the late fall. Looking at the horizon, he saw beams of sunlight shooting from openings in the clouds to the earth, which reminded him of a picture of the Lord sitting on the clouds, rays protruding from his stretched out hands as he blessed the earth, which hung somewhere in his parents front room between all his mustached grandfathers. After all these years, from a small boy getting his first piece of chewing gum from an American soldier and dreaming of going to America, he finally made it. He was driving on American soil. This was the land the soldiers had come from and where the army boots were made, his first pair of leather shoes.

Had he been destined to come here, to be part of and grow with this nation that had fought for freedom since its beginning and which had opened its arms to millions of people like him? Were these sunbeams actually symbolizing and blessing his welcome to his final destination? Somehow, since the first time he left Holland, he felt at home. Here his children would grow up and have their own children. Centuries from now, no one would even remember their Dutch heritage, but all these descendants would have some part of him in their genes. Somehow, he knew that his urge for living space on this earth had ended, but it also was the beginning of his growth and security for him and his family in this country with limitless opportunities for willing and hard-working people. Nothing and nobody would stop him from reaching his goals. What these goals were, he didn't know yet, but it didn't matter, because he would explore every opportunity that was open to him.

At dawn, he stopped in a small village somewhere between Detroit and Chicago. After eating a hearty meal in a local restaurant, he would spend the night in a small motel in the village center. Before going to sleep, however, he went to a small saloon adjacent to the motel. He sat down at the corner of the bar, ordered a glass of beer, and watched and listened with interest the locals, who mostly consisted of farm people discussing a football game.

With a loud voice, one of the men asked him something about the game, but Eric answered that he didn't know what he was talking about. When Eric mentioned that he had just arrived from Canada, the man shouted, "Hey, everybody, we have a brand-new immigrant here. This fellow is a Dutchman, and he has just arrived. Let's make him feel welcome."

Eric tried to correct the man that he actually was a Canadian now, but to no avail. Many of them came over and shook his hand, and one of the women who had kept to herself in the background came over and said, "Hey, I like your accent. Say some more. I love listening to it." Eric knew that he still had a heavy Dutch accent, but in Toronto, with its mixture of people, no one had ever mentioned anything about it.

The man with the loud voice, being slightly under the influence, was so proud about his discovery that he shouted to the bartender so that everybody could hear him, "All the drinks for my friend here are on me!" He hit Eric with his big hand so hard on his back at the precise moment when Eric took a swallow of beer that it not only shot into his throat but all over his shirt. It produced such a hefty coughing streak in Eric that he lost his breath. The man quickly calmed down but was so embarrassed by his action that he apologized over and over again not only to Eric but also to his companions, who were angry and let him have it.

It actually was a shame, because he was so embarrassed that shortly thereafter, even after Eric explained to him that it really didn't matter, he excused himself under the pretense that he had to go home anyway. He left the bar, but not before he mentioned to the bartender, "Whatever he drinks is still on me, just put it on my bill."

Eric, who had only planned to have a couple of drinks, sat there and conversed all evening long until closing time. By that time, he was so full of drinks from all the well-wishers that he stumbled, with the help of that woman who liked his accent and her husband, back to his motel. With a lot of trouble, he finally entered the room key in the door lock and fell on his bed. The next morning, he woke up with all his clothes on, including his shoes. His head was pounding so hard, as if someone was driving spikes into railroad ties with a sledgehammer. He wondered if he should drive on that day or should stay in that room, but after taking a shower and two or three cups of coffee in the restaurant of that motel, he felt a little better and decided to drive on.

He drove only a few hours that day, past the city of Chicago, and checked in early in a motel beside the highway west of Chicago. He drank one glass of wine with his dinner, avoided the bar, and went directly to his room. It was still dark the next morning when he left, and feeling a lot better than the day before, he drove straight through to Minneapolis, where he arrived in the late afternoon at the motel designated by Mr. Konrad as being the closest to the factory. He had driven more than a thousand miles since he left Toronto and was glad and tired when he finally reached his destination.

Driving to the airport in Minneapolis, he thought about all that had happened in the last couple of weeks. He was in a happy mood, because in an hour or so, Maria and the children would arrive at the airport. He had hoped for and succeeded in finding living quarters for his family before Christmas. After he arrived, he spent a few days in the motel, and Mr. Konrad had told him that he would charge all the meals and the motel room to the company until his family came over. He decided, however, to move to a less expensive motel across the road, where for less money he could have a room plus a kitchenette, where he could prepare his own meals. It didn't feel right that his company, who had spent so much money on him and his family already and who paid him a very good salary, would also be charged for the high food prices at the motel.

When Eric mentioned to Mr. Konrad the reason why he moved, Mr. Konrad answered, "You really don't have to do that, Eric, but we appreciate your way of thinking."

The first weeks at the factory, he spent most of his time on the main floor, where the machines were assembled. So as not to interrupt the engineering office constantly, the plant supervisor, who was a heavyset man, shared his office with Eric. His cubical office was located in the middle of the assembly room with windows in all four walls, which gave him a perfect vision of all the happenings on the floor. He'd been employed for many years with this company already and knew the machines inside out. Technically, he was good, but for the rest, Eric didn't know what to think about him. He wasn't unfriendly, but from the other side, he wasn't friendly either. He never smiled and had the nasty habit of staring without blinking an eye for quite some while talking to Eric, which gave him an uneasy feeling. Most of the day was spent between the assembly room, where he followed step-by-step the assembly of all the different machinery for the wood and metal industry, and the large sample room, where four or five different machines were used to run samples for customers. In the evenings, after he prepared and made his dinner, he made notes of everything he had learned during the day.

After a few weeks, he had learned enough how the machines were put together that he asked Mr. Konrad to make space for him the following week in the engineering room. This large room had eight drawing tables on each side lengthwise against the two walls. In the center, between these rows of drawing tables was a walkway, which ended at the office of Mr. Konrad. His first impressions of the American people were that, in general, they were easy to get along with. They seemed to be more open and friendly, and the engineers, in contrast to their counterparts in Canada, wore open and colorful shirts instead of white shirts and ties.

Also, the English spoken was more of a slang English than the near-perfect English used in Canada, which actually made Eric feel more at home since it felt like he was speaking his village dialect compared to the proper Dutch language. If someone made a remark about his lack of knowledge of the English language, he answered as a joke, "It is not the English language I have problems with. It's the American." Mr. Konrad was well liked by all the people for his kind, straightforward personality and his sharp mind. He had given Eric a drawing table, a high chair, and a small bookcase and assisted Eric whenever possible with his needs.

At the end of the second week, with the assistance of one of the engineers, Eric came in contact with a manager of a large new townhouse complex about a half hour drive from the plant. This manager was looking for a part-time caretaker to look after the grounds of this large complex. His services would include taking care of the swimming pool in the summertime and the snow removal in the wintertime. For his services, he would only have to pay half the rent. When on that weekend, he visited this complex consisting of about two hundred townhouses with its large number of concrete walkways, steps, flower paths, and lawns, he knew he would have his hands full. He hesitated, but the manager showed him his brand-new townhouse, with three bedrooms upstairs, a fully equipped kitchen with tile floor, a huge living room with sliding doors to a patio on the ground floor. Floors all throughout the house were fully carpeted, even the stairway and a full basement underneath it all for storage space. Eric's resistance was gone, and he accepted.

He could move in at any time, as long as he settled in before the first snow would cover the outdoor pathways. The townhouse was beautifully built, and for the first time, Eric's family would have their own place completely separated from other families. Immediately after the arrangement, he telephoned Maria and told her the good news, that she could order the moving van and that she could get ready to immigrate with the children. He did not tell her, however, how beautiful this townhouse was and that he had accepted a job as part-time caretaker. He wanted to really surprise her and the children when they arrived.

For the last couple of weeks, Maria had moved with the children back with Andre and Agnes Maasen and had left most of the household goods packed and waiting to be shipped by moving van when Eric would find living space in Minneapolis. Before he left for the United States, Eric had parted in friendship with the owner and family of the apartment building in Toronto that they lived in.

Eric felt uneasy about telling the owner he was leaving, but the owner said, "Don't worry about, that Eric. You and Maria have done a good job taking care of the building. I guess I don't want to be bothered with it anymore, and I think I'm going to sell it anyhow."

Ten days later, Eric got a call from the townhouse manager at his job, telling him that the moving van had arrived. He moved in the same day, put the furniture in its proper places, and unpacked all the boxes with the remaining household goods. That night, before he went to sleep, he sat down in the living room, which needed a lot more furniture than they possessed, and he was happy. It was quite an accomplishment—a new and beautiful place to live in, new people to be friends with, a new job, and a new country.

Arriving at the airport, he parked his car, adjusted the collar of his winter coat to protect his ears from the gushing cold wind, and walked toward the main building. In the last couple of weeks, the temperature had slowly dropped below the freezing mark, and an occasional light snow had fallen. Someone had told him that the winters in Minneapolis were even worse in temperature and amount of snowfall than Toronto. So far, he hadn't witnessed much of this, but then it was only the beginning of winter. The huge and beautiful building at the airport was already very crowded with travelers trying to beat the rush this tenth day before Christmas. After inquiring on what gate the airplane would arrive, he walked slowly in that direction since he had more than a half hour to kill yet.

Maria and the children had entered the United States and filed their immigration papers with customs at Chicago airport. From there, they flew the one-hour flight to Minneapolis. The airplane arrived on time, and Nicole, noticing her father waving at them, forced her way through the mass of departing people and jumped into the outstretched arms of her father. It was a happy reunion, and after waiting for what seemed like hours for the luggage, the whole family was finally on their way to their first home in the USA.

The children, still full of excitement, repeated over and over again the happenings of the day. Maria was more subdued. The last few days of many changes, goodbyes to all her friends, early rising that day and traveling with three small children had tired her somewhat. She inquired what the new living quarters looked like, but Eric told her, "Wait and see. I have a surprise in store for you."

The night before, on his way home from the office, he had bought some flowers, which he had placed in a vase on the coffee table in the living room. On a piece of white cardboard, he had written, "WELCOME HOME TO ALL OF YOU!"

When they turned onto the street that ran past the townhouse, which lay on a hill in the distance, Maria said, "Those are beautiful buildings there. The people who designed that surely had an eye for the surrounding beauty."

"I am glad you like the area," Eric answered, "because that is where you are going to live."

Maria couldn't believe her eyes, and she and the children, who were by now jumping with joy in the backseat, couldn't wait to arrive. The closer they came, the more overjoyed they were, and Maria had completely forgotten how tired she was.

When Eric opened the front door, for a moment, they all stood there awestruck and didn't enter until Eric, who was enjoying every moment, said, "Go in. It's ours." When Eric passed by them and walked through the living room, opening the curtains, letting the sun brighten the whole living room. As they walked through the big sliding doors to the patio, they all were breathless. Within minutes, the children, who had quickly upon Maria's demand removed their shoes, ran from top to bottom through the whole townhouse, shouting excitedly from every corner.

"Mom, look at this!"

"Mom, look at this!"

After Eric guided her through the whole house, she was so overjoyed that she hugged Eric and said, "This place is just gorgeous. It is the most beautiful place we've ever lived in, but how can we afford this place?"

"We can't," Eric answered. "That's why I took the job of part-time caretaker for this place and only pay half the rent."

"How can you do that?" Maria asked with a worried look on her face, knowing how much time and effort it had taken them in the comparably small apartment building in Toronto.

"Don't worry." He smiled. "I only have to look after the grounds. They have another family living here who takes care of the buildings."

"That sounds better," she answered. "If you think you can do it, then it is fine with me."

CHAPTER 11

Late one evening between Christmas and New Year someone knocked at the door. Eric and Maria looked surprised at each other because they wasn't expecting anyone, at least not that late in the evening. They didn't know anyone in the whole building complex yet except the manager. Even Christmas had been the loneliest time in their life together. All these years away from home, they had at least during Christmas been with friends, but this year, there was nobody, not even a telephone call. For the first time, they experienced the loneliness of immigrants in a new country not knowing anybody. It was actually harder for Maria than for Eric because he met people daily at the office. It was a cold winter, and all the inhabitants of this building complex moved swiftly in and out of their cars with an occasional fast hello on one of the walkways.

When Eric opened the door, he saw a very distinguished gentleman around six foot tall, neatly dressed, with grayish hair. He introduced himself, "I am Hank Benson. I am sorry to bother you at this late hour, but I have misplaced my keys somewhere and can't get into my place. I have heard that you are the new caretaker, and I was hoping that you had a set of spare keys. By the way, I saw you shoveling last night. I must say, you did a neat job."

"Thank you, Mr. Benson. Please, do come in and warm up a bit. In the meantime, I will put my jacket on and check which key fits your front door. It may take a while because I must have at least two hundred keys hanging on this wire behind the door." Eric and Maria introduced themselves and offered him a warm cup of coffee. "Or would you rather have a shot of brandy?" Eric questioned. "I bought a pint before Christmas, and since we've had no visitors, we still have most of it."

"Both," he answered. "I'm chilled to the bone. If you put a shot of brandy in the warm coffee and put some sugar in, it makes the coffee perfect, and it really warms you up." Without removing his winter coat, he sat down on the steps leading to the upstairs.

"That sounds good," Eric answered. "Maria, make me one too. I will go and open his door, and when I come back, I can drink it with you."

It took him quite some time and nearly frozen hands before he unlocked the door, and coming back home, he found both in a lively conversation. For more than two hours, he (Mr. Benson, now Hank) stayed there visiting. He was pleasant and showed a general interest in becoming a friend of this family. When he left, the bottle was empty, and he invited the whole family for dinner on New Year's Day.

Hank was a well-to-do man. With his father, they were in the money-lending business and had their offices somewhere in the downtown section of Minneapolis. He and his wife had been divorced for over two years, and his two sons and daughters, all in their teens, lived with their mother on their large property in another part of town.

At two o'clock in the afternoon on New Year's Day 1967, Hank walked in with a drink in his hand and asked the whole family to come over.

"The dinner will be ready at four o'clock," he said. "But it would be nice if you could come over right now so we could sit together and have a couple of drinks before dinner. The children can go into my basement and play table tennis or whatever. By the way, Eric, I am pretty good at that game, and I have a complete set up downstairs. Maybe later on, if you feel like it, we could play a couple of games."

His townhouse, which was right next door to Eric's, was well furnished, and he seemed to be a very good housekeeper. Besides a very open and friendly personality, he was also an excellent cook and produced that day a meal fit for a king. There was only one drawback, however. Eric and Maria noticed quickly that Hank had a severe alcohol problem. His favorite drink was whiskey and coke, which he mixed half and half in a large glass, and he would refilled his glass one after another.

He constantly reminded Eric, "Come on, drink up. There is more where that came from." And he showed Eric what he called his booze cabinet, which was completely stacked with liquor bottles.

The dinner he served at the big dining table in the living room using his best china and silverware showed his mastership in cooking. The flickering of the candlelight reflected into a bottle of deep dark red Bordeaux wine made this dinner, the first one served by an American friend, unforgettable. Hank was a perfect host and did everything possible to make his newfound friends feel at ease and, at the edge of showing off, let his intention known for a long-lasting friendship. He was very good with the children and played all kinds of games with them, and when it was time for them to go to sleep, he was their Uncle Hank.

After Maria and the children left, Hank invited Eric to play some table tennis with him in the basement. He was an outstanding player, and even under the influence of alcohol, he showed unbelievably quick reflexes for such a big man. They played game after game until late in the evening. At the beginning, Eric didn't have a foot to stand on and lost game after game, but as the evening progressed and Hank poured more and more liquor into his glass, Eric won a few games. The combination of the heavy drinking and losing made Hank argumentative, and Eric thought it was high time for him to leave.

In the following weeks, the Minnesota winter really showed its progressiveness. More than two feet of snow covered the area, and the temperature dropped to twenty-five degrees Fahrenheit below zero, with some evenings dropping minus thirty degrees. Since the management was not willing to buy a snowblower, Eric had to shovel the snow night after night in subzero temperature for all the walking parts of the complex. He was freezing and exhausted from shoveling, and it was hopeless. When he had shoveled around twenty yards of walkway, the winds channeled between the buildings and drove the crystalized snow like a sandstorm around him. It not only covered everything he had accomplished but, in some places, also piled it up to more than four feet high.

In every community, there seem to be some people who enjoy seeing someone suffering. Hank, on the other hand, thought it was ridiculous, and he helped Eric on some evenings. The rest of the people in these buildings didn't give a damn and didn't even remove the snow in front of their own door. When he finally came back home frozen and exhausted, the telephone would ring off the wall from tenants requesting him to come and shovel the snow again in front of their door.

When Eric told them he just had been there, some of them answered, "I don't care. It's part of the lease to have snow removal, and if it isn't removed in the next half hour, I will call the manager."

This went until late at night to be followed by the early risers the next morning. Minnesota saw an exceptionally high snow fall that year, and before the winter subsided, Eric was an exhausted man.

The friendship between Hank and Eric grew, and time permitting, they sought each other's companionship. Hank had been the only child of a well-to-do family, and at a young age, his mother had died during a car accident. Having the means to do it, the grieving father spoiled young Hank rotten with expensive gifts and an inexhaustible source of pocket money. He grew up that way, and it reflected on his behavior and character the rest of his life. Despite all he had in material things, he was a lonely man and very insecure. To compensate for that, Hank had to be a showoff. He would go out of his way for people to like him, be better, have more, and know more. Besides all these misgivings, he was a good man, and Eric enjoyed listening to his life stories, true or untrue.

Maria accepted him as a neighbor but kept her distance. She didn't particularly like or dislike him, but she didn't accept at all his drinking habits, which he tried to force onto Eric. She had a point there because Eric drank more than he used to but didn't try nor did he like to drink like Hank. As much as Hank was a lonely man in general, Eric was lonely for friendship. He had never been as close to another man as he had been with Nico, and all these years, he had missed this beautiful friendship between two men.

Hank was a sportsman, and to him, the outdoors were a second home. He had an expensive collection of hunting and fishing equipment and owned a beautiful lakeside cottage and acres of hunting ground in the wilderness of northern Minnesota. Hank also was a possessive man. He introduced Eric and Maria to all his friends and invited them to come along to their dinners and parties, but when anyone showed an above-normal interest in his newfound friend, he masterfully changed the situation.

One evening in February of that winter, his youngest son visited him, and the two were playing table tennis in the basement. Eric, hearing the exciting screams of the game, went over and took little Michelle with him. Maria didn't enjoy him being away from home that much even if it was only at the neighbor. But if he would take one of the children at least with him, it would make it a little easier on her, and she wouldn't mind as much. Both father and son were after each other on his game, and Eric watched with pleasure at the tactics they used in trying to beat each other.

Preventing Michelle from being in the way of the players, Eric gave her a pencil and a piece of paper and let her play underneath the tennis table. When time went by and both players intensified the fury of the play with long and hard smashing hits, Eric lost track of Michelle, who, without warning, walked out from under the table at the precise moment when the son from that side gave a smashing hit. Hank answered but his paddle hit the right side of Michelle's head, making a wide-open wound. Within a half hour, Hank was driving his big Chrysler, and Maria and Eric, in the back seat, were holding the blood-drenched towel over Michelle's head; she was still screaming when they arrived at a close by hospital.

When Maria and the little one separated from them and went into the emergency room to await the attending physician, Hank assisted Eric in filling out the necessary insurance forms. It took sixteen stitches to close the gap. Everyone naturally was upset by this accident, but poor Hank didn't know what to say and apologized over and over again. He promised Michelle all the ice cream she wanted and as soon as the wound had healed, he would take her to a store and buy her a new doll. Somehow it seemed to work because the little one, now getting all the attention and all these promises, eased up a bit. When they finally returned home, she had stopped crying and only wanted to know how big the doll would be.

Two days later, when Eric came home from the office and asked how the little one was doing, Maria answered, "Eric, I'm quite worried. All day long, she has been crying, and once in a while, she jerks her head as if she has a tremendous headache."

"It could be that she's starting to feel the pulling of the stitches," Eric said, "but if it isn't better tomorrow morning, I guess we better contact the doctor again."

That evening, when Maria tried to comfort Michelle in her bedroom, she noticed that a big blister deep underneath the skin was developing, covering practically the whole right side of her head. "Eric come up here and look. I don't like what I see here."

Eric rushed up the steps, and showing it to him, she said, "That doesn't look good at all. It looks like internal bleeding. No wonder the poor thing was in agony all day."

In a short time, they were back in the hospital again. Michelle, seeing the doctors and the nurses and the commotion all around her, went into a dead-scare fit, and she jerked and twisted and was hard to handle.

The attending physician said, "You two better go home and leave her with us. We will give her something to quiet her down. It will take quite some time before we will find out what happened, and then we will call you and let you know. Just don't worry. We'll take good care of her."

Michelle, seeing them leaving the room, started screaming, "Momma! Momma! Daddy! Daddy!" which cut deep into both of them. Without saying a word, they went home, each in their own thoughts.

Occasions like this were the hardest times for immigrants—not able to talk to relatives, friends, or anyone. For the first time, they missed their friends in Toronto and the close relationship that they had developed with them over the years. When they left the house, Maria told Nicole to go with Steven to Uncle Hank and stay there. When they returned Eric informed Hank what had happened, he was visibly very upset.

"That poor little thing," he said. "How is Maria taking all this?" But before Eric could answer, he continued, "Why don't you go home, Eric, and leave the children here for a while? I will play with them."

A few hours later, the physician called and informed them that Michelle would have to stay in the hospital for a couple of days. The cut in her head had been deeper than they had expected, and a large bister of fluid, which had built up between the skull and the skin, had to be drained constantly until it disappeared. Again, he told them that there was no serious danger and that Michelle was heavily sedated and possibly wouldn't wake up until the next morning. It was heartbreaking for both parents when they saw their little one the next morning lying on the big bed with high sides, her head completely covered with bandages and small tubes running down from her head and into a plastic bag hanging on the side of the bed.

A nurse, noticing how upset Maria was, said, "You must be the parents of Michelle. Don't be worried. It looks worse than it actually is. By tonight or at the latest tomorrow morning, we can take these tubes out, and if everything is all right, she can possibly go home tomorrow afternoon."

The nurse had been right. The next day, they could pick her up again, and when Hank came over that evening, he brought her a big beautiful doll as he'd promised. The wound healed very fast, and with the pressure of the built-up liquid gone, Michelle seemed to have forgotten all about the accident—until a week later when she had to have the stitches removed.

Again, she went into a rage when Maria entered the room of the doctor's office. It took two nurses and one doctor to remove her stitches. This experience had made such an impact on her that for years to follow, she would go into hysterical fits when visiting the doctor's office, even if the visit was for one of the other children. How meaningless this incident was in comparison to the cuts and bruises happening in many families with children, but for Eric and Maria, it formed a closer bond between them and Hank.

Eric worked hard at the office and made many electrical changes on the machinery, and Mr. Konrad let him know that it was worth every penny and all the trouble it had caused them to get him. There were a lot of changes to be made, and whenever possible, he would work long hours. Actually, the company didn't have to pay him extra for these hours as he was on salary, but since he worked so many hours, the company was so pleased that they awarded him overtime pay. His first miserable winter, at least for Eric, had passed, and he had made up his mind to move away from that townhouse complex. He enjoyed living by Hank, but he would never go through another winter shoveling all that snow.

In May 1968, the family moved closer to the factory and bought their first house. Mr. Konrad had been invaluable convincing the bank manager to loan Eric the money because he was without collateral except for a good steady job. Located in an old established neighborhood, the house by itself was small but clean and had a fair-sized kitchen in the back and lengthwise a living room full of windows in front. Upstairs were two bedrooms—one large and one small—and the only full-size bathroom. The open space beside the bathroom was also used as a bedroom. When only a single bed was used in that space, there was enough hall room left to walk beside the bed and into the bathroom. The basement underneath the entire house was very old with low-hanging oak beams and dirt floors. Sometime later, they found out that this house was one of the first ones built in that area; it had been leveled down to the ground on the old foundations and basement, and a new house was built, which by now was fifty to sixty years old.

It was a small but cozy house with only one handicap—anyone using the toilet had to walk through the living room upstairs. There was a slightly worn path in the carpeting of the living room from the years of traffic to the stairs. The freestanding garage, if you could call it that because it looked more like a shack than a garage, was filled with junk. Even after Eric cleaned it out and hauled about a truckload to the junkyard, he still couldn't use it for his car, because it was built way too narrow.

A nice piece of grass-covered land, a full lot size to the left side of the house was part of the bargain. All houses built on his side of the street were about six feet higher than the houses on the other side. On top beside the concrete steps leading to the sidewalk on the street was an old-fashioned gaslight mounted on a pole and was the only one still in operation. On a special occasions when Eric lit it, it would give the white-walled house a picturesque look. To the right side of the house was a tree-covered property, which belonged to the neighbor on that side. The rest of the rather short street was completely built full of small but neatly kept up houses. It took some time for Eric and Maria to get used to the stillness at nighttime. For as long as they were married, they had lived in with people or heard the noise of the neighbors through the paper-thin walls of the town-houses next to them. Even to the children, it was strange not hearing the constant "Be quiet! What will the neighbors think?" or "Don't run up and down the stairs!"

All through the years, they were used to spending their money wisely, and besides the necessary living expenses and larger house payments and insurances, they could just make it. Sometimes but not too often, the whole family would eat at an inexpensive restaurant, which was a real treat for Maria and the children just to get out of the house. Or Eric and Maria would go to a movie, but then they had to consider the extra expense of a babysitter. All in all, they were happy because they had their own home.

Hank, who didn't like this move at all but did understand their reasoning, missed his friend and called several times a week. On evenings when he was very lonely, he would jump in the car and visit them. Sticking his head inside the backdoor, he'd shout, "Hey, kids, it's Uncle Hank!"

He would be answered by three overjoyed youngsters running toward him and jumping into his arms. "It's Uncle Hank! Mom, Dad, Uncle Hank is here!"

On some Sunday mornings, Eric would visit him, but most of the time, he found him in such a stupendous hangover that even these visits became more and more sporadic. Hank was very sentimental, and Eric's moving was like a personal loss and intensified his drinking. He was doomed for destruction and would have drunk himself into the grave if he had not met Ms. Jennings.

She had met Hank at a party for one of her friends. She was ten years younger than Hank, was good-looking and full-figured woman, and had a warm smile. She didn't have the education or wisdom that Hank possessed but made up for that loss in kindness and understanding. She was immediately taken by this good-looking and well-mannered gentleman but soon discovered his drinking problem. Shortly after their meeting, when Eric visited him again on a Sunday morning and expected his living room and kitchen full of leftovers from a brawling night before, he instead found Hank clean-shaven, reading the newspaper, everything around him neat and tidy.

"What the hell happened here?" Eric opened the conversation. "I haven't seen this place like this in ages, and look at you. You look so good this morning I hardly recognize you. When I came in, I thought I was in the wrong house."

"Come on, Eric. It wasn't that bad... Or was it? Yes, I guess you are right," he said. "I really was getting heavy on the sauce. It is this Ms. Jennings, you know. By the way, her name is Connie. She doesn't like me at all when I'm drinking. A couple of glasses in the evening when she takes a glass of wine she doesn't mind, but when she sees me trying to sneak one more, she just gets up and goes home. She doesn't live too far from here, a couple of miles or so. You will meet her. She will be here shortly because today we are going for a ride to Wisconsin...to visit her brother."

"Whatever she did to you?" Eric answered while walking into the kitchen to get himself a cup of coffee. "It sure seems to be working. Again, I haven't seen you looking like that since we left and for sure not on a Sunday morning."

"Dammit, Eric, I still like to drink, but I like her too. She's a very nice and good-looking woman. Judge for yourself. I just saw her parking her car."

Moments later, she arrived and, with a friendly smile on her face, said, "Morning, Hank. My, you're looking nice this morning." And she kissed him. Hank looked kind of sheepish when Eric blinked an eye at him but immediately regained his composure and tried to introduce Eric.

But before he could open his mouth, she said, "You must be Eric. I recognize you from some of the pictures Hank showed me, but even if I hadn't seen them, I would have recognized you from the description Hank gave me. I'm very pleased to meet you." And she shook his hand.

"I am pleased to meet you too," Eric answered. "I have heard a lot about you—all good, I must confess."

After Hank poured her a cup of coffee, she turned to Eric. "You know him better than I do. What do you think about him?"

"That's not fair." Eric laughed. "Not in front of him. But I'm going to tell you anyway. He is a rotten, no good… Not really. He is my best friend."

When Eric left them that morning, he was happy not only for Hank but for himself too. In less than half a year, Hank had become, besides Maria and the children, the most important person in his life—a real true friend, something he had missed since Nico died and he thought he would never find again. And as a good friend, he was glad to share Hank with Ms. Jennings. Hank had been lonely for several years, but he surely was not a loner, and he needed feminine companionship.

Hank was a completely changed man. He was happier, more energetic, and took a lot better care of himself. When he came to visit, in the presence of Connie, he would like to have a drink all right, but instead of gobbling down one after another, he would sip once in a while, handling the glass with great dignity, showing off how proud he was at his accomplishment. He had joined a skeet shooting club some years ago; he had been quite a master at that sport. The many trophies covering the walls in his basement were witness thereof. With pride, he would show the large silver serving tray received for the second-highest scoring for the championship in Minnesota.

Several times on Saturday morning, Eric had gone with him when the club had their shoot-out. Though he was not the best anymore, Hank still had a keen eye and was highly respected by the club members. Many of the clay pigeons would practically explode within seconds after he loudly called, "Pull!" After the meet, he would let

Eric shoot down a couple of clay pigeons, if possible. Eric really enjoyed being with Hank. He liked this part very much but knew that it was too expensive a sport for him. He just couldn't afford it.

The weekend of July 4, 1967, the twosome drove over slippery dirt roads drenched with rain through the woods of northern Minnesota to Hank's cottage. A week before, Hank had called him and asked him to go with him for a long weekend fishing.

"Just the two of us. I told Connie that we should get away for a while. It would be fun, and I would really like that. You won't need anything, just your fishing license and your fishing equipment. I will take care of the rest."

"I would like that too," Eric answered, "but first I have to talk to Maria and see if she has anything planned for that weekend, but I'll call you back."

Maria wasn't at all enthused by the idea and thought that the family should do something together. Eric weighed the situation and thought that she was right, but from the other side, it would do him a lot of good to be away from the job and the family for a few days. He had been working from early mornings until late evenings, and he was getting very tired. Being away from it all with Hank would do him a lot of good, and he would enjoy it.

So he turned to Maria and said, "Maria, I know you don't like it, but I think I need this. I'm going to call Hank and tell him that we are going."

All week long, she didn't mention anything about it anymore, but when Hank arrived that afternoon, she was very curt with him. Hank noticed it but didn't say anything and tried to be as pleasant as possible. Quickly Eric loaded his fishing equipment and an extra heavy jacket into Hank's car, and they were off.

"Boy, was she ever in a lousy mood," said Hank as they turned out of the back lane onto the road. "I guess she didn't want you to go, did she?"

"No, she didn't," Eric answered. "Sometimes I don't understand her. Women are an entirely different breed. You can be married to them for years and still not understand them."

234

Hank agreed, "You work hard for your family… She is wise enough to realize that men would do anything possible for their women but once in a while, they have to be with friends and get away from it all, even if it's only for a couple of days. Let's forget about it. We are on our way now, and I promise you that we will have a beautiful time. On my way home this afternoon, the weather forecast predicted sunshine for the northern half of Minnesota, so it looks like we're going to be lucky. During the night, the weather will break, and they promise a sunny and warm weekend."

On this Friday, late in the afternoon, the highways were crowded with vacationers, thousands of campers, trailers, boats, and cars packed fully covered the roads and made traffic slow moving. For more than three hours, they had been moving along over a network of highways. With a sigh of relief, they finally exited into a small village. It had been a long ride, but a pleasant one. They had discussed women, politics, the industry in general, but it always came back to women again.

In the village, Hank stopped at a building that was a combination of a gas station and restaurant. "While the attendant is filling the tank, let's go inside and get some coffee to go." And stepping out of the car, he mentioned to the attendant, "Fill it up please. We will be right back."

It had been nice and warm in the car, so when Eric stepped out, he shivered and hurried behind Hank into the restaurant. The constant, fine, miserable rain made it abnormally cold for this time of year. The thermometer hanging on the wall of the restaurant showing fifty-four degrees. Eric stretched his stiffened body.

Hank, noticing it, remarked, "Time-wise, we didn't do so bad, but drive-wise, the worst is yet to come. For the next sixteen miles, we have to drive over treacherous dirt roads full of sharp corners, hills, and valleys."

It took nearly another hour on this road, and it was only Hank's experience that they didn't end up in the ditch on either side of the road. The rambler-style cottage with its rough cedar siding looked peaceful between the darkness of the surrounding forest when the headlights fell upon it.

"I will unlock the door, switch the inside and outside lights on, and then see if I can get the gas heater going. In the meantime, you can start unpacking, but be sure to put your heavy jacket on. This damn miserable cold temperature is not only outside but also inside the cottage, and it will take a while before the gas heater will drive the dampness out."

"My God, Hank, you brought enough groceries to feed a family for a week!" Eric said when entering the cottage.

Hank, who was sitting on his knees, trying to light the pilot of the gas heater, looked up and smiled. "Remember one thing, Eric, when you go out with old Hank, you never will go hungry. I took everything I could think of except the kitchen sink. Just put everything on the table. Damn it, I burnt my fucking fingers on this thing and still haven't gotten it going!" he shouted while throwing the burning end of a piece of paper on the floor and stamping it out with his foot.

Eric stopped in his tracks with a smile, but with a surprised look on his face, he said, "What was that? That was the first time I heard you use that word. It doesn't bother me at all. It's just that you surprised me."

"On a rough night and out here in the wilderness, you can say and do anything you please, and that's what makes it fun to be out here. For a couple of days, you can be as raw as the nature surrounding us." Then turning back to the gas heater, Hank said, "Finally, I've got the thing going. I will light the burners on the gas stove too, and the place will be warm in no time."

The cottage, consisting of a fair-sized kitchen, a large living room, and two small bedrooms, was well equipped with used non-matching but sturdily built furniture. In the middle of the living room hung a large wagon wheel on a heavy chain, which had been converted into a chandelier.

"How do you like the place?" Hank asked when he saw Eric walking toward the big window in the back of the living room.

"I love it. It's just gorgeous. I wish I could afford a place like this."

"It's yours whenever you want to use it," Hank replied. "And next time, you can bring the whole family up here and stay a whole week if you want to. The only problem is that I haven't got much of a beach. Go out on the deck and look down. You will see the lake practically underneath you. This cottage is built on a rock. From the deck, you go down twenty-eight steps to the boat dock. My beach is fairly rocky. The only beach for children is across the lake, where the guy who built the cottage there made his own beach with truckloads of sand. You won't see much tonight, but you will see it all tomorrow morning. Let's make something to eat. Are you hungry?"

"Now that you mention it..." Eric answered, "with all the excitement, I had forgotten about it. Yes, I am hungry."

"Okay then, we're going to make some hamburgers, my style," Hank said while taking the package of ground beef out of the refrigerator. "You clean some onions and slice some tomatoes while I fry the meat. To make it my style, you don't use hamburger meat. You use ground steak." And he made the patties about two inches thick and five inches in diameter. "I will make three of them," he said, "because I know you will eat a second one. Let's have a drink while they are frying. It will drive the chill out of our bones."

Never in his life had Eric eaten more delicious hamburgers than the ones Hank made. Juicy and delicious meat covered with slightly fried onions, tomato slices, lettuce, a couple pickle slices, and a touch of ketchup all piled on top of one another between two big buns then pushed together to bite height until the juices ran all over the plate and soaked the bottom half of the bun—it was so delicious that Eric practically swallowed both of them. He had to keep his head above the plate because with every bite, the juices ran down his chin. Even licking his fingers was a delicacy.

For years thereafter, the whole family liked this style of hamburger so much that on many Saturday evenings, the children would ask, "Dad, why don't you make some of Uncle Hank's hamburgers?"

The long trip, good food, warm coffee, and two more after-dinner drinks made them both tired, and around eleven o'clock, they went to bed. The next morning, Eric woke up on hearing Hank moving around in the kitchen and smelling the aroma of freshly brewed coffee. Looking outside through his bedroom window, he saw that the weather hadn't changed much. There was still a light rain, and a slightly gushing wind blew waves of small ripples on the lake.

"Morning, Hank."

"Morning, Eric. I guess you can use a cup of coffee. I will make some bacon and eggs, but I must have left a carton of groceries back at home because I can't find any bread or milk. For now, it doesn't matter. We can always use the remaining buns. Too bad the weather hasn't broken yet. We can do some fishing this afternoon or this evening. I hate to sit on the lake in this weather. You know what we can do?" he continued. "There is a small village to the north side of the lake. Through the years, I've gotten to know a lot of people in that place. We can buy the milk and bread at the small grocery store, then I'll introduce you to some of the people."

Around eleven o'clock that morning, they arrived in that little village. Hank bought a couple of loaves of bread, milk, and mustard, which he thought he'd forgotten too. A very heavy woman, nearly as wide as she was tall, welcomed Hank with a "Hi, stranger. You made it up here again, didn't you? I guess the town won't be safe for another couple of days." After Hank introduced Eric to her, she said, "Well, don't listen to me, he is a rascal, but he isn't that bad."

The noise of talking and laughing people came through the wall from the adjacent room. Hank pushed open the door with his foot, and Eric followed him into the only village bar. Five or six local farmers—distinguished by their blue and white striped overalls, mud-covered boots, and most of them with caps on their head hanging in any direction—were sitting at the bar, talking to the tiny and skinny bartender.

"Hey, Hank, it's nice to see you again!" one of the men shouted when they noticed Hank standing in the doorway. All the men seemed to know him, and when he walked over, they shook his hand and patted him on the back.

"Hey, Jim." Hank turned to the bartender. "I see your wife has lost some weight." And everyone started to laugh. "Give these bandits a drink on me. By the way, fellows, let me introduce my young Dutch friend here. He says things in a funny way, but he is a good shit."

All of them shook hands with Eric and made space in between them to sit down. Hank walked from one to the other, talking about things that happened in the past. When they all had a drink and were talking to one another, Eric looked at the tiny bartender and chuckled with the thoughts about his fat wife. Funny thoughts entered his mind seeing the two of them in their bed, and he felt sorry for the man because if she turned over, she would just squash the soul out of that little body.

It was an old dirty room. There were some oak tables with chairs around them, and the advertising plates in glass-covered pictures on the walls were so covered with dark-brown greasy dirt that later in the afternoon, Eric signed one of them with his fingernail. Other men came in, and before long, they started to play pool on a worn-out pool table.

The shouting and yelling came louder, and much too often, Eric would hear Hank yelling, "Jim, another round!"

Eric had already finished four drinks and had still another four waiting in front of him on the table where he had moved to so he could watch the pool players. He had tried playing, but he was so lousy at it that he had given it up. Around one o'clock in the afternoon, he noticed through the dirty window that the sun was shining. He tried to interrupt Hank, who was loudly debating the pool game.

Finally, he got Hank's ear and said, "Hank, the sun broke through. Let's go back and do some fishing."

"Okay, Eric, we'll go, but first I have to finish his game." He looked at Eric, having a hard time focusing his eyes, and Eric knew that it was a mistake coming into this bar.

When this game was over, there was another one and then another game. The screaming and yelling filled the smoke-covered room, and no matter how hard Eric tried to get his friend away from there, it was of no use. Finally, he gave up when later that afternoon and everyone was drunk from Hank's money, he answered him in a drunken voice, "Fuck you, Eric. I like it here, and if you don't like it, go home."

It was after seven o'clock that evening when, with help from Jim, the bartender, Eric got Hank, who couldn't stand on his legs anymore, back into the car and found his way back to the cottage. Hank was lying on the backseat, completely out. As they came around the bend and he saw the cottage, Eric's heart stopped.

The cottage was on fire! Or at least it *looked* like it was.

Grayish smoke poured out from one of the open windows in the living room and from underneath the front door. Pushing the car pedal to the bottom, he raced to the cottage and hit the brakes so hard when he arrived that Hank fell off the backseat. He didn't wake up. When Eric swung the door of the cottage open, the heavy smoke and an unbelievable stench drove him back. He waited a couple of minutes, drenched his handkerchief in a pool of water, which he held in front of his nose and mouth, and tried to enter again.

The stench and the smoke that watered his eyes were so heavy that he didn't dare go in any farther. With quick glances around, he noticed no fire and that the build-up of smoke had somewhat subsided through the open door. He entered again and this time noticed that the smoke came from the stove in the kitchen. Then he remembered that Hank that morning had put a whole bag full of turkey gizzards and liver on the stove in a pan full of water and had said that he would slowly boil them until they got back. All the water had boiled away, and all that was left was a big black smoky mess. He turned the stove off, dropped the handkerchief to the floor, and with two towels wrapped around the hot kettle, ran with it outside and threw the whole smoking thing into the woods.

He had inhaled some of that smoke and the unbelievable stench, and with tearing eyes, he sat on a tree stump, coughing and heaving. When he felt up to it, he walked back in and opened every window, but then he had to run out again for fresh air and to empty his stomach. All during that time, Hank was still lying on the floor of the car. For two hours, Eric sat outside, letting the light breeze through the windows do its job. It was not until dawn when he finally pulled Hank out of the car and dragged him into his bedroom.

He was still completely out but must have noticed something because with unfocused eyes, he looked at Eric for a moment and said, "What the hell is the stink around here?" But then closed his eyes, rolled over, and went back to sleep.

Instead of eating Hank's famous wild rice goulash, his own rec-
ipe that was hard baked to the bottom of the kettle and still laying
in the middle of the woods, Eric made himself a sandwich from a
hamburger bun to settle his stomach and sat outside on the deck,
listening to the sounds of the forest around him. There was still a
strong odor surrounding the cottage, but it had one advantage—the
mosquitos didn't like it either. They normally would have made it
impossible for Eric to sit outside at this time of the evening.

He was angry, not so much at Hank, although he was very disappointed in him, but more so that he had been unable to get him
out of that bar after a few drinks. Knowing his problem, he should
have been more forceful. That Hank had yelled at him, he ignored,
because good friends should be able to yell at each other once in a
while and still maintain friendship.

*Just forget about it. There is always tomorrow. Hank will be sorry
and full of apologies by then.*

The first sunrays coming through the screen of the open window on Eric's face woke him up. He got up and, standing in front of
his window, took a couple of deep breaths of the fresh morning air.
He stared over the mirrorlike lake. The slowly dissipating morning
fog made the opposite shoreline barely visible. Except for the calling
of a loon in the far distance, it was very peaceful, and he stood there
for quite some time, observing nature in its fullest beauty, not daring to make a sound that would break the stillness. The aluminum
fishing boat tied to the dock lay motionless as if it were frozen in the
water.

A duck with her tiny two- or three-week-old ducklings slowly
swam by, constantly alert. It was impossible to count the forever-moving, crisscrossing, and always eating ducklings, but Eric figured that
there had to be ten or twelve of them. Once in a while, one of the
little ones strayed off too far, but one quack of the forever-watching
hen made the young one run over the water, its tiny feet operating
like the wheel of a fast-moving paddleboat, back to the flock again.
Mother hen quacked a couple of times in appreciation when the little
one arrived.

Trying to avoid making a sound so as not to wake up Hank, he went into the kitchen, drank a glass of orange juice, took his fishing equipment, and walked down the steps to the waiting fishing boat. He pulled in the minnow bucket, which was floating on the water, and tied to the boat and inspected the bait. Some of the small fish—shiners they were called—had died, and Eric threw them in the lake. He took the oars and rowed about thirty yards from the dock and threw the anchor so that Hank could see him when he woke up. After connecting a big red and white float and a lead weight to his line, he hooked a shiner back on the dorsal fin and threw it into the water. He lit a cigarette and watched the float slowly moving pulled by the minnow.

He looked back to the shoreline. How beautiful it was out here. He had had seen many pictures of northern Minnesota, but as he sat on that calm water in the warm sun and seeing all these white birch trees contrasting with patches of green pine trees, he realized how truly breathtaking it was. The light-brown grayish color of the cottage seemed to have the same color as the rock underneath it, and only the sharp reflection of the sun on the windows made someone at a distance aware that it was a cottage.

When he looked back at his float, it was gone. He didn't know how long it had been under because he had set the line free on the reel so that the bait would have no restrictions. Hank had told him on the way up that there were a lot of northern pikes in the lake and that he should get the minnow and pulled the float under then let him go for a while and give the pike time to swallow before setting the hook. The float came close to the surface again but was immediately pulled under. Eric couldn't wait any longer. He flipped the lever of the ratchet on the reel, pulled the line up a couple of yards, and with both hands, jerked the rod backward. Immediately, he felt that the hook was set and the fish trying to escape, but to no avail. It swam in all directions and once in a while would pull some more line out. Keeping constant tension on the line, Eric exhausted the fish and, after a couple of minutes, scooped it out of the water with his net. It was a nice fish, a northern pike around four pounds, and after tying it to a small chain connected to the boat, he threw it back in the water again.

He caught three more pikes, all around the same size. He looked at the sun since he had forgotten to put on his watch that morning and figured it to be around ten or eleven o'clock already. No signs of life had come from the cottage, and he wondered if Hank was still sleeping.

I better row back and wake him up, he thought. *Otherwise, he will sleep away most of this beautiful day.* After he had tied the boat to the dock again, he called Hank a couple of times to show him the fish he had caught that morning, but since there was no answer, he dropped the fish and chain back in the water and walked up the steps, making extra noise to notify Hank he was coming. He walked into the cottage and noticed immediately that Hank's bed was empty.

A note was lying on the kitchen table: "Good morning. I went back to the village because we still forgot the milk and the bread yesterday. I will be back shortly."

It was not until after two o'clock that afternoon when Hank returned. As Hank stepped out of his car and took a grocery bag from the backseat, Eric noticed immediately from the moves that he made that he was unsteady on his legs. Trying to walk abnormally straight, Hank walked into the cottage.

"Morning!" he shouted. "Did you find my note? How was the fishing?"

"Yes, I found the note, and the fishing was good. I caught three northern, but it isn't morning anymore. It's after two o'clock already."

"Already?" he answered. "Gee, I stayed longer than I expected. I needed a couple of Bloody Marys to get me over this damn hangover. Sorry about that. That was a real boomer we put on yesterday. I can't remember coming home."

"No wonder," Eric answered and laughed. "I had quite an experience last night." And he told Hank what had happened.

"I figured that when I got up this morning. The house still smells awful. Where did you put the kettle?"

"Oh, I threw it outside," Eric replied. "I'll go get it."

"Yes, do that. In the meantime, I will make some sandwiches. I guess you must be hungry from sitting all morning on the lake."

Finding the kettle where he had thrown it the night before, Eric knocked it against a tree a couple of times, and most of the black stuff fell out. Walking back in again, he saw Hank setting the table, but Eric noticed immediately that he had made himself another drink.

Noticing Eric looking at the drink, Hank said, "I need them for the hangover. Should I make you one too?"

"No, thank you. I've had enough yesterday, and so did you. It is too early in the day to start now."

After a late lunch, they drank their coffee at the deck. "Was I obnoxious yesterday? Sometimes I get that way when I'm drunk, as you well know."

"Not more than usual. You're just impossible to deal with when you are in that state. Let's forget about it. It is such a beautiful day. Why we don't go fishing?"

"I know what we'll do," Hank replied. "You go fishing for another couple of hours. I still don't feel like it, but in the meantime, while you are fishing, I will make you the biggest dinner you've ever seen. I will call you when it's ready. I will make it an early dinner. Then we still have time left to fish all evening. They bite better in the evening anyhow."

Around five o'clock, Hank called out that the dinner was ready. All afternoon, Eric had tried different places, but it seemed like the fish had taken a siesta. As Hank had promised, he had prepared a delicious dinner—two huge steaks covered with sautéed mushrooms, cauliflower covered with a cheese sauce, and boiled potatoes, followed by a piece of cheesecake for dessert. It was delicious, but it would have been more joyful if Hank had stopped drinking.

After dinner, Eric finally got him to go fishing with him, but by that time, Hank was in such bad shape that when stepping into the boat, he lost his balance and nearly fell into the water if Eric hadn't gotten ahold of him. Eric caught one northern pike, but it wasn't much fun fishing with Hank. As Hank sat in the warm evening sun, his head would drop and he would fall asleep.

When the sun started to disappear on the horizon, they went back, and Hank continued to drink all evening.

Eric was angry now. "Hank," he said, "we are supposed to have a nice time out here in the wilderness doing fishing and just having fun together, but you haven't done anything else except drink. If I had known that before, I would have stayed home."

"What do you mean?" Hank replied. "We came here to have some fun, and I did go fishing with you, didn't I? There is still tomorrow morning. We can fish for a couple of hours before we go back to the city. If I had gone fishing with you this afternoon, I wouldn't have been able to prepare that meal for you."

"Honestly, Hank," Eric replied, "I must say that meal was delicious, but I would have preferred to have gone fishing with you and had some more cold cuts for dinner."

With a big grin on his face, he answered, "Some people are never satisfied, but wait till tomorrow morning. Then I'll show you how you can really catch these fish around here."

The sharp rays of the sun reflecting on the water had tired Eric's eyes, and also he had received a slight sunburn. After sitting and talking for a while and having a few drinks with Hank, who didn't seem to stop drinking anyhow, they both fell asleep in their chairs and went to bed. The next morning, Eric woke Hank up. He growled and wanted to go back to sleep.

"Come on, Hank. It's beautiful weather, and you promised me you would go fishing with me this morning. I'll go in the kitchen and make some coffee," Eric said.

Hank didn't want to get up, but he did anyhow. He walked in a daze as he came into the kitchen, didn't say much, and drank his coffee. Eric knew that he felt lousy, but he also knew that if he went fishing by himself, Hank would start drinking again. So he put the remaining coffee in a thermo flask and said to Hank, "Let's go." Hank grumbled something but followed him anyway.

Once on the water, Hank started feeling better, and the cool morning air brought him back to life again. Before leaving, Eric had connected the small outboard motor to the boat, and now trolling instead of still fishing, they had good success. Within three hours, they caught nine pikes. The first one was a beauty of about ten pounds, which Hank had caught. When they finally got it onto the chain, Hank was excited and said, "I told you I would show you how to fish these waters." The fresh air, black coffee, and good fishing had brought Hank back to his usual self again.

Shortly before noon, they returned back to the cottage and cleaned the fish they had caught that morning, and together with the fish Eric had cleaned the day before, they packed them with the leftover ice cubes out of the refrigerator in the cooler and put it in the trunk of the car. The smell still hanging in the cottage was absorbed in the woods, and before locking the doors, Hank left some of the windows just a crack open.

"This way," he said. "When we come back next time, it will be all gone." Hank had not touched a drink that day, and the ride back to Minneapolis was again pleasant. Eric, who by now was enjoying himself, was very careful not to bring it up.

Coming close to Eric's home, however, they noticed a lot of tree branches and debris lay by the road. As they came closer, they realized it was even worse than they'd seen from afar, and turning into Eric's street, they noticed that the whole neighborhood had suffered.

"They had a tornado here!" Hank shouted. "It must have happened a couple of days ago, because they've cleared the roads already."

Passing by the house to turn into the back lane, Eric saw that the big maple tree with its wide branches, which had shaded the front of his house, had been rooted out of the ground and had fallen against the house. One big branch had gone right through the roof and into their bedroom. Eric was worried, but when they parked the car beside the garage, Steven, followed by Maria, came out of the house.

While running toward them, he said, "Dad, Uncle Hank, you should have been here. We had a tornado. Did you see that tree? It fell right in the house!"

"Is everyone all right?" Eric turned to Maria while rubbing his hand through Steven's curly hair.

"Except for a broken roof, we are all right. It scared the living daylights out of me. It happened Saturday night," she said very calmly. "But I'll tell you the details later. Come in."

One of his neighbors, he noticed, was hit very hard. Of all the beautiful trees, he had, only two were still standing. One of them had its crown completely twisted off. One of the trees had fallen right alongside his garage.

Eric thought, *That's a shame. If it had fallen one foot farther, it would have taken that old shack with it and the insurance would have had to pay for a new garage.*

When he came inside, he saw Michelle and Nicole playing in the living room as if nothing had happened. "My god, you seem to be very cool about all this," Eric said to Maria.

"Now I am," she said. "You have to realize it was Saturday evening when it happened, and it is now already Monday, so I am all ready used to it. We couldn't contact you. You told me there was no telephone in the cottage. But didn't you listen to the news over the radio?"

"No," Hank replied. "We were most of the time fishing."

"Well, let me tell you what happened. The rain stopped sometime Saturday afternoon, but then the winds started rushing. Around six o'clock, I looked outside, and there was an eerie gray-greenish sky. I knew we were in for some very bad weather. The winds were rushing stronger and stronger, and I saw the trees leaning over. Then at once I heard something like a train racing at high speeds coming closer and closer. I grabbed the children and rushed into the basement. We were just in time because moments later, there was a high rumbling and whistling sound and the house seemed to vibrate. It seemed as if it was going to be pulled off its foundations! We heard cracking and breaking all around us. It must have been the trees of the neighbors that came down. We were all very scared, but I kept my composure for the children's sake. It was all over in about ten or fifteen minutes, and when we finally came out of the basement and looked outside, we saw what had happened. We were lucky we had a flashlight downstairs because during that time, the lights went out. Later, I noticed that a branch from one of the neighbor's trees had broken one of the electric wires coming to the house outside in the back."

"When did they come and connect it up again?"

"They?" she continued. "*I* did it. I have seen you working so many times with wires that I took the ladder out of the garage on Sunday morning, put a pair of gloves on, and with your insulated tools, pulled the wire and connected it together again."

"Jesus, Maria, you could have been killed yourself!" Hank interrupted.

"Not when you know what you're doing," she said and smiled. "It was not the lights I was worried about, but the food in the refrigerator. I handled everything very calmly. But yesterday afternoon, somehow I started shaking like a leaf. I guess it must have been the aftereffect. You know, Eric, if it had happened later during the night and I had been asleep, that branch would have killed me. It just touched the bed. You can't see it anymore. One of the neighbors came with a chainsaw and cut off just below the roof."

Now getting over it, Eric joked, "When I saw that tree lying in the house I thought, I know she didn't want me to go away this weekend fishing, but I didn't think she would get that angry."

After drinking a cup of coffee and unloading Eric's things and the fish out of the car, Hank thought it was better for him to go home because he was wondering what happened to his place, but Maria put him at ease and told him that the tornado only touched down in that area and no damage was reported anywhere else.

When Hank was gone Eric went over and talked for a while to his neighbor who was cutting trees with a big chainsaw, and moments later, they removed the branch top out of the roof. Eric covered the hole with a plastic sheet.

After a few days, the roof was repaired, and all went back to normal again. However, Hank was back to heavy drinking. He lost his girlfriend, and also Eric slowly lost his friend to alcohol.

Approximately one year later, Eric received a call from Hank's son that his father had only been two weeks in the hospital when he died from liver failure.

CHAPTER 12

✠

One of Eric's coworkers, Richard, had asked him if he would visit him that evening because his electrical stove was defective. When Eric was working on the stove, a friend arrived, and both men had a conversation in another room. The visitor introduced himself to Eric as Nick Fasher. He could not stay long because he had choir practice that evening. Eric, who had been in choir before in Holland, asked if he could come to one of the practices.

"Okay," Nick said. "Come here next week Monday then. I'll take you with me."

One week later, Eric visited and joined the choir.

The applause faded, and neatly row after row, they marched from the stands backstage. Everyone congratulated one another for a job well done. The welcome noise of the applauding people who filled the orchestra hall to the last seat had drowned when the last man had arrived backstage and closed the door behind him. The 1969 fall concert had come to a successful end, and every member of this large male choir felt relieved. Since September, they had been practicing week after week for this concert. For the last few weeks, they had rehearsed two or three times a week, and all their efforts paid off.

Mr. Faltor, who had conducted this choir for several years, had shaped with great effort more than one hundred voices from an ear-piercing noise in the beginning of the rehearsals to a superbly directed, gorgeous, harmonious male choir, which led to a perfect two-hour long concert. This great and large orchestra hall had been sold out to the last seat, most due to the effort of each singing member. The crowd had showed its appreciation with a standing ovation at the end of each of their outings this Saturday evening and Sunday afternoon.

At the end of each concert, they sang "Silent Night" for the encore. It was already early December. The stage director dimmed the lights to complete darkness at the ending of this beautiful melody and then turned the hall into full brightness after the last note had been brought down to a mere whisper. The crowd exploded. Eric, like the rest of the singers, was tired, not so much from the singing but more so from standing on his feet for more than two hours on the foot-high risers neatly packed together. Not only were his feet killing him, but his left side was practically numb.

Old John, standing beside him on the back row of the baritone section and who was still an active member for more than fifty years, was really too old to stand on his feet for all that time, and for the last hour, Eric had kept him from going to his knees with his left arm. He was a friendly old fella, kind of a loner who didn't want to give up this only pleasure he had left in life. This was Eric's first concert with this choir. It existed already more than eighty years. Eric did not know at that time the he still would be a singing member fifty years later. He would travel with this choir to several places in Europe, Canada, and USA.

Before this male chorus, Eric and Maria had no friends to speak of. However, within a couple of years, they were invited to many personal activities of the members. Maria loved the majestic sound of this large male choir, and for every concert, she would dress like the old style going to an opera. Eric always got a seat for her on the balcony, middle front row. After the concert, they would have dinner with other members and their wives.

One evening, after practice, some of the members got together for a couple of pints of beer in a small bar across the practice location. One of the members and Eric had their birthday celebration. It was a very cold and snowy night, but it was nice and warm inside the bar. They had one beer after another, and when Eric left, he felt no pain whatsoever. Normally, it would take about twenty minutes to travel to his home; however, the snowstorm had increased to a blizzard.

Within two miles from home, it was that bad that he could not see the side of the road. All traffic very slowly crawled along. Eric was behind a very large truck. His eyes were focusing, but as long as he could stay between, the two inner red lights of the many he saw on this truck, he would be okay.

About one half mile to go, he drove straight into a ditch beside the road, still behind the truck.

The truck driver came to the back and asked Eric to lower the window. "You stupid son of a… Why did you follow me into the ditch?

Eric didn't know what to answer, but finally, he said, "I just stayed between your red lights." Eric locked the car and made it home by foot. Half frozen and covered with snow, he stumbled into the kitchen door.

"What happened?" Maria asked. "I was getting very worried. Where is your car?"

"In the ditch," Eric answered.

Maria noticed that he could not focus too well and told him to go to bed. "Tomorrow we will get your car home."

CHAPTER 13

⚜

Around the midsixties, the race for space travel between the USSR and the USA was on. Eric watched all available information on television with great interest. He always was interested in all the unknowns of space and science technology. Allan Sheppard of the USA was the first to reach the Earth's outer limits and return safely back. However, the Russian Yuri Gulgaren beat the USA by being the first person to circle the Earth in outer space, followed by John Glen, who circled the Earth at least three times.

In 1969 Neil Armstrong and his crew were the first men to land on the moon, where he announced, "The *Eagle* has landed."

The whole Earth was watching when Neil stepped down the ladder of his space craft and said his famous words, "One small step for man, one giant leap for mankind."

Eric's eyes were glued to the television as he watched the event. He said to Maria, "We are watching history in the making."

A few years later, Eric had the honor of meeting Mr. Armstrong in Houston, Texas, on a business meeting.

He had flown to Houston early one morning and had checked into a motel. His meeting with the customer was the next morning at 10:00 a.m. In the later afternoon, he went to the bar in the motel to enjoy a drink and relax. It was a horseshoe type of bar and was quite empty except for one customer in a gray suit. Eric said hello, and the person answered accordingly. Eric noticed that this man looked familiar.

When this person made a visit to the restroom, the bartender said to Eric, "Do you know this person?"

"He looks familiar, but that's all."

Then he whispered to Eric, "That is Neil Armstrong. He has a meeting here tomorrow."

Upon his return, Neil stopped by Eric and asked him, "Where are you from? I detected an accent when you were talking to the bartender."

"Today I flew in from Minneapolis, but originally, I immigrated from Holland."

"Okay," Neil said to the bartender. "Give this Dutchman a drink from me."

Naturally, Eric returned the gesture. They sat together, and Eric said, "Neil, you must be bombarded with questions a thousand times about your history-making trip, so I will not bother you about it. But I had to ask, though, were you never scared during this whole trip?"

Neil answered, "Sure we were scared. We are human, you know, but throughout our lives, we've flown jets in wars and learned to do what has to be done under pressure."

They had a good time together, and Neil and Eric became pals for the evening. Eric mentioned to him that Steven, at his young age, wanted to be a jet pilot when he grew up. Neil asked the bartender for a piece of paper and wrote, "To Steven. I wish you all the best in becoming a jet pilot. From Neil Armstrong, the Moonman."

After some drinks together, Neil said, "Eric, there is a small Western-style bar with a blue neon light on the front. Should we walk over there and check it out?"

This bar was an old bar full of people and smoke with a guy in worn Western clothing and guitar trying very hard to be heard. The two took a small table on one of the side walls because there was no space at the bar anymore. After a few beers, one of the servers recognized Neil. He took the microphone from the singer and, in a loud voice, called out, "Quiet, quiet, we have a very famous person here tonight. Over there, on the wall sits none other than Neil Armstrong."

For the next half hour, we were overwhelmed with well-wishers. They asked Neil to say a few words on the microphone. By that time, Eric and Neil had drunk so many beers that they were in a splendid mood.

When Neil took over the microphone, he said in a blurred voice, "I really thank you guys for honoring me, but the man you don't recognize is our first man in pace, Allan Sheppard, sitting here right beside me."

Eric could not believe his ears, but before he knew what was going on, all the people crowded around him. In no time, the table was completely full of glasses of beer.

When the noise of the well-wishers quieted down, Eric said to Neil with a smile on his face, "You son of a bitch, you could have gotten me in some real trouble."

"Why? They don't know any better. And didn't we have fun?"

Shortly thereafter, again under loud well wishes, they left the bar. Both men, arm in arm to keep from falling, made it across the street back to the motel. They promised each other that they would meet for breakfast the next morning, but nothing came of that.

CHAPTER 14

All three children had been born in Canada; therefore, they were Canadian by birth. In 1965 both Eric and Maria filed for their Canadian citizenship. It was not easy. First, both had to study a lot about all the provinces and their economy and about the judiciary system. It was not possible at that time to have two citizenships, so it was for both very hard to alter being Dutchmen to Canadian. However, their children were Canadians, so Eric and Maria found it necessary to change their citizenship.

It was a completely a different story when, after being in the USA for the requested five years, Eric actually started the process of becoming a US citizen. When he met the first Americans at the end of WWII, he was about eleven years old. It was his dream when he grew up to become an American. He would be the only one in his family, because all three children were under the age of sixteen. This meant that if both parents would become American citizens, the children would also lose their Canadian citizenship, so Eric and Maria decided that Maria would remain Canadian and have the three children listed on her passport. Both thought that it was the children's birthright to be Canadians and that they could choose for themselves when they were over sixteen years old. It was also not allowed to have two or more citizenships at that time. It was much harder to become a US citizen than a Canadian.

Eric had to study for over a half year. He had to know all the states, their capitals, the major products, the governmental judiciary and governing system, and a lot more. When he was ready to take his test, he discovered that by now he knew much more about the

United States than most people. He received information that on September 2, 1972, he would have his examination. To graduate, he would sit across from a judge and answer his questions about the United States of America. It was easier than he thought. The judge asked him a lot of simple questions, and it was over in no time at all. He noticed that if he hesitated with an answer, the judge would kindly assist by asking Eric, "Could it be this…?"

Someone once told Eric a good joke about going for citizenship: "There was this old lady from Italy who, after living many years in the United States, waited to be a citizen. When she came in front of the judge, she was very nervous and couldn't answer any of the questions. She had lived in Italy during WWII, so the judge thought she would know his last question. He said to her, 'Do you know any famous American generals?' She answered immediately, "*Si*, General Motors and General Electric." The judge smiled and told her, 'You passed.'"

Eric was informed that a month later, he would take the oath to the United States with about thirty more applicants in the state capitol building in St. Paul, Minnesota.

His whole family went together to witness this special occasion. It was for the second time—first as a Canadian and now as an American. With his right hand over his heart, he stood there with many people of different countries and different styles of living. He actually felt a tear running over his cheek when he thought about Holland and Canada. He had loved both countries, and both had become a large part of his life. After the oath, they all sang the national anthem with many different dialects, but they all meant well.

After all was over, Eric stood there for a moment and thought, *Finally, after nearly thirty years, my wish has come true. I'm an American.*

Out of gratitude to all three countries, he installed three big flagpoles and hung the American flag on the tallest pole in the middle, the Dutch on the right, and the Canadian on the left side. The reason was that he had been for most of his life a Dutchman, so its flag had the most honored side, to the right of the American.

A newspaper man had seen the flags, and after a short interview with Eric, he took a picture of Eric and the flags and wrote an article in the local paper under the heading "Man that Honors Three Flags." For many years, the flags were also used in the neighborhood as a direction finder, like "If you see these flags, you go to the right [or left]."

CHAPTER 15

✠

Because of his increased income, Eric and Maria started to talk about moving to a larger home. Eric had mentioned to his local barber, who was also a part-time realtor, that if he could find a reasonable priced home "on water," Eric would be interested. His longtime dream had been to live on a lake. One day, the barber informed him that he found such a location, and together with Maria and the children, Eric met with the barber, who then drove them to take a look at this home.

It was farther out of Minneapolis's city limits than they thought it would be. When they drove around a corner, Eric saw a "For Sale" sign on a very small house.

He said to the barber, "That house is even smaller than the one we live in now."

"No, no," he answered. "The house is the one you see on the end of the street."

Then Eric and Maria saw a huge new brown house with no neighbors but beautiful woods on both sides. The closest neighbor was about two hundred yards down the road.

They looked at each other, and then Eric said, "Are you sure that this house is in our price range?"

"Just wait," he answered. "Let's first see the inside before you make a decision."

It was a large split-level home. Upstairs was the main living quarter, with the dining room, kitchen, and living room in one large open space; there were three bedrooms and a bathroom. A sliding door opened to a deck overlooking a small lake on his backyard.

Beautiful oak wood was used on all trimmings and kitchen cabinets. The downstairs was not finished at all and would have to be finished by the new owner. It was a lovely home, and the children loved it, but both Eric and Maria knew that this place was way out of their range.

"Don't be so quick with your answer," the barber said again. "The builder is in big trouble. He built several big homes all over this area, and he has not sold one in two years. You can call him directly." And he gave Eric the telephone number.

The next day, Eric called him, but as expected, the asking price was three times higher than they could afford. A half year later, the builder called again and lowered the price to two times Eric had offered. So again, Eric had to decline.

He told him, "Sorry, but I just can't afford it."

Approximately four months later, he called Eric again and asked, "Are you still interested? I need money now. You can have it for two thousand dollars more than your offer."

In 1974 they purchased the house, and they knew that this dream home would be theirs, if possible, for the rest of their lives.

CHAPTER 16

✠

E ric was not at all happy anymore at his job. When he was
hired, they had offered him the position of vice president of
sales in the time to come. However, the company was purchased by a large conglomerate, and they brought in their own management personnel.

Unexpectedly, a large manufacturer of electronic machinery
contacted Eric that they had an opening for director of international
sales. Their products were marketed over Canada, US, and Mexico.
They were expanding and wanted to cover the whole industrial
world. At Eric's meeting with the president (whom he liked immediately), he was told that if he accepted this position, he would for the
first two months study all their equipment, and then he would have
to travel all over the world to set up representatives (agents). The
salary they offered was larger than Eric even had hoped for, but the
constant traveling would be very hard on his family. He was expected
to travel for two weeks and then work in his office for two weeks and
would continue to set up and maintain this network.

Coming home, he discussed this position in detail with Maria,
but she had to agree that this high increase in salary would also raise
their standard of living. They would be able to get the house finished
in no time. They finally agreed, and Eric accepted the position.

During the two months of studying all their equipment, prices,
and the competition, Eric contacted the consulate of many countries. With this information, he started with Asia and, in a very short
time, had arranged appointments with a few large distribution companies. On his first trip, he would meet with agents in Hong Kong,

Bangkok, and Singapore. Most large companies in the world have at least two or three persons in sales and/or management who would know some of the English language. Eric had no problem conversing with them because he knew from his own experience that they translated it all in their minds. So he would speak very slowly, leaving out most of what he called the small words. For instance, if he normally would say, "It is going to be a beautiful day tomorrow," he would instead say, "Tomorrow nice weather."

Eric also had the advantage over many world travelers; he had what was known as a cast iron stomach, and throughout all his travels, his host would love it and would take Eric to many different high-rated dining places to show off their special local food. One thing Eric insisted on was that they would order the same food for him as they themselves would eat.

While he was in Hong Kong, after meeting with the management of several interested companies, Eric decided on the one that was a large company and already an agent for several manufacturers and experienced in international sales and service. They represented many lines of machinery and related equipment but had no competitive line as the one Eric represented. With their large network of salesmen, they would cover Hong Kong and China for Eric. The vice president of this company, Mr. C. K. Tang, met Eric at the Hong Kong airport and, after a light dinner, drove Eric to a very beautiful hotel reserved by Mr. Tang.

It had very large rooms overlooking the harbor. At that time, Hong Kong was still under British control, who had purchased this city from China for one hundred years. On Eric's first visit, only a few years were left before Hong Kong would return to China. C. K. Tang's first name was very difficult to pronounce, so they both decided to just call him CK. CK was about Eric's age and already a very smart businessman. It seemed like both had a lot in common and became good friends. In years to come, they both would travel together all over Hong Kong and China.

Doing business in China was very different. All meetings with Chinese potential customers had to be arranged by CK through a governmental agency at least one month before Eric would arrive.

For instance, CK's sales department would get several companies in the Chang Hai area that were interested in Eric's products. These companies would contact a local governmental office, who would then arrange for one representative of each company to meet with CK and Eric on one day in one locality especially used for such meetings.

These meeting rooms were very somber—old metal collapsible chairs and tables, no tablecloths, and no curtains on the windows. It made it very difficult for Eric to give his sales speeches. There sales literature was in English. A sales meeting would take all day instead of a few hours because the people present spoke practically no English. CK had to translate not only the products but also their questions.

When they had a weekend together, CK and Eric would visit places like the majestic Forbidden City in Beijing, the Great Wall, and the tomb of the last emperor of the Ming Dynasty. CK drove Eric back to the airport after this first meeting, and both knew that they would do a lot of business together.

Within a five-year time period, Eric traveled to all industrial countries, and his products were sold through fifty-one agents. Because of his relentless travel and hard work, the company increased its sales from fourteen to sixty-eight million. By now, the network was increasing such that Eric needed assistance, and three more traveling sales engineers were employed, who were all managed by Eric. The president, who was very pleased with Eric's accomplishments, increased his salary accordingly.

It was, however, very hard on Eric's family. Whenever there was any activity at school, church, or sports activities, Eric could not be there. When he returned home, the children would inform him of all the things they did without him, and he felt sometimes that he was a stranger in his own home.

On one of his trips through Asia, Eric visited Hong Kong again. During a dinner meeting, CK asked Eric, "Why don't you start your own company?"

"My own company?" Eric replied. "In what?"

"Let me explain," CK answered. "All over the world, there are many companies who are looking to have some of their products or parts manufactured for a lower price than they can do themselves. This is where you come in. You have at the present fifty-five agents all over the world. These agents could become your company's agents. Through these agents, they would send to you by fax [e-mail had not been invented yet] all information and specification, and your company would send this information to other agents."

"It sounds interesting," Eric replied. "Let me do some thinking about that. But why would these companies come through me? There are large import/export companies who could handle that."

"Not so," CK replied. "Like you said, large companies are too large and expensive for the small manufacturers and, in general, have not the technical knowledge for this kind of business."

When Eric returned home, he and Maria discussed this idea in detail. She was not at all in favor of it, because Eric would have to quit his present job. He had a very good income, including all insurances. It made no difference how Eric tried. Maria thought that it was too risky for their family.

"What if it doesn't work at all? How would we live?" she said.

Eric relented and let it go for a month or so. However, it did stay in his mind. Finally, he said to Maria, "I know that you are right, but I have a suggestion. We don't have to start this right now. What would you say if we open a new bank account and save enough money so that in case this business is not successful in one year, we will have enough to live on?"

Still Maria was not sure, but when Eric mentioned that he would not have to travel that much anymore, she gave in. After a few years, it was time to start their own business.

CHAPTER 17

⳨

First, Eric had a meeting with the president and informed him of his plans. He had been not only his employer but also a good friend in all those years. Eric was afraid that his friend would be very upset. However, it turned out that he was very pleased with Eric's decision. He thought that this was a wise decision, and he wished Eric all the luck in his new venture.

"You have done an outstanding job for us. All is well organized, and I am sure that we can maintain it. I would like for you to do me one favor, however. I would like for you to be one of our board of directors. We need your experience."

Eric agreed. He had also contacted all the present agents, and fifty-one out of fifty-five accepted to be Eric's agent.

For many years, Eric and Maria became very successful in international trading. A large laboratory in Tokyo, Japan, contacted Eric to visit them on his next trip to Japan. The day of his arrival, he was invited to dinner. The evening went very well, and except for some personal information, no business was discussed. In Japan, there was very seldom a one-to-one meeting. All important meetings were group meetings, which would be held the next day. That evening, they drank a lot of sake, and Eric listened with pleasure to the Japanese language spoken all around him. One word, however, stuck in his mind: *ah sohdeska*, which sounded to Eric like *aso diska*. He didn't know what it meant, but it sounded nice.

The next morning was the big meeting. Sitting at a large table in a beautiful conference room on the fifth floor was the president and several of his top management personnel. They manufactured very high-precision measuring instruments and had contacted Eric to be their agent to cover the USA, Canada, and Mexico. This would be for Eric and Maria an additional division to their trading company. Eric had studied the market for these instruments and also his competition in his marketing area, so he was very informed about this for his new business. During the meeting, Eric was very surprised about their knowledge of the English language, but after three hours of discussions, they couldn't come to an agreement.

So Eric stood up and said, "I thank you, gentlemen, for this meeting and our pleasant dinner last night, but I think that this meeting is over. I will return to the USA tomorrow, if possible."

The president, who had studied in Germany, replied in German, "Mr. Oosterbeek, please let me speak with my people. Could you please leave us for a moment?"

Eric agreed and walked to one of the windows overlooking part of Tokyo. While they were talking back and forth in Japanese, Eric remembered the night before, and without thinking, he said, "Aso diska." It was the word he had heard several times. It was as if he had thrown a bomb on the conference table. He saw the shock on their normally very controlled faces.

"Oh! Oh, you speak Japanese?" one asked Eric.

Being a good salesperson, Eric answered "A little bit." He was invited back to the table and had an agreement in no time at all. Later, he discovered what he had said was "Ah sohdeska," which meant "Is that right?" Several years later, he and his very good Japanese friend would still laugh about this incident.

In the many years of traveling, Eric came to the conclusion that most people all over the world—even with different religions, habits, language, etc.—are kind. Whenever Eric needed help, there was always someone who would help him.

Someone had asked Eric, "What do you think is the most important thing to be successful in international business?"

Without hesitation, Eric answered, "A smile. If you are friendly to people, they are friendly to you. The only thing you never discuss is religion and politics. Also, you better study all available information about every country you want to visit, because small mistakes can make the difference between success and failure. Also, people are very pleased that you know about their way of living. For instance, in Japan, it is really offending if you sit with one leg over the other because you would show the bottom of your shoe, which is taboo. All floors in Japan are super clean, so you have to get used to constantly removing your shoes. They will always provide you with slippers. To be able to eat their food is a real advantage."

Upon his return from a long trip, Maria and the children couldn't wait for Eric to open his luggage because he always came home with presents and, for Maria, some fine jewelry.

CHAPTER 18

He loved the many places he visited. Each had its own beauty, but some stood out in his mind. He thought that for him, the two most beautiful cities in the world were Singapore and Prague.

Singapore had flower arrangements all over the city and gorgeous parks. It was a very exhausting trip (thirteen hours flying to Tokyo—three hours at the overfull Narita airport and then another six and a half hours from Tokyo to Singapore). Because of this, Eric would rest the next day after his arrival in his hotel.

One of the clerks told him that very close by was a very large and beautiful park. It was huge and full of flowers and waterfalls. He spent a few hours in the park, and on his way out, he noticed a young man who had a woven basket and was holding a snake about three to four feet long in each gloved hand.

Eric walked to him and asked, "Are you selling snakes?"

"No," he said. "I prepare and fry them for a very reasonable price."

Eric laughed and said, "Are these poisonous snakes?"

"Sure," he answered. "But the poison is in their mouth and not in the body. Can I prepare one for you?"

"Okay," Eric answered. "If other people can eat it, so can I."

"Here, hold each one right behind the head." Eric wasn't sure about that, but he did it anyway. When he had one in each hand, the man said, "Move your arms a little bit closer to you and higher." Eric did as told, but it scared him to death when the man took both tails of the snakes and guided them around Eric's neck. Eric was about to scream, but the man said, "Don't be scared. They cannot harm you as long as you hold on to the heads."

The snakes twisted around his neck. He felt very strange, but not uncomfortable. Quickly the man took a photo of Eric and his two snakes (which Eric would show around for many years afterward). After that, the man returned one snake to the basket and pushed the head of the other snake through a sharp nail on a wooden board. The snake died instantly. Then with a sharp knife, he opened and cleaned the snake, cut it into small pieces, and fried the pieces in a wok over a small gas burner. He used some butter and some black sauce and, after a few minutes, put it on a plastic plate and gave it to Eric. When Eric tasted the first pieces, he was very surprised. The taste was between chicken and fish—a little oily but good tasting.

The other most beautiful city for Eric was Prague in the Czech Republic. This city was full of art. There were statues all over, which were a pleasure for the eyes around each corner.

While he was in Russia, upon his agent's advice, Eric took a few days off and purchased a train ticket from Moscow to Omsk to Tomsk Irkutsk around the Baikal Lake to Vladivostok. It was a several days' ride, so Eric had purchased accommodation in a sleeper car. After a while, the scenery was very boring. Except for the cities, the only thing he saw were hundreds of miles of birch and pine trees. It was a stop train, and the last section had cars with practically no seats. To Eric's surprise and pleasure, the train stopped in nearly all small villages and picked up village people in all colors of dress with their goats, sheep, geese, and vegetables, going or coming from the villages to sell their wares. It was without saying the most beautiful part of the trip. Eric had seen so much of the world that he could entertain friends and neighbors for hours with his stories.

One of the worldwide marketing trips Eric would always remember was when he attended an international meeting organized in Damascus for manufactures to represent their technical product for the Arabian manufacturing industry. Eric received an invitation to attend.

A very high-class hotel with meeting rooms was reserved for the attendees. Everything was organized perfectly. Eric had provided previously to the community his flight plans and arrival time. When he arrived, the luggage department people with large signs showed several names and welcomed the arrivals and directed them to limousines to bring them to the hotel. On arrival, Eric noticed that this was the most luxurious hotel he had ever stayed in. The meeting was scheduled for the second day after his arrival. After a good night's sleep and breakfast, Eric left the hotel for a walk around the block.

This was a completely different world. All around the hotel were small merchants showing their wares while shouting, one louder than the next, for attention of the passersby. All kinds of products strange to Eric were shown. He loved their clothing, which were white or black, mostly long togas with small round hats or turbans.

The meeting was scheduled to start the next day at 10:00 a.m. in the very large meeting room. Before entering, everyone had to sign his or her name in and would receive a tag on a small chain showing his or her name and the company he or she represented. Several attendees were stationed behind the door to assist everyone to their seat on the very long meeting table. At one end of the room was a small podium with a microphone, where every representative would give a short speech about their products. The meeting was conducted in the English language, but earphones with translators were available to all seats for the translation of other languages. On the left side of Eric sat a person from Switzerland, and on his right was an Arabian person dressed in beautiful cream colors to go with an embroidered head gear. Eric guessed that he was around fifty-five to sixty years old. He introduced himself as Sheik Abdul (the rest Eric could not understand).

From the moment they introduced each other, there was an immediate bond between Eric and the sheik. Beside his Arabic, he also spoke very clear and understandable English. During the morning meeting, when there was a chance, they whispered questions and answers to each other. He seemed to be a highly respected person because when both walked together to the lunch facility, many peopled bowed to him.

At approximately 2:30 p.m., Eric was called to make his speech. He had prepared a sheet with items he would talk about and also the experience he had in international trading.

When Eric returned to his seat, the sheik shook his hand and said, "Well done, young man. Well done."

At the end of the afternoon, the sheik asked Eric if he had any plans for the evening.

"No, I do not," Eric replied.

"I would be honored if you would join me tonight at my home for dinner," the sheik answered. "I'll have my chauffer pick you up at this hotel at 7:00 p.m., if this is okay with you."

"I am very honored for your invitation," Eric said, and they parted.

Precisely at 7:00 p.m., the sheik's chauffer arrived at the hotel in a black stretch Mercedes and opened the door for Eric. It was a real luxurious car with soft beautiful seats and a fully stocked bar in the middle of. The driver was separated from his guest by a sliding glass window. After approximately a half-hour drive, the driver stopped in front of a huge magnificent mansion, a real Arabic mansion Eric had only seen in some movies. The cream color nearly matched the sheik's clothing.

The weather was beautiful, and the sheik was sitting in a chair on a pad leading through his gorgeous landscaped garden, waiting for Eric. They shook hands, and Eric tried to pronounce his surname, but the sheik interrupted him and said, "You have a problem pronouncing my name, and I yours. So if you do not mind, from now on you call me just Abdul, and I call you Eric. It will make it a lot easier to converse." Eric happily agreed.

Abdul walked Eric around the mansion because he noticed Eric's enthusiasm about this wonderful layout. On the right side and separate from the mansion was a long one-story building. In Eric's imagination, that would be the stable for many beautiful Arabic horses.

He asked Abdul, "Is that building for your horses?"

Abdul smiled. Without saying a word, he walked to the building and motioned to Eric to follow him. He pushed a button, and a very large door slid open. "These are my horses," he said with a smile on his face.

The sight took Eric's breath away. Inside this room was a line of the most beautiful and expensive automobiles Eric had ever seen—Ferraris, Mercedes, Cadillac, Lincoln, and many other brands, all shiny new and in different colors.

"This is my hobby," he said. "However, I have no driver's license. But I have several drivers who also take care of my 'babies.'"

Then Abdul showed Eric the inside of the mansion, which had many rooms, one more beautiful than the next. All over there were gilded or pure gold or silver items. The floor in the large hallway was shiny black marble beautifully engraved with the owner's family emblem and filled with gold.

Abdul guided Eric into one room, which was a fully stocked bar with a big pool table in the middle. While having a drink, Abdul was very down to earth and showed all this as very normal.

Eric asked him, "Has this beautiful mansion been in your family for ages?"

He answered, "Yes, but most of this comes from the earth." When Eric must have looked puzzled, he smiled and said, "Oil. My father and grandfather purchased large sections of land when oil was discovered under this land." Then he enquired about Eric's life. When Eric told him about all his travels worldwide, his interest was very high and couldn't stop asking about these countries Eric visited and his experiences there.

One member of his staff entered the room and informed them that dinner was served. The dining room was large with a very long, low oval table surrounded by many thick cushions. An older lady entered, and Abdul introduced her as his number-one wife. The driver informed me later that he had two wives but many ladies in his harem. The harem was in another section of the mansion and was closed off from visitors. Only male offspring of his number-one wife would inherit his title and investments. But if the number-one wife didn't give birth to a male child, the male child of the number-two wife would be in line for inheritance.

The lady that entered the room was very shy. She bent her head slightly and left after an elaborate dinner and a few after dinner drinks. Abdul's number-one son arrived and introduced himself as

Marrid (again the last name was hard to pronounce, like his father's). His father was kind and easy to be with, but Marrid seemed to be a hard and unkind person. Eric didn't like him, but he thought that he came here for business. It turned out that Marrid was interested to be an agent for Eric's products. Eric had only scheduled his trip for the meeting and would leave the next day. He promised to return after a month to introduce his product and pricing to Marrid and his sales personnel.

After Marrid left, Sheik Abdul and Eric had one more drink, and Abdul asked, "Eric, when you return next month, please arrange to stay a few days longer. By the way, since you haven't been in this country, besides the sales meeting, what would you like to see or do?"

Eric thought for a moment and said, "Abdul, it is maybe too much to ask, but would it be possible to visit a Bedouin tribe in the desert? I have read lots about them, but only saw them in movies."

"There is a tribe about half a day's ride by automobile. I've known the chieftain for many years, and I will have one of my drivers accompany you. He not only knows where they are located but also speaks their language."

After a real friend's handshake, Eric was driven back to the hotel. After returning to the United States, he immediately started making arrangements to return to Saudi Arabia. Approximately five weeks later, Eric returned. He had planned to stay a week—three days for the meeting and the remaining three days for the time Abdul had asked him and also to make a trip in the desert to stay with the Bedouins for one day and night.

The sales meeting was a disaster.

Eric had asked Marrid at their first meeting if he represented a competitive manufacturer to Eric products and Marrid answered, "No, we do not."

The meeting went well for two days. The sales personnel appeared to be very interested, and Eric thought that he had discovered a very good agent. However, on the third day, Eric made a trip to the toilet, but on his way of returning to the meeting, Eric opened the wrong door and entered a room separate from the room Eric was shown to that morning. This room was full of crates and boxes that were full of equipment from his competitor. Eric was very angry and disappointed. He immediately stopped the meeting and requested an answer from Marrid about his discovery.

But Marrid rudely said, "What is in that room is none of your business."

Eric immediately gathered all his sales information and asked to have someone give him a ride back to the hotel. With a very rude face and without a handshake, Marrid abruptly left the room. One of the salesmen drove Eric back to the hotel. The same evening, as arranged before, Eric was picked up from his hotel and driven to Abdul's mansion.

Abdul was very upset and apologized for his son's behavior. "Eric, I hope that this will not interfere with our friendship and that you are not going to cancel your trip to the Bedouins, which I have arranged for you."

"No," Eric answered, "it has nothing to do with our friendship, and I really look forward to meeting these dessert people."

The next day, at about noon, Eric was picked up at his hotel by a chauffeur named Arrad, who drove a covered Jeep with extra big ribbed tires. The dessert was different than Eric had imagined. It was not all sand, and large areas were covered with sharp rock the size of a child's head. It was not easy to drive over these rocks, and Eric was sure that his whole body would come apart. But soon they drove through beautiful dunes of sand, and now it was obvious why the Jeep had such strange tires. They drove until approximately 9:00 p.m.

Then the driver stopped and said, "Now we eat, rest, and sleep until tomorrow morning. I will wake you up."

By now, Eric noticed how hot the dessert was in the daytime and how really cold it was at night. He was shivering.

Arrad said, "We will build a fire and have some warm dinner. I brought some thick sleeping bags and will sleep beside the Jeep."

Arrad seemed to be very at home in the desert. In the back of the Jeep, he carried wood for the fire and cooking equipment for the dinner. In no time at all, Arrad had dinner ready; it consisted of mashed potatoes, goat meat, and a strange but good-tasting vegetable.

He also made some very strong coffee. When Eric took a big swallow, he nearly had to spit it out. It tasted like a poisonous thick black drink. Arrad, who was a quiet but nice man, laughed and said, "I guess you have to learn to drink Arabic coffee. You cannot drink it. You sip it."

Afterward, they crawled into their sleeping bag, which was nice and warm. Eric didn't wake up until he heard Arrad relieve himself early in the morning, using the whole dessert for his toilet. Around noontime, Arrad showed Eric a dark spot on the horizon.

He said, "Our destination."

The spot became larger and larger, and as they came closer, Eric saw people moving but also got a sniff of animal dung and humans. All at once, they were surrounded by people all in black clothing and riding on horses and camels. They guided Eric and Arrad through a row of tents to a huge tent in the middle of the tribe. A very large man, also in black elaborate clothing, was waiting and, after some greetings, opened the flap of his tent to welcome his guests into his domain.

The inside was more beautiful than Eric had expected. Large leather-covered pillows surrounded a low table. The whole floor was carpeted in beautiful rugs. Eric knew immediately that this was the chieftain's domain. For some time, Arrad and the chieftain spoke in Arabic to each other while hot tea was served. Eric knew immediately that they were conversing back and forth about him because the chieftain constantly looked in Eric's direction. The chieftain did not seem to like what he was hearing from Arrad because his face got somber and his voice sounded angry. Finally, when he got the chance, Arrad explained that the chief had not agreed that Eric would stay with them for a few days. However, when Arrad showed him all the gifts he carried in the back of the Jeep, the chief quickly changed his mind and welcomed Eric with a big smile on his face.

The chief showed Eric around the congregation that existed of approximately four hundred people, including women and children and huge herds of goats, horses, and camels. Nearly one half of their living area was surrounded by an oasis, which spread into the distance. The oasis was covered with palm trees and underbrush and had a large spring-fed pool. Arrad did a wonderful job translating to Eric all that the chief was explaining. Eric was amazed how these people lived completely isolated from the modern would without cars, computers, TVs, or any way of corresponding with the outside world. They lived happy lives.

Dinner was served outside by women whose faces were covered. The chieftain and his staff were seated separately but surrounded by the remaining people who were singing and laughing all through the meal. The chieftain had Eric seated on the right and Arrad on the left side of him. The food consisted of a mixture of goat meat and other ingredients, unfamiliar to Eric, in a large cast iron container. Also, a heap of bitter-tasting herb surrounded the pot. The chieftain showed Eric how to eat this thick nearly black and gluewy food. He took a small branch of the herb and, with three fingers of his right hand, scooped the mixture out of the container and guided it to his mouth. All his staff members and Eric and Arrad followed. It tasted strange, but Eric had tasted worse food in his worldwide travels.

After dinner, his staff members left, and the chieftain showed very high interest in Eric's travels that Arrad had told him of. Eric had to show him with a stick in the sand what the world looked like. In two large circles, Eric engraved the continents on one side and the other side of the world. The chieftain had a very inquisitive and sharp mind and asked a lot of questions for nearly two hours. By now, the chieftain really liked Eric because several times when bending forward to observe Eric's drawings, he put his right arm on Eric's shoulder.

Later in the evening, by the fire, he said something to Arrad that caused a chock on Arrad's face. The chieftain indicated to Arrad to translate to Eric. Arrad, now very nervous, explained that the chieftain told him that because of his great friendship, he would give one of his wives to Eric for the night.

"Before you answer," said Arrad, "think carefully, because this is the greatest gift he'd ever given that I know of, and he will not accept a negative answer."

The chieftain called one of his staff and whispered something in his ear. The man looked surprised but left and returned with six ladies. Not only were they unattractive but also had a smell that disagreed with Eric's senses. Eric had noticed that at some time during his stay, the whole congregation had laid down their prayer mat and, sitting on their knees bending over, had prayed to Allah.

This gave Eric and idea. He told Arrad, "Please translate to the chieftain exactly what I am going to tell you. I noticed today that his people are very religious, which I highly appreciate. I am also a very religious man, but in my religion, a man can only have one wife. It would be very sinful to have another woman. Please tell him"

Arrad very nervously explained to the chieftain what Eric had told him. At first, the chieftain showed a mixture of disbelief and anger, but then he slowly stood up and, in a loud voice, told his people Eric's answer and that he was extremely happy to have met such a highly religious man who could and would not accept his offer. A lot of them cheered, but maybe not the six ladies, who put their veils back over their—Eric thought—sad faces. Eric would not sleep much that night because of all the noise of the animals and babies crying around him.

The next morning, the chieftain asked Eric if he had ever ridden a camel. When Eric said no, he answered, "Okay, let us teach you." At first, Eric felt very comfortable on top of the camel. He noticed, however, that the gait of a camel was different from that of a horse. A horse walked by moving the opposite front and back leg at the same time, but the camel used both legs on one side and then both legs on the other side at the same time. Everything went well while walking, but then one of the men hit the camel with his stick. The camel jumped forward and ran as fast as he could, Eric holding on for his life. In about a half mile, because of the strange motion, Eric's stomach gave way, to the laughter of the other riders. They quickly stopped the camel. Eric slid off the beast and walked back.

Later that afternoon, they said goodbye to Eric's new friends and jumped in the Jeep to return home. The chieftain gave Eric a good hug and told him that he was always welcome. When they left, the men, with both arms in the air shouted, some kind of farewell, while the women, standing on top of a dune, gave a high-pitch wailing sound that Eric could hear for quite some time.

Arriving at Abdul's mansion, Eric had to tell about his experience. When he finished, Abdul asked him, "Did you really enjoy that?"

"I enjoyed quite a lot. This is an experience I will never forget."

The next day, Eric continued his trip to Calcutta, India, for a meeting with his agent.

Abdul and Eric stayed in contact for nearly a year. The correspondence slowly faded until Eric did not receive any answer to his last letter.

In early January 1987, Eric was visiting his agent in St. Louis, Missouri. The meeting with the sales personnel was interrupted by the president, who informed him that his wife was on the telephone with an emergency message.

Eric went to his office to answer. "Hi, Maria. What's up?"

"Paul, your brother just called," she answered. "He said that your mother is in the hospital and could die within a few days. If you want to see her alive, then you better stop the meeting and see if you can get a flight from where you are to Holland. If so, then inform Paul of your arrival so he can pick you up."

"Okay," Eric answered. "As soon as I make the arrangements, I will give you a call back." And he hung up.

The president immediately told his secretary to make the first possible arrangement for Eric's flight to Holland. She got him on a flight that would leave in two hours to New York and then an overnight flight to Amsterdam. She also told Eric that within an hour after his arrival, there was a small airplane available from Amsterdam to a city close to Paul's home, which would arrive there in one and a half hours.

"Okay," Eric said. "Please make the reservation."

Eric had enough clothing in his luggage because he had planned to work with the agent's sales personnel for a few days before he left St. Louis. He contacted Paul and informed him of his time of arrival. During the drive from this small airport to the hospital, Paul informed him that Martha, already for a long time had trouble with diabetes and was having kidney problems. Finally, her kidneys were shutting down. She had asked the other three children not to inform

Eric. She said that this would only cause unnecessary worry; her son could not do anything about it anyhow.

Arriving at the hospital, they immediately went to Martha's room. Surprisingly to Eric, she seemed very awake and was surprised that Eric was there. They hugged each other for quite some time.

Then Martha said, "I am very happy that you came all the way from the United States to visit me, but it really wasn't necessary. I will only be a couple of days in this hospital."

Eric and Paul were with her until late afternoon. Naturally, Martha wanted to know everything about his whole family. John, Eric's father, and Johan and Elly arrived. After some hugging, Eric and Paul left for some dinner. Johan promised them that if anything happened, he or Elly would call Paul immediately. After hugging his mother and promising to return the next morning, they left. John had been staying with Elly the last few days, and it was as if he could not accept what was happening. After a small dinner, Eric went with Paul to his place.

"I do not understand what is going on," Eric said. "You have me come here all the way in a rush, and it seems to me that mother is not dying at all."

"I was quite surprised myself how she was today compared to yesterday. Maybe your visit gave her some extra boost. However, the doctor told us that her body was shutting down and her death will be inevitable in a few days."

Eric was tired and went early to bed. At two o'clock the next morning, Paul woke him up with tears in his eyes and told Eric that Elly had called and that their mother had died. Immediately, they dressed and drove to Elly's home. Johan and Paul went to the hospital, but Eric and Elly stayed home. Eric knew that if he visited his mother now, he would always remember her death face instead of her kind and smiling face that he was used to.

His father was sitting beside the kitchen stove, having a cup of coffee. He was talking as if nothing had happened, and Eric knew that the loss of Martha was too much for him to bear. Even at the funeral, he acted as if this funeral was not for the person he had loved so much for such a long time. Eric stayed for one more week and, during that time, talked a lot with his father about the good old times. But most of the time, his father's brain drifted away. When Eric left, he knew that it would be the last time he would see his father alive. All the way home, it was a very sad flight for Eric.

He was right. John died in August 1988. He had slowly faded away. Eric went to the funeral. Sitting there, he thanked them both for being his beloved parents and for the most wonderful and loving time he had spent with them. All that he was had come from them, and he would never forget them.

The oak tree had lost two of its most beautiful branches.

For several years, Eric had gone deer hunting with two of his neighbors. One of the neighbors has an old friend who owned a small cottage and forty acres of woods located on one of the many lakes, about a three-hour drive north of Minneapolis.

The three were the only ones allowed to hunt on this property. For several years, they shot many deer in these virgin woods. Eric had purchased some books on butchering and smoking venison (deer meat). Mixing some ground venison with pork made delicious hamburgers and breakfast and summer sausage when smoked. He also cut steaks and chops from the remaining venison. Every year, they gave some venison to the old owner and his wife, which they greatly appreciated. Eric liked the old man, and the two had many conversations together—sitting by a campfire, drinking beer. On one of the evenings, the old man asked Eric if in the future he would like to purchase these woods, which was actually a separate property from the cottage.

Eric answered, "Yes, I would, but it all depends on when and at what price."

The old man laughed and said, "I will contact you whenever I plan to sell, and I promise to make you a good deal."

Two years later, Eric got a call from the old man, wanting to know if he still wanted the woods. It was at a low price, and after discussing the woods as an investment with Maria, they purchased them. Now, they were owners of woods, which were nearly as large as the centrum of the village Eric grew up in.

Eric purchased an older house trailer that was in very good condition. The trailer owner not only delivered it with a large tractor to the location, but also gave Eric a large wooden deck—the full length of the trailer.

In the following two years, Eric had electric power installed and a well drilled for water. The trailer became another home for him. Besides hunting, Eric would spend some weekends in the woods, just to relax from his sometime exhausting business. Maria went with Eric to the woods only one weekend, but she was not an outdoor person and did not enjoy the wild woods the way Eric did. However, she did not mind at all for Eric to trample the peaceful woods and listen to the sound of the wild life, while sitting on an old tree stump. Eric figured out many big business deals in the woods because he could think and concentrate without any interruptions.

Eric had spent a couple of weekends "up north," as he called his property in the woods, because Maria had gone home to Holland for a month. They could not go together because of their business. During that time, Eric had sold a large special measuring instrument to a company in Atlanta, Georgia. A technician from the Japanese manufacturer also flew to Atlanta, where Eric met him, to install the large instrument. The following day, after arriving in Atlanta, Eric got a pain in his left cheek, which became worse as the day went on. He could not sleep that night, so the following day, he went to a medical clinic close by. The doctor informed him that he had a very bad sinus infection and prescribed him some medicine. The company arranged a flight back to Minneapolis the next day, which was Friday. On Saturday, the pain was not as intense as it had been, and Eric thought it must have been a sinus infection like the doctor said. However, on Sunday morning, while drinking a cup of coffee, he suddenly felt a strange sensation in his entire face, and the coffee ran down his chin and all over his shirt. He had lost all muscle control in his face. He could not move his lips to talk anymore; he just made strange sounds. When he looked in the mirror, he saw a very strange face. At that time, his daughter, Michelle, arrived at the house because they were supposed to go to brunch together. As soon as Eric opened the door, she immediately knew that something was wrong and said, "Dad? What happened?"

He struggled to answer her, saying, "Stroke."

Michelle wanted to call an ambulance, but Eric shook his head *no* and walked to her car in the driveway. Michelle drove him to the emergency room of the hospital close by his house. After a lot of testing and an MRI, the doctors concluded that it was not a stroke, but he had some kind of an infection. Eric had to stay in the hospital for several days, while they gave him large amounts of different antibiotics. The hospital had sent blood samples to a laboratory, and they figured out he had "Lyme disease." Eric must have been bitten by a wood tic (a small bug that carries the Lyme disease) while he was up north at the woods. Eric was released from the hospital, but for two weeks, he had to return to the hospital every day to get antibiotic injections. His face was still somewhat paralyzed, and one big problem was his eyes, he could not close his eyelids. He had to use eye drops consistently. His eyes got infected, and he had to use special ointment and kept his eyes closed with Band-Aids at night and during the day; because of that, he could hardly watch television or read anything.

His face muscles were still not normal, and eating was difficult. His cheeks had no muscle strength yet, so everything he chewed would go between his teeth and cheeks. He had to hold his lips closed with one hand, and with the other hand, push each individual cheek. Eric sent an e-mail to all his customers, explaining what had happened and that he could not answer the phone and would return their requests or concerns by e-mail.

Since this infection was not life-threatening, Eric had not notified Maria in Holland. He thought, *Let her have a nice vacation. She can't help me get better anyway.* After another week, his voice slowly returned, but when he met Maria at the Minneapolis airport, she immediately asked him if he had a dental appointment that morning. She said he was talking very strangely. Eric laughed, and between him and Michelle, they informed her of what had happened over the last few weeks. Maria was very angry at first but calmed down when

Eric explained, "I knew that you would return immediately, but you really could not have done anything to help."

A month later it was all history again. This event forever changed Eric's feelings about his woods. It was not the same anymore, and he did not visit the woods any longer, except for hunting.

CHAPTER 19

✠

One day, Eric and Maria went to a bookstore to pick up a book Maria had ordered. While she was waiting in line by the cashier, Eric walked through the store. One large table was filled with books for sale. He picked up a book titled *All You Want to Know about Pottery*. It was full of beautiful pictures and step-by-step instructions of how to make pottery. Eric purchased it, and while reading at home, he thought that this could be something for him.

After studying the book, the first thing was to find a potter in his neighborhood. There was one listed in the telephone book, but when Eric visited him, he came to the conclusion that he was not a real potter because he would purchase already made and first fired pottery. But he had an old wheel and some clay and asked Eric to practice. However hard Eric tried, the small bowls he made were not concentric. One side was always thicker than the other.

One day, while having his hair cut, he complained to the barber that he tried so hard but was not successful in pottery.

"Eric, that man who just passed you in the hallway is a well-known master potter," the barber told him. When Eric ran outside, the person had driven away already. The barber told him, "He doesn't advertise in the telephone book, but he paid by check, so I have his name and address. Here, his name is Doug Brennen."

The next day, Eric drove to this address, which was only a ten-minute drive. When he parked his car on the driveway, he saw a man waving at him behind the window on the bottom of his two-story home. He waved Eric to walk to the back of his house. Eric walked to the back and down a stairway and shook hands with Doug.

"What can I do for you?" Doug asked. "Do you want to buy some pottery?"

"No, no," Eric answered. "I was told that you are a world-famous potter. I would like to have some lessons."

Doug laughed and said, "Come in, and tell me what you know about pottery."

Eric told him the whole story, from purchasing the book to the first eccentric pottery. Doug's studio was filled from wall to wall with hundreds of gray pottery. Eric could not believe his eyes, seeing so much beauty all around him.

"Are they all finished?" Eric asked.

"You are right," Doug answered. "You don't know much about pottery. After I make them, they are still wet, so they have to dry for a few days. Those are the ones you see here. Then they go into the kiln for the first time for what is called bisque firing. After bisque firing, they are glazed with the color you want and again are fired at very high temperature in our big gas fire kiln in that small building in the backyard. But more of that later. First, show me what you can do before we go any further."

Doug had four electric-controlled potter wheels, all speed-controlled with a foot pedal on the floor.

"Take a chair behind this wheel," he said.

When Eric sat down, Doug put an old shirt over him and said, "You need to put some old clothes on. In the beginning, you will be covered with clay." Without saying another word, he made a ball of soft clay about five inches in diameter and threw it approximately in the middle of the wheel.

Eric pushed down the speed controller, and the wheel turned slowly. He tried with his two hands to center the clay ball on the wheel, but to no avail. "You see?" he told Doug. "I just cannot do it."

"No one can center that ball with this speed. Push your damn foot down to higher speed."

Eric did, and within a few seconds, the ball centered itself.

"Now," Doug continued, "wet your left hand and hold it softly against the ball on the left side. Now put your right-hand thumb on the top in the middle so that the thumb does not move. That is the center. Now slowly push your thumb down into the clay as far as you can. Now push your thumb slowly outward. There is the beginning of your first bowl."

Eric could not believe what he had just done. Eric stayed with Doug for over two hours and told Doug how much he wanted to learn. He also told him that he traveled all over the world but that he needed a hobby in his spare time to relax.

"How much do you charge per hour if you want to teach me?"

"I'll tell you what. You can come here as much as you want. I will not charge you a penny, as long as you tell me the stories of all your travels."

Eric's first bowl, which had a beautiful twisted handle, he made for Maria. It was glazed white with blue painted tulips on it. She was very pleased, and she cherished this bowl for the rest of her life. In no time, Eric made some beautiful pottery, and Doug, who was very surprised, told Eric that he had a natural feeling because no one that he knew could learn that fast. They stayed friends for many years, and Eric made a lot of pottery.

CHAPTER 20

†

Eric and Maria worked hard for several years and, during this time, took several vacation trips to Holland. However, because of the business, both could not travel together. Eric would visit his lifelong mentor, the oak tree, which had grown into a tree with the bottom branches nearly two feet wide. Johan and Eric had long forgotten their animosity for each other while they were children and had come a lot closer together over the years. Both, Johan and Paul had studied languages and were teachers at individual colleges. Elly had married a young engineer. All three had their own families now and it was a real pleasure when all four got together when Eric visited Holland. John and Martha had been very proud of their children's accomplishment. When John walked with Eric through the village, he would proudly say to some of the people "This is my son from America."

On one of Maria's trips, she noticed some pain in her left breast. After returning home, she made an appointment with her longtime physician. He checked her out and told her that it was only nerves. She trusted him, and for over one year, he kept on telling her that it was only nerves. Eric, who was very upset with her because he didn't believe this doctor, told her several times to visit another doctor. When one of the neighbor ladies who was Maria's closest friend agreed with Eric, she finally made an appointment with another doctor. When this doctor checked her out and took some biopsies, he informed her that she had breast cancer but that it was very likely that he did not have to remove the left breast. Two weeks later, she had the cancer removed, and after a few days in the hospital, she returned home.

However, this was only the beginning of worse things to come.

After this operation, she had to take chemotherapy for several months. Every time, Eric would bring her to the hospital and would sit with her through the whole process. She was very tired after each visit, and most of the time, she would have an upset stomach. She bore all this like a trooper and seldom complained, but when her beautiful gray hair started to fall out, she lost it and cried. By bunches, the hair came out. Eric felt very sorry for her and tried to help her as much as possible.

He did not travel at all during this time. Their business just had to wait. Maria would wear a shawl, but on her last visit, a nurse told her that they had several wigs available in another part of the hospital. First, Maria didn't want to hear of it, but at Eric's persistence, she finally decided jut to take a look at them. One of the many wigs they had available had the same gray color and was very nicely curled as her actual hair had been. She liked it, and Eric made her smile when he told her that she looked even better than before.

That same night, Eric took her for dinner at a first-class dining place, and for the first time in a long time, she felt very good. It was a successful evening. She knew that her hair would grow back, so for now, this wig was okay. It made her very happy when one lady she had not seen for a long time greeted Maria with "Hi, girl. How are you? You have a new hairdo. It really looks good on you."

It seemed like his oak tree was losing some more of its large branches again, because within two years, an even worse calamity happened.

On Sunday mornings, Maria and Eric would read for a few hours. The house was quiet, and both enjoyed that very much. Everything was good. The cure for the cancer had been successful. Their son, Steven, was in the air force as an airplane mechanic and had married a nice girl in Rhode Island, close to the base. Nicole was now also married and had two children (the joy in Maria and Eric's life); she and her children had moved to California. To Eric and Maria, this was a setback. Their youngest child, Michelle, who was still single, had moved into an apartment but was within minutes' drive from her parents' home.

On one Sunday morning, while they were reading, Maria told Eric, "There is something wrong with my eyes. I see black spots in front of me."

Eric, a little concerned, answered, "It could be your eyes. When did you have them checked lately? Remember, we are both now in our seventies, and things can go wrong like an old car engine. Let's make an appointment with an eye doctor tomorrow."

They visited an optometrist, and after a careful examination, the doctor informed her that it was not the eyes that was wrong with her. There could be something wrong with her blood. This doctor called a hospital close by and set up an appointment for the next day. In the hospital, after a blood check and a very painful bone marrow extraction, they were informed that Maria had leukemia. Upon hearing this, Maria made a horrible scream because she knew that this could be a death sentence.

Eric, who sat beside her on the bed, had never heard her scream like that and was really shocked. He did not know that leukemia was a form of cancer, so he said to Maria, "Honey, we went through a lot together in our life. We will get through this one also." When Eric was alone with the specialist, he informed him that this was cancer and a very serious one.

"To start, I will prescribe some pills, and she has to come to our laboratory for a blood check every two weeks, more times in the future."

"What do you mean in the future? Is it that dangerous?"

"Mister Oosterbeek, I will be straightforward. Your wife has only a few years left, at the most five years."

Upon hearing this, Eric had to hold on to the doctor because he nearly fainted and his knees went very lame. Eric took Maria for a two-week vacation to Holland. It was not the same as previous trips, because Maria knew that she was dying and that this would be the last trip to Holland and the last time that she would see many of her siblings.

One day, about a year into Maria's illness, she went shopping. (She still could and wanted to do things by herself.) Eric just came home after making pottery all morning at his by-now best friend,

Doug Brennen, the master potter. As soon as he came inside the door, he heard the telephone ringing.

When he picked up, Steven's wife said just like that, "Eric, Steven is dead. He killed himself last night."

Eric had to sit down. He first thought that this was a joke, but then no one would make a joke like that. After a long time of stillness, Eric finally got his voice back.

He asked, "What happened?"

She answered, "He was working on his car in the garage, which was normal and into the late hours. This morning, I noticed that he had not come to bed, and I went to the garage to find him. There he was, lying on the floor, dead with his pistol beside him."

When Maria came home, Eric told her to sit down because something terrible had happened. When he finally told her, she said nothing for quite some time and then started crying first very softly and then started to shake so hard that Eric had to hold her to keep her from falling down.

She kept on saying, "Not Steven, not my boy."

His ashes were sent to them because his wife thought that he should go home. She never went to the funeral, but nearly the whole male chorus Eric still belonged to came and made this parting special.

After this, Eric and Maria were never the same. For Eric, a large branch had broken on his inner tree, but for Maria, it was the end. For one more year, she suffered the agonizing pains in her bones of the increasing leukemia, and now she had to have blood transfusion nearly every third day. Eric took care of her for everything she needed. She slowly faded away. About two weeks before Christmas 2009, her oncologist told her that he could do no more and that her end was near.

"Is there anything I can do for you?" he asked her.

Maria answered, "Can you keep me alive until after Christmas? I still would like to make Christmas dinner for my family."

This dinner had always been her special dinner of the year. The dining room table, which was seldom used, would be filled not only with her best food but also with all the silver bowls and all the silverware she had kept in a beautiful wooden box, which was her pride and joy. After dinner, Eric warmed up the car and, with a heavy blanket around her, drove her through the neighborhood, watching all the Christmas lights. They spent New Year's Eve together, but by now, Maria was very weak. Eric had ordered a hospital bed, which he put in the living room, so she could watch the outside through the large windows.

The last she said to Eric, when she woke up from her coma, which by now had become constant, was a very weak "Eric, I see beautiful orange flowers outside."

There was only snow, so Eric answered, "Honey, Steven did that. He is making a path for you to him."

She smiled and went into a deep coma. For two days, Eric sat beside her, holding her hand. He thought about all the fifty-three years they had spent together. He knew that he would miss her thoroughly.

On Friday, January 8, 2010, at approximately 5:00 p.m., Eric watched her take her last breath. His nearly lifelong love and companion was gone.

CHAPTER 21

☩

For several years after Maria's death, Eric operated the business by himself. He was amazed how much Maria had been involved with the company. Even after all that time, international letters and by now the more popular e-mails were still addressed to her. He cut back on the international trading but kept the sales and repair of the instruments from Japan.

Some years later, Eric still was very lonely. On a Sunday afternoon, he sat in his big chair overlooking the lake. It was dark and had been raining already for two days.

He thought, *Will I sit here in this beautiful big house all by myself?*

He stayed in contact with Michelle, but it was not the same.

He looked at Maria's picture and said, "Honey, I miss you. Is there something you can do for me?"

It was as if his request was answered. A few minutes later, the doorbell rang, and one of his best friends from the choir walked in. Eric told him how lonely he was, and his friend suggested that it was about time to meet a lady companion.

"You don't have to get serious. It's just to have one to take for dinner sometime. Eric was not at all interested, but he slowly changed his mind when his friend carried on.

His friend asked, "What can be worse than sitting here by yourself every day?"

"Yes, I think that you are right, but how do you think I will meet a lady friend? You think that I walk down the street, carrying a big sign above my head, saying, 'I want to meet a lady'?"

His friend laughed and answered, "Eric, you are still living in the past. Already for several years, there are organizations on television for people to meet. Let's go on your computer, and I'll show you. There are many of them, so you can choose the one you think could help you."

They found one that was specially dedicated to elderly people. Eric signed on, and the next day, to his surprise, he received 4 pages (a total of 166) of inquiries. He quickly looked through them and decided to answer ten ladies in the range of his age. He finally decided on three ladies and, after some time of conversing, took each one individually for lunch. The information on the computer only showed a picture of the head of each person. All three showed a very friendly face.

The first one, Eric met at her home to take her for lunch. She was unbelievably wide in the hips. The second was very slim, nearly skinny. She owned three companies, and her mind was obsessed with them. The third was very beautiful, Mexican descent, but Eric had never seen so many black decayed teeth in one mouth. It was a real disappointment for him, so he decided to cancel his agreement the following Monday.

However, on the Sunday prior to his cancellation, he looked once more at a new list of ladies. Then he noticed one very friendly-faced lady, and Eric took one more chance of finding a companion. After a week of conversing, they met in person. They both liked and enjoyed each other.

Her name was Jane Decker. Eric had finally found a companion. She had a beautiful home, and her husband had died a long time ago. Also, like Eric's son, Steven, her son had taken his life. Right from the beginning, there was a bond between the two. Eric lost his loneliness, and his sun began to shine again.

But his tree was not finished with him yet. At the start of March 2016, Eric felt a strange feeling in the back of his throat. He first thought that a fishbone was embedded there because he had eaten some fish a week before. He went to the clinic, but his doctor could not find anything wrong. They decided, that if Eric still felt the same after two weeks, he should see a specialist. Nothing changed, so Eric visited this nose-and-throat specialist. Eric sat in a sort of barber's chair, and the doctor found a small spot at the back of his throat and took a biopsy two days later. After four days, he informed Eric with the very good news that it was not cancerous. Eric was so happy with this news that he invited his lady friend for a long weekend to San Francisco.

The doctor set up an appointment for two weeks later to check the healing of the biopsies. "Everything looks okay," he said. "It was nicely healed."

"That can't be so," Eric answered. "I still have the same feeling. You took a biopsy on the back, but to me it feels like it's in the middle, more to the right side of my tongue."

The doctor looked quite annoyed. "Okay, lean back in the chair, and I will look again." After a thorough investigation, he said, "Yes, you are right. There is a small spot. I missed last time. I am very sorry, but we have to take another biopsy."

Three days later, he informed Eric that it was cancer but that it was too small for an operation. Eric also didn't need chemo treatment, but they could treat it with laser. From a special plastic screen, they made a mask of his face and shoulder, which would keep his head when tied down in the same position for every treatment. The oncologist informed him that he would have thirty-five laser treatments.

"Why so many?" Eric asked.

"Because around the small area we will be bombarding with the laser, you have your teeth, saliva glands, taste buds, etc. So we cannot use the full laser."

"Will it be very painful?" Eric asked.

"Well, I will give it to you straight. The first half of the treatment, you will not feel it, but after that, the pain will start and will increase as we go along. By about the twenty-fifth, it will be so painful that you will not be able to swallow your normal food and will have to drink only liquid food that you can purchase at any pharmacy. You will have to drink five small bottles of it a day to keep up with your nutrition and vitamins."

In the hospital, Eric lay down on a moving bed, with his head secured under the plastic mold. When he was moved into position, the huge machine started humming, and the top part started to turn over Eric's head. After a few seconds, the humming became very loud, and Eric knew that the laser was turned on. This lasted for a few seconds, and then it was switched off. The whole procedure lasted only thirty seconds. But he would have to go through with this five days a week for seven weeks.

As the doctor had mentioned, by about the twentieth week, the pain started. By the twenty-fifth week, he could only swallow liquid food. The doctor informed him that many of his patients with a similar condition by now could not bear this excruciating pain any longer and had a feeding tube installed in their stomach, but Eric thought that as long as he still could swallow his saliva, however very painful, he could swallow the liquid food. The last two laser sessions were the worst. The laser was burning on top of already burned and raw flesh at the end.

After the last treatment, it took another two weeks before he finally could eat some soft food again. But it had no taste because his taste buds had suffered a lot. Nothing tasted good or not at all. It took more than a year before his sense of taste came back, but it was never the same. He also lost most of his saliva glands, which never returned. Eric had to carry water or mouth spray with him all the time. With the laser treatment and over one year of having no appetite for food, he lost nearly sixty pounds of his body weight. Slowly his weight increased, but he enjoyed being slim now. He kept this increase to a minimum.

For a few years, everything was back to normal, or so he thought. His reduced business was doing well, and he had been very lucky with the cancer on his tongue. He still missed Maria, and too late he discovered how busy she must have been. All through the years of their business, besides taking care of the children, all the cooking, cleaning and washing clothes, she had handled the office part perfectly all at the same time. Now he had to do most of this by himself.

Every two years, he would take a vacation to Holland, and also every two years in between, he would travel to Japan for business and some vacation. He would always visit the oak tree. Several branches had broken off, but still it stood there as the king of the woods. Every time he visited, he remembered the happy times but also the sorrows he had from the time of their first meeting.

CHAPTER 22

✠

In the year 2000, Eric was asked and accepted the honor of being the first overseer position of protector for his village, Shooters Gild. In the southern part of Holland, Germany and Belgium there were hundreds of similar gilds.

These Shooters Gilds went back for many centuries and originated when a few young men got permission from the local authorities to carry rifles to protect their village churches during the night hours from stealing and rampages. There were no streetlights, and people in general were poor. Wintertime was the worst, because most young men could find no available jobs during that time period and would steal anything they could get their hands on. Eventually, they formed gilds and would have shooting contests with neighboring gilds to determine who were the best riflemen. They formed organized groups with drum and flute corps and beautiful uniforms and marched through the village on special occasions. The leaders of each group consisted of a tambour major, commander, several officers, and even a general, all dressed accordingly.

Every gild was named after a saint. Eric's village gild was named St. Bernard. The whole summer and fall, large groups of gilds marched together for special activities and to win prizes for shooting, marching, and the most beautiful king and queen. On one Sunday in fall, on St. Bernard's Day, a king was crowned. The days before this outing, a large bird, approximately two feet by one foot, was cut out of a piece of very old and hard wood. A slim tree about fifty feet high with branches removed was installed in a special meadow reserved for this outing. The bird was tied down on a steel pin on top of this pole.

Each member would shoot at that bird with a specially made, very heavy single-shot gun. The bore and bullets (from lead) were of approximately one inch in diameter, and each member had his turn. The person who shot the last piece off the bird would be the new king. If he had a wife or girlfriend, they would be queen for the year. Three ladies, each with a flower in their hands, would be standing by in case the new king had no wife or girlfriend. The first lady who could tie her flower onto his jacked would be the new queen.

After Eric accepted his title of protector, which was a high position in the gild, he made his visits to his village during this time to witness this event. He was honored by the whole gild. The title of protector was to assist the gild wherever possible in case of financial or other problems.

CHAPTER 23

᛭

Only one year after his cancer episode, Eric developed another major problem—his heart. In October 2017, while in Japan, he developed some pain in his chest while walking from a train station to his motel with one of the Japanese sales managers. Not to get him worried, Eric asked him if they could stop for a moment because his left hip was giving him problems. After a few minutes, the pain subsided, and they continued to the motel. Eric did not think that it was serious and soon forgot all about it. But when walking from the airplane to the luggage department upon arrival back in Minneapolis, he again got a similar pain and had to rest in a chair for a few minutes until the pain had subsided again. He arrived on a Friday and made a doctor's appointment for the following Monday.

After listening to Eric heart, the doctor said, "Eric, have you ever had a stress test?"

"No," Eric answered. "I've had no trouble with my heart. Why should I?"

"Well, at your age, I think it is best that you have one. I will make an appointment for you next week."

Eric thought that he would be back from taking this test in about an hour, so he didn't lock the front door. The stress test consisted of walking at a good speed on an inclined conveyor belt while having sensors all over his chest, connected to a computer and monitored by a nurse. About halfway through the test, the nurse stopped the conveyor belt and told Eric to take a seat.

"I have to see the doctor," she said. "I will be back in a moment."

Eric was still out of breath when the doctor entered the room and said, "I am sorry, Mr. Oosterbeek. Your heart is in bad shape. You must have noticed that."

"No," Eric replied. "Except for the pain in my chest a week ago during my trip to Japan, I haven't noticed anything. However, whenever I went for a walk, I noticed that I had to stop several times, but I blamed it on my age."

"We will take an X-ray of your heart so we can determine the damage."

After studying the X-rays, the doctor informed him that he had a blockage in four arteries ranging from 60–80 percent. He would have to stay in the hospital for some more tests and to prepare for his operation the next morning. Eric immediately called his daughter, Michelle, and Jane.

The next morning, the heart surgeon came into his room and said, "We first considered to install some 'stints' to open up these arteries, but after a more in-depth look, my assistant and I came to the conclusion that the arteries were in such bad shape that we decided to do open-heart surgery to bypass those blockages. Before we do that, however, we need you to sign this permission, because this is a major operation."

Eric was now very concerned, but he finally said, "If it has to be done, do it." And he signed.

The next day, about 1:00 p.m., they took Eric into the operating room.

One doctor sat on the right side, and the one standing on the left side leaned over and said, "Are you okay? We will start shortly."

It sounded to Eric that the doctor's voice came from a far distance, but he answered, "I am fine. Just keep me alive."

The next thing Eric remembered was that he woke up in a room with a nurse telling him, "It is about time that you wake up. I was getting worried. The operation went very well, but the doctor will see you tomorrow morning to give you more of the details."

An hour later, Michelle and Jane came into the room. Both were very concerned and wanted to know how he was doing.

"I am fine at the present. I have no pain," he said and showed the big piece of tape over the length of his entire breastbone.

"We were so worried," Jane said. "During the whole operation, we were sitting in the waiting room downstairs, waiting for the news."

Eric smiled and answered, "Yes, I am glad it is over, and I am still alive."

He must have closed his eyes because he heard Jane say, "Let's go, Michelle. He needs his sleep now."

Eric didn't sleep too much because every three to four hours, a nurse would take his vital signs and give him some pills. At 9:00 a.m., the surgeon came into his room and explained to Eric the details of the operation.

"When we opened up your chest, we immediately discovered that your arteries were in a very bad shape. In all my thirty years of heart operation, I've never seen a heart with such bad arteries and the person still walking around and even shoveling snow, as you told me. For a moment, my assistant and I were not sure if we should continue or just close your chest again. We even took close pictures to send to the university. It was very dangerous, but we decided that the only chance you had to stay alive was for us to continue."

They had taken a vein out of his left leg (a kind of spare vein), which they then divided into pieces and bypassed all the obstruction of the four arteries.

"Actually, it went better than we had expected. You are one very lucky man," the surgeon concluded.

"Thank you very much," Eric answered. "I guess that you heard me just before the operation when I had said, 'Just keep me alive.' How many stitches did you use to close my breastbone together?"

The surgeon smiled and answered, "We don't use stiches anymore. Now we close the chest with glue, a kind of superglue."

After the surgeon left, Eric thought about all the close encounters with death he'd had in his life. *I guess this is not my time yet.* Maybe he was like his oak tree. Its branches had come off, even big ones, but it still survived.

From the first day after the operation to the hearth, he had to walk with the assistance of a nurse one hallway at the time, and on the fourth, he walked slowly around his whole floor. On the fifth day, after a doctor's visit, he was allowed to go home. After a few months of taking it easy, he was back to his full capacity again.

However, he was not finished yet. After approximately six months, Eric woke up one night, perspiring heavily. It seemed that it had not subsided. He went back to the hospital, and there they discovered that his heart was fibrillating. The top half was not in sync with the bottom half. The doctors decided that Eric should have a pacemaker. It was only a small operation, and Eric could return home the same day.

CHAPTER 24

After three years of health problems, Eric felt strong enough to travel to Holland for a well-earned vacation. The day after his arrival at his brother Paul's, he went for a walk to the woods to visit the oak tree. Coming closer, he noticed that something was wrong. In the area where the oak tree was supposed to be was an apartment building.

This couldn't be. He must be in the wrong area!

After some checking, Eric came to the conclusion that his several-centuries-old pal and mentor had been removed by a building that would last not more than fifty years. Eric was heartbroken. For several days, Eric visited the area where his tree had been a part of his life. The tree had been there while Eric was overwhelmed with sadness but also celebrated with him the happy moments in his life.

To reduce his sadness, Eric purchased a very young oak tree, and walking far into the woods, he planted it in an open spot. "I hope that you grow big and strong and have a long life, and maybe sometime in the distant future, you will be the mentor to a person who needs you in desperation like I did."

The End

ABOUT THE AUTHOR

Willim T. Walraven was born in Holland (the Netherlands). He studied electro-hydraulic engineering and became chief engineer and plant manager for a large automated machinery manufacturer in the USA. After several years of also being technical assistant to the sales department, he was promoted to vice president of international sales and marketing with the primary duty of organizing a worldwide distribution network.

Many years he traveled all over the world, setting up agents. He then started his own successful business in international trading. He resides in Minneapolis, Minnesota, USA.

CPSIA information can be obtained
at www.ICGtesting.com
Printed in the USA
FSHW010208010920
73385FS